Windows XP for Starters

THE MISSING MA

Windows XP for Starters
THE MISSING MANUAL

Exactly what you need to get started

David Pogue

POGUE PRESS™
O'REILLY®

Beijing · Cambridge · Farnham · Köln · Paris · Sebastopol · Taipei · Tokyo

Windows XP for Starters: THE MISSING MANUAL

by David Pogue

Copyright © 2006 Pogue Press. All rights reserved.
Printed in the United States of America.

Published by O'Reilly Media, Inc., 1005 Gravenstein Highway North, Sebastopol, CA 95472.

O'Reilly books may be purchased for educational, business, or sales promotional use. Online editions are also available for most titles (*safari.oreilly.com*). For more information, contact our corporate/institutional sales department: (800) 998-9938 or *corporate@oreilly.com*.

Printing History:
November 2005:   First Edition.

 This book uses RepKover™, a durable and flexible lay-flat binding.

ISBN: 0-596-10155-4
[M]

TABLE OF CONTENTS

The Missing Credits xiii

Introduction. 1
About This Book 3
Basic Terms 6
About MissingManuals.com. 7

PART ONE: THE WINDOWS XP DESKTOP

Chapter 1: The Very Basics 11
What Is Windows, Anyway? 12
Working Windows Smarter. 14
    The Right Mouse Button Is King 14
    Summon a Wizard 15
    There's More Than One Way to Do Everything 15
    You Can Use the Keyboard for Everything 16
    You Could Spend a Lifetime Changing Properties 18
    Every Piece of Hardware Requires Software 20

Chapter 2: The Desktop and Start Menu. 21
Logging In 23
    Workgroups vs. Domains 23
The Elements of the XP Desktop 24
The Start Menu 24
Start → Log Off. 28
Start → Shut Down (Turn Off Computer) 30
Start → All Programs 32
    The Startup Folder 34

Start → Search. 36
    Finding Files and Folders 36
    Managing the Found Files and Folders 41
Start → Help and Support 44
Start → Control Panel. 45
Start → My Network Places. 45
Start → My Computer. 45
Start → My Music, My Pictures 45
Start → My Recent Documents. 47
Start → My Documents 47

Chapter 3: Windows, Folders, and the Taskbar 49
Windows in Windows. 50
    The Task Pane 52
    Sizing, Moving, and Closing Windows 55
    Working with Multiple Windows 57
The Desktop Window Overhaul 58
    Icon and List Views 59
    Standard Folder Views 64
Window Toolbars 64
    The Standard Buttons Toolbar 65
    The Address Bar 66
    The Links Toolbar 67
The Taskbar 68
    The Notification Area 69
    Window Buttons 71
Taskbar Toolbars 74
    Quick Launch Toolbar 74

Chapter 4: Organizing Your Stuff. 77
Creating a Folder 78
The Folders of Windows XP 78
    What's in the Local Disk (C:) Window 80
    Your Account Folder 83
    Navigating My Computer 84
    Navigating with Windows Explorer 84

Life with Icons. 88
   Renaming Your Icons 88
   Icon Properties 90
Copying and Moving Folders and Files. 91
   Highlighting Icons 91
   Copying by Dragging Icons 93
   Copying by Using Copy and Paste 95
The Recycle Bin. 98
   Restoring Deleted Files and Folders 98
   Emptying the Recycle Bin 100
Shortcut Icons. 101
   Creating and Deleting Shortcuts 102
Burning CDs from the Desktop. 102

PART TWO: THE COMPONENTS OF WINDOWS XP

Chapter 5: Programs and Documents 109
Launching Programs. 110
Switching Programs 111
Exiting Programs 114
When Programs Die 114
Saving Documents 117
   The Save File Dialog Box 117
   Saving into My Documents 118
   Navigating in the Save Dialog Box 119
   Navigating the List by Keyboard 122
   The File Format Drop-Down Menu 123
Closing Documents. 123
The Open Dialog Box. 124
Moving Data Between Documents. 125
   Cut, Copy, and Paste 125
   Drag-and-Drop 126
Filename Extensions. 130
   Displaying Filename Extensions 130
Installing Software 132
   The Pre-Installation Checklist 132
   Installing Software from a CD 133

Installing Downloaded Software 135
Installing Preloaded Software 135
Installing Windows Components 136
Uninstalling Software 137

Chapter 6: Pictures, Music, and Movies 139
Digital Photos in XP 140
Hooking Up Your Camera 140
Fun with Downloaded Pictures 144
Scanning 153
Windows Media Player 154
The Lay of the Land 154
Playing Music CDs 155
Copying CDs to Your Hard Drive 156
Organizing Your Music Library 160
Burning Your Own CDs 162
Playing DVD Movies 164

PART THREE: WINDOWS ONLINE

Chapter 7: Getting on the Web 169
How to Get Online 170
Cable and DSL 170
Wireless Networks 171
Establishing a New Dial-Up Internet Account 172
The Connection Icon 176
Manually Plugging in Internet Settings 178
Via Dial-up Modem 178
Via Cable Modem, Network, or DSL 179
Dialing Up to the Internet 180
Manual Connections 180
The Notification Area Icon 181
Automatic Dialing 181
Disconnecting 183
Surfing the Web 185

Internet Explorer. 186
  Browsing Basics and Toolbars 186
  Internet Explorer Toolbars 188
  Status Bar 192
  Explorer Bar 192
  Ways to Find Something on the Web 193
  Tips for Better Surfing 194
  Ditching Pop-Ups and Pop-Unders 200

Chapter 8: Outlook Express 6. 201
Setting Up Outlook Express 202
Sending Email 202
  Mail folders in Outlook Express 203
  Composing and sending messages 205
  The Address Book 211
  Attaching Files to Messages 211
Reading Email 212
  How to Process a Message 213
  Opening Attachments 219
  Message Rules 222

PART FOUR: BEYOND THE BASICS

Chapter 9: Printers and Other Hardware 229
Installing a Printer. 230
  Existing Printers 230
  USB Printers 231
  Network Printers 231
  The Printer Icon 234
Printing. 236
  Printing from Applications 236
  Printing from the Desktop 240
  Printing from the Internet 241
Controlling Printouts 241
Printer Troubleshooting. 244
Hardware 245

Connecting New Gadgets 246
    Using the Add Hardware Wizard 247
The Device Manager. 250
    Red X's and Yellow ?'s: Resolving Conflicts 252
    Turning Components Off 254
    Updating Drivers with the Device Manager 254

Chapter 10: The Control Panel 257
Navigating the Panel 259
Accessibility Options 262
Add Hardware 263
Add or Remove Programs. 264
Administrative Tools 264
Automatic Updates. 264
Bluetooth Devices. 264
Date and Time. 264
Display 266
Folder Options 269
Fonts. 269
Game Controllers 269
Internet Options 270
Keyboard 271
Mail 271
Mouse 272
Network Connections. 274
Network Setup Wizard. 274
Phone and Modem Options. 274
Power Options. 275
Printers and Faxes 277
Regional and Language Options 277
Scanners and Cameras. 277
Scheduled Tasks 277
Security Center 277
Sounds and Audio Devices 278
Speech 278

System 279
    General Tab 280
    Computer Name 280
    Hardware Tab 280
    Advanced Tab 283
    System Restore Tab 283
    Automatic Updates Tab 283
    Remote Tab 283
Taskbar and Start Menu... 283
User Accounts.. 283
Windows Firewall... 284
Wireless Network Setup Wizard 284

Chapter 11: Help, Maintenance, and Backups 285
Navigating the Help System 286
    Help Home Page 286
    Search the Help Pages 288
    Help Index 290
 "What's This?": Help for Dialog Boxes 290
Getting Help from Microsoft..................................... 292
PC Maintenance: Internet Security............................... 294
Security Center 295
    The Windows Firewall 296
    Virus Software 299
    Spyware Cleaners 300
Automatic Updates... 301
Microsoft Backup 305
    Backup Hardware 306
    Creating a Backup Job 307
    Restoring with Microsoft Backup 312

PART FIVE: LIFE ON THE NETWORK

Chapter 12: User Accounts 319
Introducing User Accounts 321
Setting Up Accounts 322
    Administrator Accounts 324

Limited Accounts 324
Adding an Account 325
Editing an Account 326
The Forgotten Password Disk 331
Deleting User Accounts 334
Setting Up the Logon Process 335
"Use the Welcome Screen" 335
"Use Fast User Switching" 337
Shared Folders 340

Chapter 13: The Home Network 343
The Network Setup Wizard 344
"Before you continue" 345
"Select a connection method" 347
"Select your Internet connection" 348
"Give this computer a description and name" 348
"Name your network" 348
"Ready to apply network settings" 348
"You're almost done" 348
Testing the Network 351
Simple File Sharing 354
The Shared Documents Folder 355
Sharing Your Own Folders 357
Notes on Sharing 360
Hiding Folders 361
Accessing Other Computers 361
My Network Places 362
Working with Network Files 364
At the Desktop 365
Using Start → Search 365
Inside Applications 365

Index 367

THE MISSING CREDITS

About the Author

 **David Pogue** is the weekly computer columnist for the New York Times, an Emmy-winning correspondent for CBS News Sunday Morning, and the creator of the Missing Manual series. He's the author or co-author of 37 books, including 16 in this series and six in the "For Dummies" line (including Macs, Magic, Opera, and Classical Music). In his other life, David is a former Broadway show conductor, a magician, and a pianist.

News and photos await at *www.davidpogue.com*. He welcomes feedback about his books at *david@pogueman.com*.

About the Creative Team

Nan Barber (editor) is O'Reilly's associate editor for the Missing Manual series and has worn every hat from copy editor to co-author. She lives in Boston and never doubted for a moment that both the Macworld Expo and the Commissioner's Trophy would someday come back home. Email: *nanbarber@mac.com*.

Wendy Cholbi (editor) has been a freelance writer, editor, and Web site creator for the past 10 years. She works from her Southern California home, where she lives with her husband, two children, two cats, and year-round hummingbirds. Email: *wendy@cholbi.com*.

David A. Karp (technical editor, previous edition) is the author of nine power-user books, including the bestselling *Windows XP Annoyances for Geeks* and *eBay Hacks* (both from O'Reilly).

Rose Cassano (cover illustration) has worked as an independent designer and illustrator for twenty years. Assignments have ranged from the nonprofit sector to corporate clientele. She lives in beautiful Southern Oregon, grateful for the miracles of modern technology that make working there a reality. Email: *cassano@highstream.net*. Web: *www.rosecassano.com*.

The Missing Manual Series

Missing Manuals are witty, superbly written guides to computer products that don't come with printed manuals (which is just about all of them). Each book features a handcrafted index; cross-references to specific page numbers (not just "see Chapter 14"); and RepKover, a detached-spine binding that lets the book lie perfectly flat without the assistance of weights or cinder blocks.

Recent and upcoming titles include:

Access for Starters: The Missing Manual by Kate J. Chase and Scott Palmer

AppleScript: The Missing Manual by Adam Goldstein

AppleWorks 6: The Missing Manual by Jim Elferdink and David Reynolds

Creating Web Sites: The Missing Manual by Matthew MacDonald

Dreamweaver 8: The Missing Manual by David Sawyer McFarland

eBay: The Missing Manual by Nancy Conner

Excel: The Missing Manual by Matthew MacDonald

Excel for Starters: The Missing Manual by Matthew MacDonald

FileMaker Pro 8: The Missing Manual by Geoff Coffey and Susan Prosser

FrontPage 2003: The Missing Manual by Jessica Mantaro

GarageBand 2: The Missing Manual by David Pogue

Google: The Missing Manual, Second Edition by Sarah Milstein and Rael Dornfest

Home Networking: The Missing Manual by Scott Lowe

iLife '05: The Missing Manual by David Pogue

iMovie HD & iDVD 5: The Missing Manual by David Pogue

iPhoto 5: The Missing Manual by David Pogue

iPod & iTunes: The Missing Manual, Third Edition by J.D. Biersdorfer

iWork '05: The Missing Manual by Jim Elferdink

Mac OS X: The Missing Manual, Tiger Edition by David Pogue

Office 2004 for Macintosh: The Missing Manual by Mark H. Walker and Franklin Tessler

Photoshop Elements 4: The Missing Manual by Barbara Brundage

QuickBooks: The Missing Manual by Bonnie Biafore

Quicken for Starters: The Missing Manual by Bonnie Biafore

Switching to the Mac: The Missing Manual, Tiger Edition by David Pogue and Adam Goldstein

Windows XP Home Edition: The Missing Manual, Second Edition by David Pogue

Windows XP Pro: The Missing Manual, Second Edition by David Pogue, Craig Zacker, and Linda Zacker

INTRODUCTION

- ▶ **About This Book**
- ▶ **Basic Terms**
- ▶ **About MissingManuals.com**

FOR MANY YEARS, the evolution of Microsoft Windows ran along two different tracks. First, there were the home versions: Windows 95, Windows 98, and Windows Me. These were the Windows for everyday individuals. They were compatible with just about everything on earth, including games of every description—but where stability was concerned, they weren't what you'd call Rocks of Gibraltar.

Second, there were the corporate versions of Windows: Windows NT and Windows 2000. These versions of Windows rarely froze or crashed, and they featured industrial-strength security. However, they weren't anywhere near as compatible as the home versions of Windows. If you tried to run the Dora the Explorer CD-ROM at work, for example, you were out of luck (if not out of a job).

This schizophrenic approach to the evolution of Windows had its share of drawbacks. For example, it meant twice as much work for software companies, who had to ensure compatibility with both systems. For you, the PC fan, it was even worse: you had to read the fine print on every program or game you bought to make sure it would run on your computer. And it was entirely possible to get confused when sitting down in front of a PC running a different version of Windows.

The goal of Windows XP was simple: combine the two versions of Windows into a single new operating system that offers the best features of both.

For the most part, Microsoft succeeded. If you're used to one of the home versions, you may be surprised by some of the resulting changes; under the colorful, three-dimensional new skin of Windows XP Home Edition lurks Windows 2000, which includes some of its beefy security features. This book will help you get through them.

If you're accustomed to Windows 2000 or Windows NT, you'll probably be happy to hear that XP Professional is built on the same bulletproof frame. All you have to get used to are XP's greater compatibility with a wide range of hardware and software, and Windows' new look (which you can even turn off, if you like).

Either way, you've entered a new age: the unified Windows era. Now you, Microsoft, and software companies can get used to the notion that everybody is using the same Windows. There are still two different *editions* of Windows XP—Professional and Home Edition—but they're not really two different operating systems (see the box below).

Professional Edition vs. Home Edition

It's *mostly* true that there's really just one Windows XP. The Professional and Home editions look alike, generally work alike, and are based on the same multigigabyte glob of software code.

But as with a pizza, insurance policy, or Toyota Camry, you can pay a little more for a few extras. Most of them are useful primarily to professional corporate network nerds and, accordingly, not covered in this book. If you're a small-business owner who's purchased Windows XP Pro, you'll eventually want to pick up a copy of *Windows XP Pro: The Missing Manual, Second Edition*, which has detailed coverage of all those advanced features.

About This Book

Despite the many improvements in Windows over the years, one feature hasn't improved one iota—Microsoft's documentation. Windows XP includes no printed guidebook at all. To learn about the thousands of pieces of software that make up this operating system, you're expected to read the online help screens.

Unfortunately, as you'll quickly discover, these help screens are tersely written, offer very little technical depth, and lack examples and illustrations. You can't even mark your place, underline, or read them in the bathroom. In Windows XP, many of the help screens are actually on Microsoft's Web site; you can't see them without an Internet connection. If you're unable to figure out how to connect to the Internet in the first place...you're out of luck.

Not only that, the help screens don't exactly give you an objective evaluation of the system's features. They don't tell you how well something works, or if it's even the right feature for what you're trying to do. Engineers often add technically sophisticated features to a program because they *can*, not because you need them. You, however, shouldn't waste your time learning features that don't help you get your work done.

The purpose of this book, then, is to serve as the startup manual that should have accompanied Windows XP. In these pages, you'll find step-by-step instructions for using every Windows feature you need to hit the ground running with your PC.

Windows XP for Starters: The Missing Manual is the ideal first book for newcomers to the PC game as well as advanced beginners who want to learn more. If you're a seasoned Windows jockey, on the other hand, you may want to check out *Windows XP Pro: The Missing Manual* or *Windows XP Home Edition: The Missing Manual*, both of which are comprehensive guides to all the features of Windows XP, from basic to advanced.

 Note: This book is based on *Window XP Home Edition: The Missing Manual* (O'Reilly) and *Windows XP Pro: The Missing Manual* (O'Reilly). Those books are truly complete references for the Windows operating system, covering every feature, including geeky stuff like network domains, NTFS permissions, and other things you'll probably never encounter—or even want to. But if you get really deep into Windows XP and want to learn more, either Windows XP Missing Manual can be your trusted guide.

About the Outline

This book is divided into five parts, each containing several chapters:

▶ Part 1, **The Windows XP Desktop,** covers everything you see on the screen when you turn on a Windows XP computer: icons, windows, menus, scroll bars, the Recycle Bin, shortcuts, the Start menu, shortcut menus, and so on.

- Part 2, **The Components of Windows XP**, is dedicated to the proposition that an operating system is little more than a launch pad for *programs*. Chapter 5 describes how to work with applications in Windows—launch them, switch among them, swap data between them, use them to create and open files, and so on.

- Part 3, **Windows Online**, covers the special Internet-related features of Windows, including the wizards that set up your Internet account, Outlook Express (for email), and Internet Explorer 6 (for Web browsing).

- Part 4, **Beyond the Basics**, is all about plugging printers and other gadgets into your PC, setting system-wide preferences with the Control Panel, and getting online help.

- Part 5, **Life on the Network**, honors the millions of households and offices that now contain more than one PC. If you work at home or in a small office, these chapters show you how to build your own network; if you work in a corporation where some highly paid professional network geek is on hand to do the troubleshooting, you won't need to read these chapters.

About → These → Arrows

Throughout this book, and throughout the Missing Manual series, you'll find sentences like this: "Open the Start → My Computer → Local Disk (C:) → Windows folder." That's shorthand for a much longer instruction that directs you to open three nested icons in sequence, like this: "Click the Start menu to open it. Click My Computer in the Start menu. Inside the My Computer window is a disk icon labeled Local Disk (C:); double-click it to open it. Inside *that* window is yet another icon called Windows. Double-click to open it, too."

Similarly, this kind of arrow shorthand helps to simplify the business of choosing commands in menus, as shown in Figure I-1

Figure I-1. In this book, arrow notations help to simplify folder and menu instructions. For example, "Choose Start → All Programs → Accessories → Notepad" is a more compact way of saying, "Click the Start button. When the Start menu opens, click All Programs; without clicking, now slide to the right onto the Accessories submenu; in that submenu, click Notepad."

Basic Terms

You'll find very little jargon or nerd terminology in this book. You will, however, encounter a few terms and concepts that you'll encounter frequently in your computing life:

- **Clicking.** This book gives you three kinds of instructions that require you to use your computer's mouse or trackpad. To *click* means to point the arrow cursor at something on the screen and then—without moving the cursor at all—to press and release the clicker button on the mouse (or laptop trackpad). To *double-click,* of course, means to click twice in rapid succession, again without moving the cursor at all. And to *drag* means to move the cursor while pressing the button continuously.

- **Keyboard shortcuts.** Every time you take your hand off the keyboard to move the mouse, you lose time and potentially disrupt your creative flow. That's why many experienced computer types use keystroke combinations instead of menu commands wherever possible. Ctrl+B, for example, is a keyboard shortcut for boldface type in most word processing programs, including Microsoft's.

    When you see a shortcut like Ctrl+S (which saves changes to the current document), it's telling you to hold down the Ctrl key and, while it's down, type the letter S, and then release both keys.

- **Choice is good.** Windows frequently gives you several ways to trigger a particular command—a menu command, *or* by clicking a toolbar button, *or* by pressing a key combination, for example. Some people prefer the speed of keyboard shortcuts; others like the satisfaction of a visual command array available in menus or toolbars. This book usually lists all of the alternatives, but by no means are you expected to memorize all of them.

About MissingManuals.com

You're invited and encouraged to submit corrections and updates to this book's Web page at *www.missingmanuals.com.* (Click the book's name, and then click the Errata link.) In an effort to keep the book as up to date and accurate as possible, each time we print more copies of this book, we'll make any corrections you've suggested.

Even if you have nothing to report, you should check that Errata page now and then. That's where we'll post a list of the corrections and updates we've made, so that you can mark important corrections into your own copy of the book, if you like.

In the meantime, we'd love to hear your suggestions for new books in the Missing Manual line. There's a place for that on the Web site, too, as well as a place to sign up for free email notification of new titles in the series.

Safari® Enabled

 When you see a Safari® Enabled icon on the cover of your favorite technology book, that means it's available online through the O'Reilly Network Safari Bookshelf.

Safari offers a solution that's better than e-books: it's a virtual library that lets you easily search thousands of top tech books, cut and paste code samples, download chapters, and find quick answers when you need the most accurate, current information. Try it for free at *http://safari.oreilly.com*.

PART ONE: THE WINDOWS XP DESKTOP

Chapter 1   The Very Basics

Chapter 2   The Desktop and Start Menu

Chapter 3   Windows, Folders, and the Taskbar

Chapter 4   Organizing Your Stuff

CHAPTER 1:
THE VERY BASICS

▶ What Is Windows, Anyway?

▶ Working Windows Smarter

IF YOU'RE NEW TO WINDOWS, you've got to start with the fundamentals. Don't worry—this chapter won't make you memorize a bunch of jargon. Instead, it gives you a solid understanding of what Windows XP does and how to use it. In fact, even if you're not so new to Windows, a little background information will help you feel at ease with the program you're staring at on the screen.

Be prepared to encounter the following terms and concepts over and over again—in the built-in Windows help, in computer magazines, and in this book. Along the way, you'll pick up some basic operating principles—like right-clicking and keyboard shortcuts—that will make every moment you spend at your PC more efficient and productive.

What Is Windows, Anyway?

Windows is an *operating system*, the software that controls your computer. It's designed to serve you in several ways:

▶ **It's a launching bay.** At its heart, Windows is a home base, a remote-control clicker that lets you call up the various software programs (called *applications* in the trade) you use for work or play. When you get right down to it, applications are the real reason you bought a PC.

Windows XP is a well-stocked software pantry unto itself. As you'll see later in this book, it comes with such basic programs as a Web browser, email program, simple word processor, and calculator. There's even software to download, print, and edit photos from your digital camera and play music and movies on your PC.

If you're like most people, sooner or later, you'll buy and install *more* software. That's one of the luxuries of using Windows: you can choose from a staggering number of add-on programs. Whether you're a left-handed beekeeper or a German-speaking nun, some company somewhere is selling Windows software designed just for you, its target audience.

▶ **It's a file cabinet.** Every application on your machine, as well as every document you create, is represented on the screen by an *icon* (see Figure 1-1). You can organize these icons into little onscreen file folders. You can make backups (safety copies) by dragging file icons onto a floppy disk or blank CD, or send them to people by email. You can also trash icons you no longer need by dragging them onto the Recycle Bin icon.

▶ **It's your equipment headquarters.** What you can actually *see* of Windows is only the tip of the iceberg. An enormous chunk of Windows is behind-the-scenes plumbing that controls the various functions of your computer—its modem, screen, keyboard, printer, and so on.

Figure 1-1. Your Windows world revolves around icons, the tiny pictures that represent your programs, documents, and various Windows components. From left to right: the icons for your computer itself, a word processing document, a digital photo (a JPEG document), a word processor program (Word), and a CD-ROM inserted into your computer.

UP TO SPEED

Service Packs

As you probably know, Windows is a creature that constantly evolves. Every few weeks, Microsoft issues another bundle of tiny patches: drivers for new add-ons, patches for bugs, seals for newly discovered security holes, and so on.

But once a year or so, the company rolls all of these minor updates into one mama patch called a Service Pack. All PCs sold since the fall of 2004 come with Service Packs 1 and 2 pre-installed. This book assumes you have such a machine. Either way, you'll want to get to know Windows XP's Automatic Updates feature (page 301), to make sure your PC is *always* running the latest and greatest version of Windows.

Working Windows Smarter

The next few pages may well be the most important in this book. The coolest, most powerful PC on the planet can feel awkward and clunky if you're using computer techniques you learned during the first Bush administration. Even if you have a favorite way of doing something, make this your mantra: never stop learning. There's probably a way to do it better and faster in Windows XP. Fortunately, remembering just a few simple principles usually helps you find a better way every time.

The Right Mouse Button Is King

One of the most important features of Windows isn't on the screen—it's under your hand. The standard mouse has two mouse buttons. You use the left one to click buttons, highlight text, and drag things around on the screen.

When you click the right button, however, a *shortcut menu* appears onscreen, like the ones shown in Figure 1-2. Get into the habit of *right-clicking* things—icons, folders, disks, text in your word processor, buttons on your menu bar, pictures on a Web page, and so on. The commands that appear on the shortcut menu will make you much more productive and lead you to discover handy functions you never knew existed.

This is a big deal: Microsoft's research suggests that nearly 75 percent of Windows users don't use the right mouse button, and therefore miss hundreds of time-saving shortcuts. Part of the rationale behind Windows XP's redesign is putting these functions out in the open. Even so, many more shortcuts remain hidden under your right mouse button.

 Tip: Microsoft doesn't discriminate against left-handers...much. You can swap the functions of the right and left mouse buttons easily enough.

In the Control Panel window (page 272), open the Mouse icon. When the Mouse Properties dialog box opens, click the Buttons tab, and turn on the "Switch primary and secondary buttons" checkbox. Then click OK. Windows now displays shortcut menus when you *left*-click.

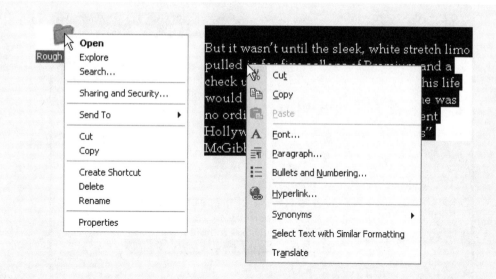

Figure 1-2. Shortcut menus (sometimes called context menus) often list commands that aren't in the menus at the top of the window. The commands shown here appear when you right-click a folder (left), or some highlighted text in a word processor (right). Once the shortcut menu appears, left-click the command you want.

Summon a Wizard

A *wizard* is a series of screens that walks you through the task you're trying to complete. Wizards make configuration and installation tasks easier by breaking them down into smaller, more easily digested steps. Figure 1-3 offers an example.

There's More Than One Way to Do Everything

No matter what setting you want to adjust, no matter what program you want to open, Microsoft has provided five or six different ways to do it. For example, here are the various ways to delete a file: press the Delete key, choose Delete from the File menu at the top of a window, drag the file icon onto the Recycle Bin, or right-click the file name and choose Delete from the shortcut menu.

Pessimists grumble that there are too many paths to every destination, making it much more difficult to learn Windows. Optimists point out that this abundance

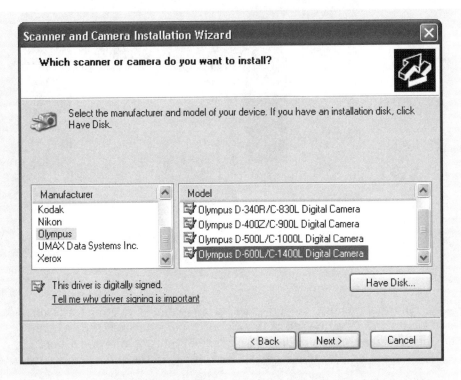

Figure 1-3. Wizards are everywhere in Windows, helping you through multi-step tasks via a series of interview screens. For example, here the Scanner and Camera Wizard is helping you install driver software for a digital camera by asking you to indicate the model number.

of approaches means that almost everyone will find, and settle on, a satisfying method for each task. Whenever you find a task irksome, remember you have other options.

You Can Use the Keyboard for Everything

In earlier versions of Windows, underlined letters appeared in the names of menus and dialog boxes. These underlines were clues for people who found it faster to do something by pressing keys than by using the mouse.

The underlines are hidden in Windows XP, at least in disk and folder windows (they still appear in your individual software programs). If you miss them, you have two options:

▶ Make them come back full-time, using the control panel's Display program (see page 266).

▶ Make them reappear only when you summon them—by pressing the Alt key, Tab key, or an arrow key whenever the menu bar is visible. (When operating menus, you can release the Alt key immediately after pressing it.) In this book, in help screens, and in computer magazines, you'll see key combinations indicated like this: Alt+S (or Alt+ whatever the letter key is).

Once the underlines are visible, you can open a menu by pressing the underlined letter (F for the File menu, for example). Once the menu is open, press the underlined letter key that corresponds to the menu command you want. Or press Esc to close the menu without doing anything. (In Windows, the Esc key always means *cancel* or *stop*.)

Pressing the Windows logo key (next to the Alt key on most recent keyboards) opens the Start menu and turns on its little underlines. Microsoft assumed, logically enough, that if you're enough of a keyboard lover to have opened the Start menu from the keyboard, you're probably going to want to use the keyboard to trigger the commands in the Start menu, too.

If choosing a menu command opens a dialog box, you can trigger its options, too, by pressing Alt along with the underlined letters. (Within dialog boxes, you can't press and release Alt; you have to hold it down while typing the underlined letter.) As you can see in Figure 1-4, it's a rare task indeed that you can't perform entirely from the keyboard.

 Tip: The Enter key always does the same thing as clicking the highlighted button in a dialog box (the one with a shadowed border).

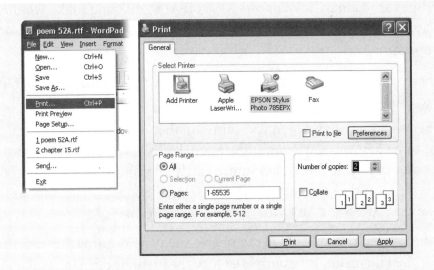

Figure 1-4. You can print documents without ever using the mouse. First, press Alt+F, which opens the File menu (left). Then type P to open the Print dialog box (right). Press Alt+C to highlight the Copies box, then type the number of copies you want. Finally, press Enter to "click" the Print button.

You Could Spend a Lifetime Changing Properties

You can't write an operating system that's all things to all people, but Microsoft has sure tried. You can change almost every aspect of the way Windows looks and works. You can replace the gray backdrop of the screen (the *wallpaper*) with your favorite photograph, change the typeface used for the names of your icons, or set up a particular program to launch automatically every time you turn on the PC.

When you want to change some *general* behavior of your PC, like how it connects to the Internet, how soon the screen goes black to save power, or how quickly a letter repeats when you hold down a key, you use the Control Panel window (see Chapter 10).

Many other times, however, you may want to adjust the settings of only one *particular* element of the machine, such as the hard drive, the Recycle Bin, or a particular application. In those cases, simply right-click the corresponding icon. In the resulting shortcut menu, you'll often find a command called Properties. When you click it, a dialog box appears containing settings or information about that object, as shown in Figure 1-5.

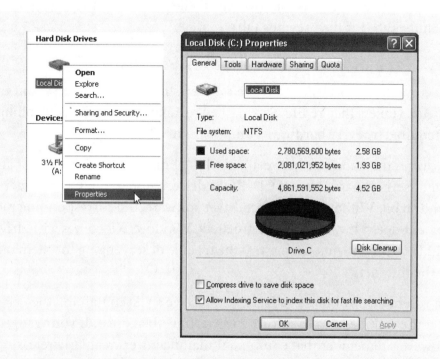

Figure 1-5. One quick way to find out how much space is left on your hard drive is to right-click the corresponding icon and choose the Properties command (left). The Properties dialog box appears (right), featuring a handy disk-space graph.

 Tip: As a shortcut to the Properties command, just highlight an icon and then press Alt+Enter.

It's also worth getting to know how to operate *tabbed dialog boxes*, of which the Properties box is a fine example. These are windows that contain so many options, Microsoft has had to split them up into separate panels, or *tabs*. To reveal a new set of options, just click a different tab. (In Figure 1-5, these are called General, Tools, Hardware, Sharing, and Quota.) These tabs are designed to resemble the tabs at the top of file folders. You can switch tabs without using the mouse by pressing Ctrl+Tab (to "click" the next tab to the right) or Ctrl+Shift+Tab (for the previous tab).

Every Piece of Hardware Requires Software

When computer geeks talk about their *drivers*, they're not talking about their chauffeurs (unless they're Bill Gates); they're talking about the controlling software required by every hardware component of a PC.

The *driver* is the translator between your PC's brain and the equipment attached to it: mouse, keyboard, screen, CD-ROM drive, scanner, digital camera, palmtop, and so on. Without the correct driver software, the corresponding piece of equipment doesn't work at all. Fortunately, Windows XP comes with drivers for over 12,000 components, saving you the trouble of scavenging for them on a disk or on the Internet.

When you buy one of these gadgets, you receive a CD containing the driver software. If the included driver software works fine, then great. If your gadget acts up, however, remember that equipment manufacturers regularly release improved (read: less buggy) versions of these software chunks. (You generally find such updates on the manufacturers' Web sites.)

CHAPTER 2:
THE DESKTOP AND START MENU

▶ Logging In

▶ The Elements of the XP Desktop

▶ The Start Menu

▶ Start → Log Off

▶ Start → Shut Down (Turn Off Computer)

▶ Start → All Programs

▶ Start → Search

▶ Start → Help and Support

▶ Start → Control Panel

▶ Start → My Network Places

▶ Start → My Computer

▶ Start → My Music, My Pictures

▶ Start → My Recent Documents

▶ Start → My Documents

2

WHEN YOU TURN ON a brand-new Windows XP computer for the first time, you're treated to a series of blue "Welcome to Microsoft Windows" setup screens. This Setup Wizard guides you through setting up an Internet account, *activating* your copy of Windows, setting up *accounts* for all the people who use the computer, and so on. If you've been through that process once, read on.

Tip: You don't *have* to create accounts for different users, but if you're interested, you can learn all about the subject in Chapter 12.

Logging In

If your PC isn't connected to any others and you're the only one who uses it, life is easy. You arrive at the Windows XP desktop without needing to log in.

Otherwise, what happens when you turn on your PC (or when you complete your first setup) depends on whether your PC is connected to some kind of network. Windows XP behaves a bit differently when the computer is on a big, corporate network than when it's on a home network. That's why what you see onscreen when you log in may not match the examples you see in magazines, books, and Web sites.

Workgroups vs. Domains

Although Windows XP works very well for home PCs, it's also designed to thrive in massively networked corporations. It has two slightly different personalities that you only really see when you're starting up each day.

When you connect your PCs, printers, and so on into a home network, Windows calls that a *workgroup*. You can share files with other machines in the workgroup by setting up an account for yourself on each machine. Some very small businesses also use a workgroup arrangement. (Chapter 13 is all about home networking.)

If you're in a larger office, you're probably part of a *domain network*, managed by a system administrator (*sysadmin* for short). This highly paid professional can set up and troubleshoot all files and security settings on all domain PCs.

If you're not sure whether your computer is a member of a workgroup or a domain, choose Start → Control Panel → System, and then click the Computer Name tab. This dialog box shows the name of your computer and the name of its domain or workgroup.

 Tip: If you set up multiple user accounts on your PC, then Windows XP acts like it's in a workgroup, even though it's not actually connected to one. So the workgroup information below pertains to you, too.

▶ **If your PC is part of a workgroup**, you may encounter the Welcome dialog box shown in Figure 2-1. Click your name in the list, type your password if you're asked for it, and click the little right-pointing arrow button (or press Enter). You arrive at the desktop.

▶ **If your PC is on a domain network,** you'll see a message saying "Press Ctrl+Alt+Del to begin" when you power up. You must press those keys to summon the logon window. Type your name in the User Name box, type your password in the Password box, and then click OK (or press Enter). You arrive at the desktop.

The Elements of the XP Desktop

Once you're past the heart-pounding excitement of the new startup logo and the Setup Wizard, you reach the digital vista shown in Figure 2-2. It's the Windows desktop, now graced by a pastoral sunny hillside that should look familiar to anyone who has ever watched "Teletubbies."

A new installation of Windows XP on a new computer presents an absolutely spotless desktop, utterly icon-free except for the Recycle Bin. Your first step in doing pretty much any task will be to click the Start button in the lower-left corner of your screen. The following pages cover the Start menu in detail.

The Start Menu

The Start menu is so important because it lists every *useful* piece of software on your computer, including commands, programs, and files. You can use the Start

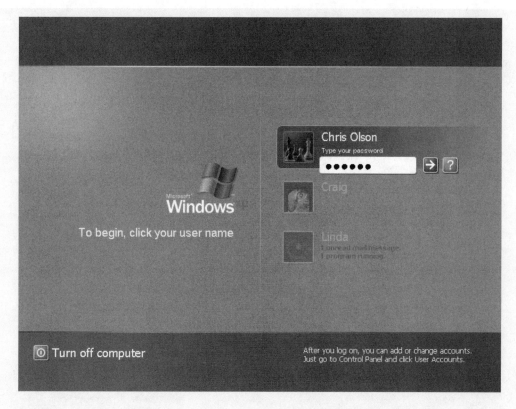

Figure 2-1. This is the logon screen you see if your PC is on a home network or has multiple user accounts, as shown here. Click your name, then type the password you created when you set up Windows.

menu to open your applications, install new software, configure hardware, get help, find files, and much more.

When you click the Start button at the lower-left corner of your screen, the Start menu pops open, shooting upward. Its contents depend on which options you (or your computer's manufacturer) have put there; Figure 2-3 illustrates an example.

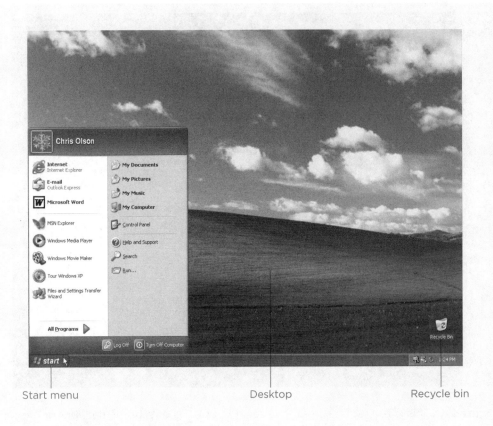

Start menu   Desktop   Recycle bin

Figure 2-2. Everything you'll ever do on the computer begins with a click on one of these three elements: a desktop icon, the Start button (which opens the Start menu), or the taskbar, which is described in Chapter 3. (The Start menu lists every significant command and software component on your PC.)

The new Start menu is divided into four chunks. One area, the *pinned items list*, lists programs you use every day and is yours to modify. Another, the *most frequently used programs list*, lists programs you use often and is computed automatically by Windows. The final two sections list Windows features and standard Windows programs. Figure 2-3 describes the function of each section.

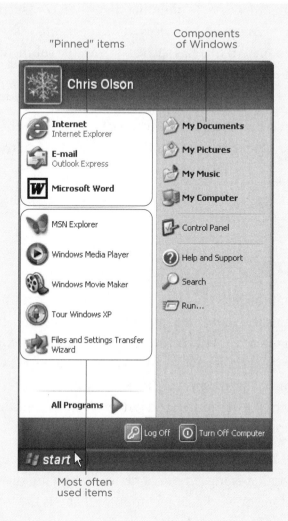

"Pinned" items

Components
of Windows

Most often
used items

Figure 2-3. In Windows XP, the Start menu is divided into several distinct sections. The lower-left section lists the programs you use most often, according to Windows XP's calculations. The right-side column provides direct access to certain Windows features and standard Windows programs.

Tip: If you're a keyboard-shortcut lover, you can open the Start menu by pressing the Windows logo key. Once it's open, you can use the arrow keys to "walk" up and down the menu (or type the first letters of the command you want) and then press Enter to "click" the highlighted command.

Start menu items graced by a right-pointing triangle arrow (such as Accessories in Figure 2-3) have *submenus*, also known as *cascading menus*. As you move your mouse pointer over an item that has such an arrow, the submenu, listing additional options, pops out to the right (you don't have to click). It's not unusual for submenu items to have arrows of their own, indicating—what else?—additional submenus.

This discussion describes the items in the Start menu from the bottom up, left to right, the way your mouse encounters them as it moves up from the Start button.

 Tip: To change your name and icon as they appear at the top of the new Start menu, use the User Accounts program in the Control Panel, as described on page 322.

Start → Log Off

This command is at the heart of Windows XP's *accounts* feature, in which each person who uses this PC gets to see his own desktop picture, email account, files, and so on (see Chapter 12). When you're logged into a network domain, this is one of the most important features of all. You should log off your computer any time you walk away from it, especially if your computer stores confidential information. If this is a home computer and it doesn't store confidential information, you can safely ignore this option forever.

Choosing this command presents one of two dialog boxes, depending on whether your computer is logged into a network domain, or whether or not you log on to a standalone or workgroup computer that has the Windows XP feature called *Fast User Switching* turned on. (You can't use Fast User Switching on a computer that logs on to a network domain.)

▶ **Switch User/Log Off.** If you see the dialog box shown at the top of Figure 2-4, then Fast User Switching is turned on (as it is on any fresh Windows XP installation for a standalone or workgroup computer). It's among the most useful new features in Windows XP, since it lets somebody else log into the computer, opening up his own world of documents, email, desktop picture, and so on. Meanwhile, whatever *you* had up and running remains open behind the scenes. After the interloper is finished, you can log on again to find all of your open programs and documents exactly as you left them on the screen.

Although this is a handy Windows XP feature, it can also be the least secure. When user accounts aren't assigned passwords, anyone can access anyone else's information as easily as clicking the person's name.

▶ **Immediate log off.** If you see the dialog box shown at bottom in Figure 2-4, either you're logged into a network domain or Fast User Switching has been turned off. When you click Log Off (or press Enter), Windows closes all open programs and then presents the classic Welcome to Windows dialog box so that the next person can log on.

Figure 2-4. Top: On workgroup computers, if Fast User Switching is turned on, this is what you see when you choose Start → Log Off. Both buttons return to the Welcome screen, but clicking Switch User leaves all of your programs open and in memory, while Log Off actually closes them.

Bottom: On domain-network computers (or any PC with Fast User Switching turned off), this starker dialog box appears when you choose Start → Log Off.

- If you click Cancel in either case, you're sent right back to whatever you were doing.

 Note: On your Windows XP standalone or workgroup computer, you turn off Fast User Switching in Start → Control Panel → User Accounts. Click the link called "Change the way users log on or off."

Start → Shut Down (Turn Off Computer)

In Windows XP, this menu item is more powerful than its name implies. Choosing it opens a dialog box that offers several variations on "shut down" (see Figure 2-5):

- **Stand By** puts your computer to "sleep." This special state of PC consciousness reduces the amount of electricity the computer uses. It remains in suspended animation until you use the mouse or keyboard to begin working again. (This feature is available only if your computer offers it *and* you've turned it on in the Power Options program in the Control Panel.) Whatever programs or documents you were working on remain in memory.

 Note: This information is stored only in memory, not on your hard drive. If your computer loses power, you lose all of the information that was stored in memory. To be absolutely safe, save your open documents before putting the PC in Stand By.

If you're using a laptop on battery power, Stand By mode is a real boon, because it consumes only the barest trickle of battery power.

- **Shut down** quits all open programs (or, in some cases, prompts you to do so), offers you the opportunity to save any unsaved documents, and then exits Windows. Most modern PCs then turn off automatically. If you're logged on to a workgroup network, this command may be called Turn Off.

 Tip: You don't have to open the Start menu to turn off the computer. Just press the power button. (If that makes the PC sleep or hibernate instead, see page 275.)

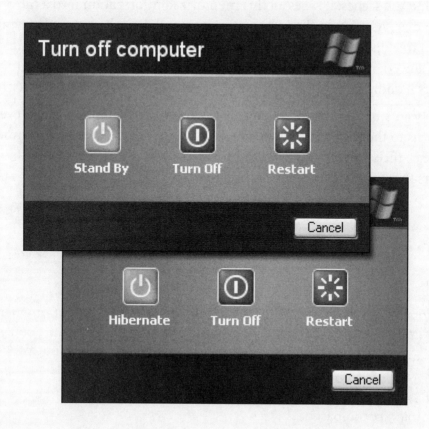

Figure 2-5. Here's the Shut Down dialog box on a workgroup PC. Press Shift to reveal the Hibernate button (bottom). If your company has a domain network, you choose these options with a drop-down menu instead of buttons.

▶ **Restart** quits all open programs, then quits and restarts Windows again automatically. The computer doesn't turn off. (You might do this to "refresh" your computer when you notice that it's responding sluggishly, for example.)

▶ **Log off** quits all programs, disconnects from the network, and then displays the Welcome screen so that the next person can log in. (The PC doesn't restart.)

▶ **Hibernate** shuts down the machine after it *memorizes* the state of your software, including all open operating system files, applications, and documents.

Behind the scenes, it saves all this memorized information into a file on your hard disk. As a result, the Hibernate command doesn't work unless you have a lot of free disk space. The more RAM your computer has, the more disk space you'll need. (As with Stand By, this feature is available only if your computer offers it and you've turned it on in the Power Options Control Panel program.)

The beauty of this feature is that when you start the computer again, everything returns to the way it was when you shut down—*fast*. The same documents appear, the same programs are running, and so on. Hibernate, in other words, offers the speed and convenience of Stand By, with the safety of Turn Off.

FREQUENTLY ASKED QUESTION

Turn Off Computer in the Start Menu

Could someone explain why the Turn Off Computer command is in a menu called Start?

The Name-the-Button committee at Microsoft probably thought that you'd interpret Start to mean, "Start here to get something accomplished."

But you wouldn't be the first person to find it illogical to click Start when you want to stop. Microsoft probably should have named the button "Menu," saving all of us a lot of confusion.

Start → All Programs

For most people, the Start → All Programs command is the most important function of the Start menu. It's the master list of every program on your computer. You can jump directly to your word processor, calendar, or favorite game, for example, just by choosing its name from the Start → All Programs menu (see Figure 2-6).

When the Start menu is open, you can open the All Programs menu in a number of ways: by clicking the All Programs menu, by pointing to it and keeping the mouse still for a moment, or by pressing the P and then the right-arrow keys on your keyboard.

Figure 2-6. The Start → All Programs menu may list the actual application (such as Microsoft Word) that you can click to launch the program. But it may also list a program group, a submenu that lists everything in a particular application folder. Some software programs install a folder on the All Programs menu, like the Office Tools folder shown here.

Note: Speaking of keyboard fanaticism: once the programs list is open, you can also choose anything in it without involving the mouse. Just type the first letter of a program's name—or press the up and down arrow keys—to highlight the name of the program you want. Then press Enter to seal the deal.

The Startup Folder

The Start → All Programs menu also lists the *Startup folder*, which contains programs that load automatically every time you start Windows XP. This can be a very useful feature; if you check your email every morning, you may as well save yourself a few mouse clicks by putting your email program into the Startup folder. If you spend all day long word processing, you may as well put Microsoft Word or WordPerfect in there.

In fact, although few PC users suspect it, what you put into the Startup folder doesn't have to be an application. It can just as well be a certain document you consult every day. It can even be a folder or disk icon whose window you'd like to find open and waiting each time you turn on the PC. (The My Documents folder is a natural example.)

Of course, you may be interested in the Startup folder for a different reason: to *stop* some program from launching itself. This is a particularly common syndrome if somebody else set up your PC. Some program seems to launch itself, unbidden, every time you turn the machine on. Fortunately, it's easy to either add or remove items from the Startup folder:

1. **Click the Start button. Point to All Programs. Right-click Startup and choose Open from the shortcut menu.**

   The Startup window opens, revealing whatever is inside.

   To delete an icon from this folder, just right-click it, choose Delete from the shortcut menu, and answer Yes to send the icon to the Recycle Bin. Close all the windows you've opened and enjoy your newfound freedom from self-launching software. The deed is done.

   To add a new icon to the Startup folder, on the other hand, read on.

2. **Navigate to the disk, folder, application, or document icon you want to add to the Startup folder.**

   Doing so requires familiarity with one of two folder-navigation schemes: My Computer or Windows Explorer. Both are described in Chapter 4.

3. **Using the right mouse button, drag the icon directly into the Startup window, as shown in Figure 2-7.**

   When you release the button, a shortcut menu appears.

4. **Choose Create Shortcuts Here from the shortcut menu.**

   Close all the windows you've opened. From now on, each time you turn on or restart your computer, the program, file, disk, or folder you dragged will open by itself.

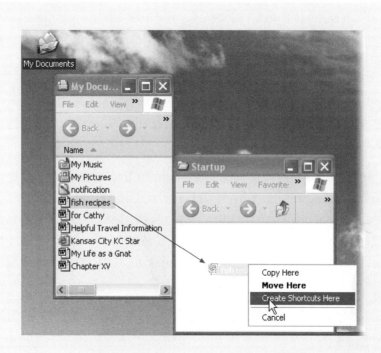

Figure 2-7. It's easy to add a program or document icon to your Startup folder so that it launches automatically every time you turn on the computer. Here, a document from the My Documents folder is being added. You may also want to add a shortcut for the My Documents folder itself, which ensures that its window will be ready and open each time the computer starts up.

Tip: To find out what something is—something in your Start menu, All Programs menu, or indeed anywhere on your desktop—point to it with your cursor without clicking. A small yellow screen tip appears, containing a text description. (If it doesn't appear, the window you're pointing to might not be the active window on your desktop. Click the window and try again.)

Start → Search

The humble Search command looks no more special than anything else on the Start menu. In Windows XP, however, it's a powerhouse that you'll probably use often. Using it, you can quickly find all kinds of computer-ish things: file and folder icons, computers on your network, Web sites, email addresses, and phone numbers.

Finding Files and Folders

If you save your files exclusively into the My Documents folder (page 47), you'll have little need to use the Search function to locate your files. You'll always know where they are: right there in that folder.

Every now and then, however, you won't remember where you filed something, or you'll download something from the Internet and not be able to find it again, or you'll install something and not know where to look for it. In those situations, the Search command is just what you need. It lets you look for a particular file or folder based on its description—by its name, size, date stamp, and so on.

Tip: To get rid of the cutesy animated dog who accompanies the Search function, either click "Turn off animated character" on the current menu, or click directly on the animated character to open up a panel allowing you to change or remove the character.

The Search command can also look for the words *inside* your files—a powerful feature if you remember typing or reading something, but not what you named the file.

Starting a search

Microsoft wanted to make absolutely sure you'd be able to find the Search command. It has provided at least six different ways to begin a search:

- Choose Start → Search.

- Press F3 or Windows key+F (that's the Windows logo key on the bottom or top row of most keyboards).

- If a disk or folder window is already open, press Ctrl+E, click the Search toolbar button, or choose View → Explorer Bar → Search.

In each case, the Search window appears, as shown in Figure 2-8.

Figure 2-8. Left: Basic Search panel, complete with Rover, the search-companion dog.

Right: If you click the desktop itself and then press F3, or if you turn on the "More advanced search options" checkbox that occasionally appears, the Search panel may look slightly different, as shown here.

Windows XP comes with a set of canned searches (listed at left in Figure 2-8) designed to help you find what you're looking for faster. Click the green arrow next to the one you want (or click the *words* next to the arrow).

Pictures, music, or video

When you click this link, the Search panel lets you choose one or more of these file types. Turn on the checkboxes you want, and type in part of the file name.

Documents (word processing, spreadsheet, and so on)

This link produces panel options designed to search only for documents—files that *you* can create or download. In other words, it doesn't bother looking through hidden files, system files, application files, and so on. And it doesn't find the names of folders at all—just files.

UP TO SPEED

Typing in the File Name

No matter which kind of search you undertake, Windows XP offers you the chance to look for a file whose name you know by typing its name into the "All or part of the file name" text box on the Search panel.

You don't have to type the entire file name—only enough of it to distinguish it from the other files on your computer. Capitals don't matter, and neither does the position of the letters you type—if you type *John*, Windows will find files with names like Johnson, Peterjohn, and DiJohnson.

You can also search for all files of a specific type, such as all Word files, by typing *.doc*—that is, an asterisk, a period, and then the three-letter filename extension of the kind of file you want (page 130). The asterisk is a wildcard meaning, "any text at all."

To narrow the search, you can enter both a partial name *and* an extension, such as *mom*.doc*. This will turn up Word files named Mom's Finances.doc, Moment of Truth.doc, and so on. (These searches work even if the filename extensions themselves are *hidden*.)

All files and folders

This is the slowest kind of search, because it searches the thousands of hidden in-system files as well as the ones that you've created yourself.

This kind of search offers a number of useful power features:

▶ **A word or phrase in the file.** Sooner or later, it happens to everyone: A file's name doesn't match what's inside it. Maybe a marauding toddler pressed the keys, inadvertently renaming your doctoral thesis "xggrjpO#$5%////." Maybe, in a Saturday afternoon organizing binge, your spouse helpfully changed the name of your "ATM Instructions" document to "Cash Machine Info," without realizing that it was a help file for Adobe Type Manager. Or maybe you just can't remember what you called something.

The "A word or phrase in the file" option searches for words *inside* your files, regardless of their names. It's extremely slow, since Windows has to read every single file, which it does only slightly faster than you could. Furthermore, this kind of search works only if you can remember an *exact* word or phrase in the missing document. Even punctuation has to match exactly.

Finally, the text you enter should be unique enough to assume it only exists in the file you're looking for; if you search for, say, *Microsoft*, Windows will find so many files that the search will be pointless.

▶ **Look in.** Use this drop-down menu if you want to limit your search to a single folder or disk. Every disk attached to your PC at the moment—your hard drive, Zip disk, CD-ROM, and so on—shows up in this list. (To search your whole computer, choose My Computer and then proceed.)

▶ **When was it modified? What size is it?** When you click one of the double-down-arrow circle buttons (like those shown in Figure 2-9), you expand the Search panel for additional options. For example, the "When was it modified?" feature lets you find only files or folders you created or changed in a certain date range (see Figure 2-9), and the "What size is it?" feature lets you screen out files larger or smaller than a number of KB you specify.

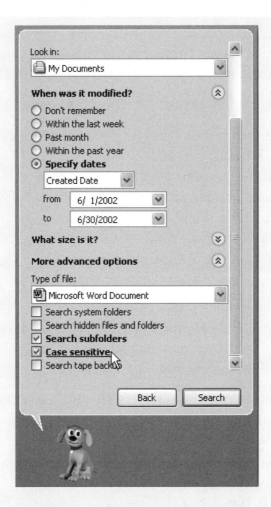

Figure 2-9. By clicking the double-down-arrow circle buttons, you can expand the Search panel considerably (shown here scrolled down so far that you can't even see the file names you're searching for). This search will find Word documents in the My Documents folder created during June 2002.

▶ **Search subfolders** is much more practical. It looks for files within folders *inside* the disk or folder you've specified. Turn this option off only when you know for sure that the file you need is in the disk or folder you're starting with, but *not* within any subfolders there. Skipping the subfolders makes the search process much faster. *Case sensitive* instructs the Search program to match the capitalization of the characters you enter; searching for files containing "dentist" won't find files containing "Dentist." And *Search tape backup*, of course, searches for the specified files on your tape-backup system, if you have one.

Windows uses the checkboxes you turn on *in addition* to any data you entered into the basic search fields.

Managing the Found Files and Folders

Once you've set up the search, click the Search button (or press Enter). As the search proceeds, the screen changes. On the right side of the window, you now see a list of files and folders whose names contain what you typed in the blank (Figure 2-10).

Figure 2-10. When you click Search, you see your results in a standard list window (page 59). Anything Windows XP finds in My Documents appears twice in the list. Repeat to yourself: "It's not my fault."

The Path to Enlightenment About Paths

Windows is too busy to think of a particular file as "that family album program in the Program Files folder, which is in the My Programs folder on the C: drive." Instead, it uses shorthand to specify each icon's location on your hard drive—a series of disk and folder names separated by backslashes, like this: *C:\program files\pbsoftware\beekeeperpro.exe*.

This kind of location code is that icon's path. (Capitalization doesn't matter, even though you may see capital letters in Microsoft's examples.)

You'll encounter file paths when using several important Windows features, including the Search command. When you choose the Search command, Windows identifies the location of each file it finds for you by displaying its path.

Using the Search Results panel

At this point, you can proceed in many different ways. A few of these ways are listed in the panel at the left side of the window (the exact assortment depends on the kind of search you performed).

▶ **Yes, finished searching.** Click to close the whole left panel (and lose the dog).

▶ **Yes, but make future searches faster.** Click this link to turn on Window's XP's Indexing Service. (To learn more, consult a book like *Windows XP Pro: The Missing Manual*)

▶ **Refine this search.** Windows XP often offers you a number of links that let you adjust the search settings you just used. For example, you may opt to perform the search again, this time including hidden and system files, or restrict the search to a different folder or disk, and so on.

▶ **Sort results by category.** Click the double-down-arrow circle button to open controls that let you sort the list—by name, date, and so on.

- **View results differently.** Click this double-down-arrow circle button to change the view of the results window—to Details, Tiles, or Thumbnails view, for example (see page 59).

- **Start a new search.** Click this option to start all over with new search parameters.

Using the results list

You can also manage the list of found files by treating the right side of the window just as you would any desktop window. For example:

- **Read all about it.** If you point to the name of a found icon, a pop-up rectangular balloon displays a little paragraph identifying the file's path, full name, modification date, size, and other information.

- **Find out where something is.** The In Folder column just to the right of an icon's name shows you exactly where it is on your machine, using the standard Windows path notation described in the box on page 42.

  You may have to widen the column to see the complete pathname; to do so, drag to the right the dividing line that is to the right of the In Folder column heading. Alternatively, point to the location information without clicking. As shown in Figure 2-10, a screen tip reveals the complete folder path.

- **Open the file.** If one of the found files is the one you were looking for, double-click it to open it. This, in fact, is what most people do most of the time when using the Search program. In many cases, you'll never even know or care *where* the file was—you just want to get into it.

- **Jump to an icon in its home folder.** If you want to view the found file in its native habitat, sitting somewhere on your hard drive, right-click the icon in the Search window and choose Open Containing Folder from the shortcut menu. The Search window instantly retreats to the background, as Windows opens the folder and then highlights the icon in question, sitting wherever it is on your hard drive.

- **Move or delete the file.** You can drag an item directly out of the found-files list onto the desktop, directly onto the Recycle Bin icon, or into a different folder, window, or disk. (For more on moving icons, and all related hazards, see Chapter 4.)

▶ **Send To, rename, or create a shortcut.** After highlighting an icon (or icons) in the list of found files, you can use any of the commands in the File menu: Send To (which lets you move the icon to one of several standard folders), Rename, and so on. (See page 101 for more on shortcuts.)

 Tip: You can also right-click a found icon to copy, move, rename, or create a shortcut to it. Just choose from the resulting shortcut menu.

▶ **Adjust the list.** By clicking the column headings of the results window, you can sort the list of found files in a variety of ways: by name, size, date modified, and so on. (You can reverse the order by clicking the column heading a second time.) You can also adjust the relative widths of the columns just by dragging the column-name dividers. And, as with almost any Windows window, you can drag the lower-right corner of the window to make it bigger or smaller.

▶ **Save the search setup.** By choosing File → Save Search, you can immortalize the search you've just set up. You might use this feature if you perform the same search each day—if, for example, you like to round up all the documents you created yesterday for backing up.

Windows XP automatically names the search file with a description it derives from the criteria you entered into the search fields, and adds the extension *.fnd* (for example, *Files Named Budget.fnd*). You can save the resulting search icon anywhere you like.

To use the search criteria again, double-click the saved *.fnd* file. The Search window opens, with your data already entered. Click the Search button to get the canned search underway.

Start → Help and Support

Choosing Start → Help and Support opens the new, improved Windows Help and Support Center window, which is described in Chapter 11. Once again, speed fans have an alternative to using the mouse—just press the F1 key to open the Help window.

Start → Control Panel

This extremely important command opens an extremely important window: the Control Panel, which houses two dozen programs you'll use to change almost every important setting on your PC. It's so important, in fact, that it gets a chapter of its own—Chapter 10.

Start → My Network Places

If your PC is part of a network, choosing this command opens the My Network Places window, which displays icons for the computers, disks, and folders other people on the office network have made available for rummaging. (For details on setting up and joining a network, see Chapter 13.)

Start → My Computer

The My Computer command is the trunk lid, the doorway to every single shred of software on your machine. When you choose this command, a window opens to reveal icons that represent each disk drive (or drive partition) in your machine, as shown in Figure 2-11.

 Note: If your PC is on a home or office network, your My Computer window will look a little different. See Figure 4-1 for some examples.

For example, by double-clicking your hard-drive icon and then the various folders on it, you can eventually see the icons for every single file and folder on your computer.

Start → My Music, My Pictures

Clearly, Microsoft imagined that most of its Windows XP customers would be multimedia mavens, decked out with digital cameras and MP3 music players. To

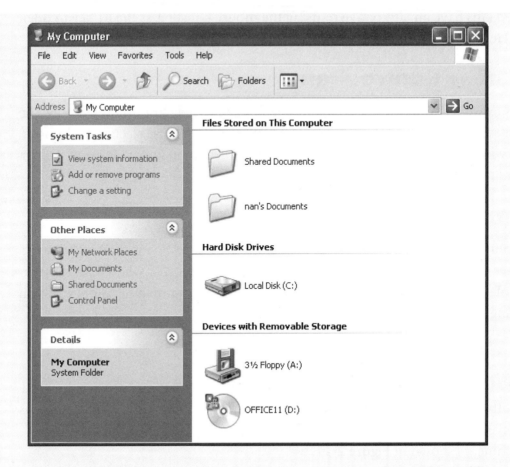

Figure 2-11. The My Computer window gives you an overview of your PC's world. You see icons representing your hard drive and any CD, floppy disk, and other internal or external drives Windows detects. If anything's in the drive, as is the case for the CD drive here, you can see that, too. Double-click the icon to read the contents.

hammer home the point, it has stocked your My Documents folder with My Pictures and My Music folders to store digital photos and music files, respectively.

If you do indeed have a digital camera or MP3 player (and it's Windows XP compatible), you'll probably find that whatever software came with it automatically dumps your photos into, and sucks your music files out of, these folders. You'll find more on this topic in Chapter 6.

Start → My Recent Documents

The My Recent Documents menu command gives your Start menu a submenu listing the last 15 documents you've opened. Using a list of recent documents can save you time when you want to reopen something you've worked on recently but you're not in the mood to burrow through folders to find its icon.

Note, however, that:

▶ Documents appear on the "recently used" list only if your applications are smart enough to update it. Most modern programs (including all Microsoft programs) perform this administrative task, but not all do.

▶ The Documents list doesn't know when you've deleted a document or moved it to another folder or disk; it continues to list the file even after it's gone. In that event, clicking the document's listing produces only an error message.

Of course, there's another easy way to open a document you've recently worked on. To start, simply launch the program you used to create it. Many programs maintain a list of recent documents at the bottom of the File menu; choose one of these names to open the corresponding file.

Start → My Documents

This command opens up your My Documents folder, which is designed to hold the data files you and your programs create.

Of course, you're welcome to file your documents *anywhere* on the hard drive, but most programs propose the My Documents folder as the target location for newly created documents.

Sticking with that principle makes a lot of sense for three reasons. First, it makes navigation easy. You never have to wonder where you filed some document, since all your stuff is sitting right there in the My Documents folder. Second, this arrangement makes backing up easy, in that you can drag the entire My Documents folder right onto a Zip disk or blank CD.

Third, remember that Windows XP has been designed from the ground up for *computer sharing*. It's ideal for any situation where different family members, students, or workers share the same PC. Each person who uses the computer will turn on the machine to find her own separate, secure set of files, folders, desktop pictures, Web bookmarks, preference settings—and My Documents folder. (More about user accounts in Chapter 12.)

UP TO SPEED

The Not-My-Documents Folder

Whenever you log on, Windows XP provides a My Documents folder just for you. (It actually sits in the My Computer → Local Disk (C:) → Documents and Settings → [*Your Name*] folder.)

This feature can be confusing if you're not expecting it. For example, if you stop by the computer after somebody else has logged in, none of your stuff is where you expect to find it—specifically, in the My Documents folder. That's because the computer no longer opens your documents folder when you choose Start → My Documents.

If this happens to you, check the name that appears at the top of the Start menu. It identifies who's currently logged on—and whose documents are showing up in the My Documents window.

CHAPTER 3:
WINDOWS, FOLDERS, AND
THE TASKBAR

▶ Windows in Windows

▶ The Desktop Window Overhaul

▶ Window Toolbars

▶ The Taskbar

▶ Taskbar Toolbars

WINDOWS GOT ITS NAME from the rectangles on the screen—the *windows*—where every computer activity takes place. You look at a Web page in a window, type into a window, read email in a window, and look at the contents of a folder in a window—sometimes all at once. But as you create more files, stash them in more folders, and launch more programs, it's easy to wind up paralyzed before a screen awash with cluttered, overlapping rectangles. Fortunately, Windows is crawling with icons, buttons, and other inventions to help you keep these windows (and the folders in them) under control. The taskbar along the bottom of your screen is another enormously helpful tool, as you'll see later in this chapter.

Windows in Windows

There are two categories of windows in Windows:

- **Desktop windows.** These windows, sometimes called Windows Explorer windows, include the windows that open when you double-click a disk or folder icon. This is where you organize your files and programs.

- **Application windows.** These are the windows where you do your work—in Word or Internet Explorer, for example.

Nonetheless, all windows have certain components in common (see Figure 3-1):

- **Title bar.** This top strip displays the name of the window. Drag it like a handle when you want to *move* the window on the screen.

- **Minimize button.** Click this box to temporarily hide a window, shrinking it down into the form of a button on your taskbar (page 68). You can open it again by clicking that button. *Keyboard shortcut:* Press Alt+Space bar, then N.

- **Maximize button.** Click this button to enlarge the window so that it fills the screen, gluing its edges to the screen borders. At this point, the maximize button turns into a *restore down* button (whose icon shows two overlapping rectangles), which you can click to return the window to its previous size. *Keyboard shortcut:* Press Alt+Space bar, then X.

 Tip: You can also maximize or restore a window by double-clicking its title bar.

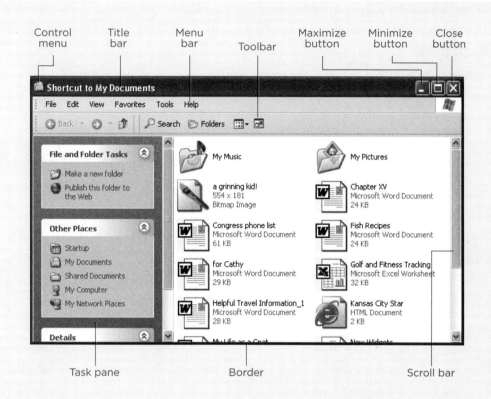

Figure 3-1. All windows have the same basic ingredients, making it easy to become an expert in window manipulation. This figure shows a desktop window—a disk or folder—but you'll encounter the same elements in application windows.

▶ **Close button.** Click the X button to close the window. *Keyboard shortcut:* Press Alt+F4.

▶ **Menu bar.** Click a menu title (such as File or Edit) to open a menu, revealing a list of commands available for that menu in this window. *Keyboard shortcut:* Press Alt+[underlined letter in menu], or press F10 to activate the menu bar in the active window and *then* press the underlined letter.

▶ **Toolbar.** Some windows offer rows of one-click shortcut buttons as equivalents for the menu commands that Microsoft thinks you'll use frequently.

- **Scroll bar.** A scroll bar appears on the right side or bottom of the window if the window isn't large enough to show all its contents (as described in the box on page 53).

- **Address bar.** This bar lets you type in a Web address or the address of a folder on your PC; when you press Enter or click Go, that Web page (or a list of the contents of that folder) appears.

- **Control icon.** The icon next to the title is actually a menu that offers commands for sizing, moving, and closing the window. You can double-click it to close a window. Otherwise, it's not very useful, because its commands duplicate the other doodads described here.

- **Borders.** You can change the size of a window by dragging these edges. Position your pointer over any border until the pointer turns into a double-headed arrow. Then drag inward or outward to reshape the window. (To resize a full-screen window, click the restore-down button first.)

Tip: You can resize a window in both dimensions at once just by dragging one of its corners. The diagonally striped ribs at the lower-right corner may suggest that it's the only corner you can drag, but it's not; all four corners work the same way.

The Task Pane

At the left side of every desktop window is a special, independent blue panel. For novices in particular, it's one of the most useful new features in Windows XP.

The programmers at Microsoft were clearly frustrated at having built so many interesting features into Windows that nobody knew existed. Most of these features appeared only when you right-clicked something—a folder, file, or whatever. But by Microsoft's research, as many as 75 percent of Windows users never right-click *anything.* They've been missing out on all of these features.

The idea behind the *task pane,* therefore, is to unearth the list of features that once lurked (and still lurk) inside shortcut menus. The contents of this blue

Scroll Bar Crash Course

Scroll bars are the strips that may appear at the right side or bottom of a window. The scroll bar signals you that the window isn't big enough to reveal all of its contents.

Click the arrows at each end of a scroll bar to move slowly through the window, or drag the square handle (the thumb) to move faster. (The position of the thumb relative to the entire scroll bar reflects your relative position in the entire window or document.) You can quickly move to a specific part of the window by holding the mouse button down at the location on the scroll bar where you want the thumb to be. The scroll bar rapidly scrolls to the desired location and then stops.

If your mouse has a little wheel on the top, you can scroll (in most programs) just by turning the wheel with your finger, even if your cursor is nowhere near the scroll bar. You can turbo-scroll by dragging the mouse upward or downward while keeping the wheel pressed down inside the window.

Finally, keyboard addicts should note that you can scroll without using the mouse at all. Press the Page Up or Page Down keys to scroll the window by one "windowful," or use the up and down arrow keys to scroll one line at a time.

panel change depending on the kind of window you're viewing (Figure 3-2), but the idea is always the same: to wave a frantic little software flag in front of your eyes, so that you'll notice some of the possibilities that are only a click away.

In a standard desktop window, for example, the task pane lists frequently sought commands like "Make a new folder," "Publish this folder to the Web," and "Share this folder" (with other people on your office network). Below that list of File and Folder Tasks is a box (Other Places) that offers one-click links to frequently accessed locations on your PC: My Computer, My Network Places, and so on.

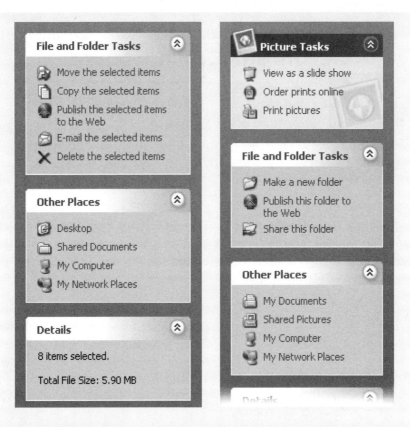

Figure 3-2. Left: The task pane is divided into blocks: tasks at top, places below that, file and folder info below that. If the pane becomes too long, you can collapse sections of the pane by clicking the round buttons.

Right: The tasks you see pertain to the folder you click—My Pictures, in this case.

Finally, at the bottom of every desktop task pane is a Details area. If you click a file icon, this panel displays its size, name, type, modification date, and (if it's a picture) dimensions. If you click a disk icon, you're able to see how full it is and how much it holds. If you select several icons at once, this panel shows you the sum of their file sizes—a great feature when you're burning a CD, for example, and don't want to exceed the 650 MB limit.

Depending on the *template* that's been applied to a folder, you may also see special multimedia task links: "View as a slideshow" and "Print this picture" for graphics files, "Play All" and "Shop for music online" for music folders, and so on.

Sizing, Moving, and Closing Windows

Any Windows window can cycle among three altered states. The buttons that resize windows are labeled back in Figure 3-1, and the full descriptions are right here:

▸ **Maximized** means that the window fills the screen. Its edges are glued to the boundaries of your monitor, and you can't see anything behind it. It expands to this size when you click its maximize button—an ideal arrangement when you're surfing the Web or working on a document for hours at a stretch, since the largest possible window means the least possible scrolling.

When a window is *maximized,* you can restore it (as described below) by pressing Alt+Space bar, then R.

▸ When you click a window's **minimize** button, the window disappears…but not completely. It's merely reincarnated as a button on the taskbar at the bottom of the screen. You can bring the window back by clicking this taskbar button, which bears the window's name. Minimizing a window is a great tactic when you want to see what's in the window behind it.

▸ A **restored** window is neither maximized nor minimized. It's a loose cannon, floating around on your screen as an independent rectangle. Because its edges aren't attached to the walls of your monitor, you can make it any size you like by dragging its borders.

 Tip: Double-clicking the title bar alternates a window between its maximized (full-screen) and restored conditions.

Moving a window

Moving a window is easy—just drag the title bar. Usually, you move a window to get it out of the way when you're trying to see what's *behind* it. However, moving windows around is also handy if you're moving or copying data between programs, or moving or copying files between drives or folders, as shown in Figure 3-3.

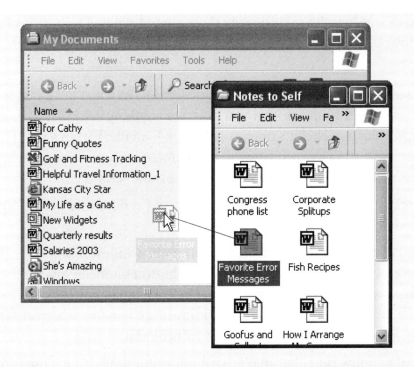

Figure 3-3. Creating two restored (free-floating) windows is a convenient preparation for copying information between them. Make both windows small and put them side by side, scroll if necessary, and then drag some highlighted material from one into the other.

Closing a window

You can close a window in any of the following ways:

▶ Click the close button (the X in the upper-right corner).

▶ Press Alt+F4.

- Double-click the Control icon in the upper-left corner.

- Single-click the Control icon in the upper-left corner, and then choose Close from the menu.

- Right-click the window's taskbar button, and then choose Close from the shortcut menu.

- In desktop windows, choose File → Close.

- Quit the program you're using, log off, or shut down the PC.

Be careful: in many programs, including Internet Explorer, closing the window also quits the program entirely.

 Tip: If you see two X buttons in the upper-right corner of your screen, then you're probably using what Microsoft calls an MDI, or *multiple document interface* program (see page 113). The outer window represents the application itself; the inner one represents the particular document you're working on.

If you want to close one document before working on another, be careful to click the inner Close button. Clicking the outer one exits the application entirely. If you have multiple documents open within one application, you can close the active document by pressing Ctrl+F4. The program may ask if you want to save the document before closing it, but nothing is certain, so get in the habit of pressing Ctrl+S before you press Ctrl+F4.

Working with Multiple Windows

Many people routinely keep four or five programs open at once, like a calendar, word processor, Web browser, and email program. Others (computer-book authors, for example) regularly work in just one program, but have several document windows open at once, representing several chapters. Clearly, learning how to manage and navigate a flurry of overlapping windows is an essential Windows survival skill.

Active and inactive windows

When you have multiple windows open on your screen, only one window is *active,* which means the following:

▶ It's in the foreground, *in front* of all other windows.

▶ It's the window that "hears" your keystrokes and mouse clicks.

▶ The title bar is vivid blue, and the background (inactive) window title bars are a lighter, more faded blue.

Of course, just because a window is in the background doesn't mean that it can't continue with whatever assignment you gave it—printing, downloading email, and so on. If a background program needs to pass a message to you (such as an error message), it automatically pops to the foreground, becoming the active program. When you respond to the message (usually by clicking OK), Windows XP sends the program *back* to the background.

To activate a background window, click anywhere on it. If other windows are covering up the background window, click its name on the taskbar (described on page 68).

You can also rotate through all the open windows and programs by pressing Alt+Tab. A little panel appears in the center of your screen, filled with the icons of open folders and programs; each press of Alt+Tab highlights the next in sequence. (Alt+Shift+Tab moves you one backward through the sequence.) Upon releasing the keys, you jump to the highlighted window, as though it's a high-tech game of Duck Duck Goose.

Of course, you won't become a true Zen master of window juggling until you've explored the multiple-window command center itself—the taskbar (see page 68).

The Desktop Window Overhaul

Windows' windows look just fine straight from the factory: all the edges are straight, and the text is perfectly legible. Still, if you're going to stare at this computer screen for half of your waking hours, you may as well investigate some of the ways these windows can be enhanced for better looks and greater efficiency. As it turns out, there's no end to the tweaks Microsoft lets you perform.

Icon and List Views

You can view the files and folders in a desktop window in any of several ways: as small icons, jumbo icons, a tidy list, and so on. Each window remembers its own view settings.

To change the view of a particular open window, choose one of these commands from its View menu (or from the little icon-filled desktop-window icon on the toolbar): Filmstrip, Thumbnails, Tiles, Icons, List, or Details. Here's a brief rundown:

▶ **Filmstrip view,** new in Windows XP, creates a slideshow right in the folder window. It's ideal for working with digital pictures, as you can see on page 145.

▶ **Thumbnails view** shows you a small preview of the document, making it, too, great for viewing folders full of photos. See Figure 3-4 for an example.

▶ **Files view,** also new to Windows XP, is a more readable improvement on the old favorite Icons view. It shows icons alphabetically in vertical columns, with details just to the right. Figure 3-1, for example, shows a window in Tiles view.

▶ **Icons view** sorts icons horizontally in rows, displaying only their names. The window at right in Figure 3-3, for example, happens to be in Icons view.

▶ **List view** earns its worldwide popularity by packing the most files into the space of a window. The window at left in Figure 3-3 is a good example of List view.

▶ **Details view** is similar to List view, except that it has additional columns revealing the item's size, its type, and the date and time it was last modified.

Some of these views are new in Windows XP. Filmstrip view, for example, is a home run for anyone with a digital camera or scanner. It turns the folder window into a slide show machine, complete with Next and Previous buttons

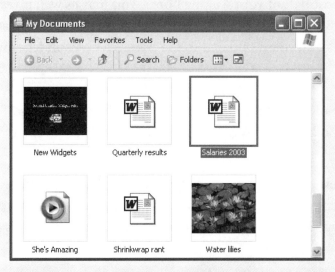

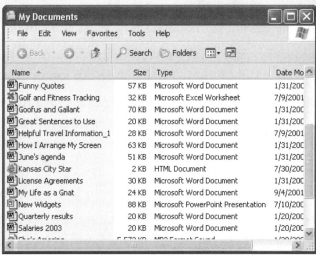

Figure 3-4. As you can see throughout this chapter, Windows lets you see your windows in many different ways. For example, Thumbnails view (top) gives you a preview of what you're clicking—and gives your mouse a nice, big target. Details view (bottom), by contrast, shows you the greatest amount of information about each item, making it dense and harder to read.

beneath an enlarged picture, as well as buttons that rotate the image on the screen. (You get this view automatically when you open your My Pictures folder.)

 Tip: In Filmstrip view, try right-clicking inside the large image of your photo. The resulting shortcut menu offers a number of very useful options, including Rotate commands, "Set as Desktop Background," and Send To (which lets you fire off the picture to somebody by email).

Changing the sorting order

Windows XP starts out arranging the icons alphabetically in two different groups. Folders come first, followed by the list of loose files in a second group.

But you don't have to be content with an alphabetical list. Windows XP is wildly flexible in this regard, letting you sort a window's contents in any of 32 ways.

To change the sorting criterion, choose View → Arrange Icons By, and then choose from the drop-down menu. The sorting possibilities listed here depend on which *columns* you've made visible in Details view (described in the next section). Generally, though, you'll find these options:

▶ **Name** arranges the files alphabetically.

▶ **Type** arranges the files in the window alphabetically by file *type*, such as Word documents, applications, JPEG files, and so on. (Technically, you're sorting files by their *filename extensions*; see page 130.)

▶ **Size** arranges files by size, smallest first. (Folders are unaffected; Windows never shows you the sizes of folders in its list views.) In the My Computer window, this option says Total Size and lists your disks by their capacity.

▶ **Free Space** is an option only in the My Computer window. Needless to say, it shows you how much space is left on each of your disks.

▶ **Show in Groups** is a fascinating enhancement in Windows XP. In any view except Filmstrip and List, it superimposes *headings* on your sorted list of icons, making the window look like an index (see Figure 3-5). When sorting the list by size, for example, the headings say Tiny, Small, Medium, and Folders. When sorting by modified date, you see headings called Yesterday, Last week, Earlier this month, and so on. It's an inspired idea that makes it much easier to hunt down specific icons in crowded folders.

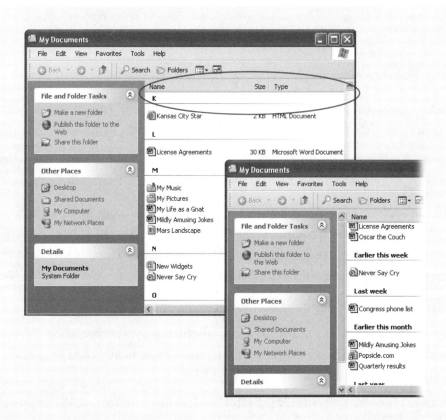

Figure 3-5. Show in Groups is a useful new view option (available in all views except Filmstrip and List) that superimposes a set of "filing tabs" on any window (circled), with headings that reflect the date, size, name, type, and so on. It's perfect for scanning a crowded list. This example shows sorting by name (left) and by modified date (right).

- **Auto Arrange,** available only in Icon and Tile views, isn't actually a sorting method; it's a straightening-up method. It rearranges the icons so they're equally spaced and neat. You can use this command on the desktop, too, which is one way to avoid CWDS (Cluttered Windows Desktop Syndrome).

- **Align to Grid** is slightly different. Whereas Auto Arrange always keeps icons or tiles in a tight, equally spaced clump, Align to Grid snaps dragged icons into position against an invisible underlying grid, even if they're scattered across the broad space of an open window (instead of clustered together in the upper-left corner). In other words, this feature is generally useful only when Auto Arrange is turned off.

Tip: You can't reverse the sort order of your icons (from Z to A, for example), except in Details view, described next.

Manipulating the Details view

You gotta love Details view. Clearly, Microsoft does: it's endowed Details view with much more flexibility and power than the other views.

First, there's the obvious advantage of being able to see the size and date of the objects in neat columns, as shown in Figure 3-4. Second, you can sort the contents by file size, type, or date simply by clicking the appropriate column heading. Click the same heading again to reverse the sort order.

Third, you can rearrange the column sequence just by dragging their headings horizontally. You can adjust column widths just by dragging the vertical divider bar (between column headings) from side to side.

Finally, you can manipulate the columns in a number of ways:

- To add more columns to the window, providing even more information about each icon, right-click any column heading and choose column names from the resulting drop-down menu. As you'll quickly discover, many of these column headings are useful only in folders that contain certain kinds of files—Date Picture Taken is for digital photos, Album Title is for music files, and so on.

▶ For even more control over the columns, choose View → Choose Details to open a dialog box where you can turn on the checkboxes beside the columns you want. You can even determine their sequence just by clicking a column name and then clicking Move Up or Move Down (although, as noted above, it's much easier to drag the column headings in the window yourself).

Once you've opened the Choose Details window, you *could* change the width of a column by editing the number at the bottom in the "Width of selected column (in pixels)" text box—but that's for geeks. It's much more natural to adjust column widths just by dragging the vertical divider bar.

Standard Folder Views

Now that you've twiddled and tweaked your system windows into a perfectly efficient configuration, you needn't go through the same exercises for each folder. Windows XP can immortalize your changes as the standard setting for *all* your windows.

Choose Tools → Folder Options → View tab. Click the Apply to All Folders button. When Windows XP asks whether you're sure you know what you're doing, click Yes.

At this point, all of your disk and folder windows open up with the same view, sorting method, and so on. You're still free to override those standard settings on a window-by-window basis, however.

And if you change your mind *again,* seeking to make all of your maverick folder windows snap back into line with the original standard settings, choose Tools → Folder Options → View tab and click the Reset All Folders button.

Window Toolbars

On the day it's born, every Windows XP desktop window has a standard *toolbar* across the top (see Figure 3-6). A toolbar is simply a strip of one-click buttons like Back, Forward, Search, and so on.

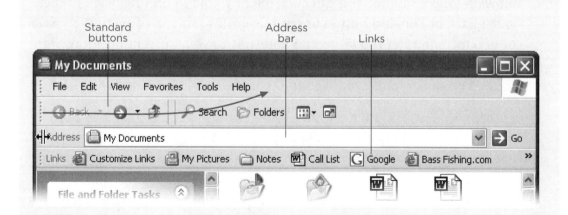

Figure 3-6. Here are the three basic toolbars that you can summon independently for any desktop window. By dragging the vertical left-side handle of a toolbar, you can place two or more bars on the same row, or even in the menu bar (arrow).

But by choosing View → Toolbars, or right-clicking a blank spot on a toolbar and pointing to Toolbars on the shortcut menu, you can add or hide whichever toolbars you like, on a window-by-window basis. Three different toolbars are available from the View menu: Standard Buttons, Address Bar, and Links.

 Tip: As anyone in the U.S. Justice Department could probably tell you, the Internet Explorer Web browser is deeply embedded in Windows itself. These window toolbars are perfect examples: they appear not only in desktop windows but also in Internet Explorer when you're browsing the Web.

The Standard Buttons Toolbar

This toolbar helps you navigate your desktop (or the Web). The desktop version contains buttons like these:

▶ **Back, Forward.** On the Web, these buttons let you return to Web pages you've just seen. At the desktop, they display the contents of a disk or folder you've just seen.

But wait—there's more! You can click the tiny down-pointing black triangle on the Back or Forward button to see a drop-down menu of every Web page (or desktop window) you visited on your way to your current position. Similarly, if you point to one of these buttons without clicking, a tooltip indicates which Web site or folder you'll go to if you click.

 Tip: These Back and Forward buttons work exactly the same in both Internet Explorer and the Windows desktop.

▶ **Up.** This button, short for "up a level," displays the *contents* of the folder that contains the one you're examining. If you're looking at the contents of, say, the Idaho folder, clicking this button would open the USA folder that contains it.

▶ **Search.** Opens the Search panel described on page 36. *Keyboard shortcut:* F3.

▶ **Folders.** Hides or shows the master map of disks and folders at the left side of the window, re-creating the two-panel Windows Explorer navigational display described in the next chapter.

▶ **Views.** Opens a short menu listing the different window views: Tiles, Thumbnails, Details, and so on. In other words, it duplicates the View menu on the menu bar. (More details about these views begin on page 59.)

The Address Bar

In a Web browser, the Address bar is where you type the addresses of the Web sites you want to visit. At the desktop, the Address bar obeys your commands in all kinds of ways. Here's what you can type there (pressing Enter afterward):

▶ **A Web address.** You can leave off the *http://* portion. Just type the body of the Web address, such as *www.sony.com*, into this strip. When you click Go or press Enter, the icons in your desktop window are replaced by the actual Web page you specified. Suddenly you're in Internet Explorer.

- **A search phrase.** If you type some text into this strip that isn't obviously a Web address, Windows assumes that you're telling it, "Go online and search for this phrase."

- **A folder name.** You can also type one of several important folder names into this strip, such as *My Computer, My Documents, My Music,* and so on. When you click Go or press Enter, that particular folder window opens.

  The little down-arrow button at the right end of the Address bar is very useful, too. It offers a list of the primary locations on your PC (My Computer, My Documents, your hard drives, and so on) for instant location jumping.

In each case, as soon as you begin to type, a drop-down list of recently visited Web sites, files, or folders appears below the Address bar. Windows XP is trying to save you some typing. If you see what you're looking for, click it with the mouse, or press the down arrow key to highlight the one you want and then press Enter.

The Links Toolbar

At first glance, you might assume that the purpose of this toolbar is to provide links to your favorite Web sites. And sure enough, that's what it's for—when you're using Internet Explorer.

Although few realize it, you can drag *any icon at all* onto the toolbar—files, folders, disks, programs, or whatever—to turn them into one-click buttons. In short, think of the Links toolbar as a miniature Start menu for places and things you use most often.

To add your own icons, just drag them from the desktop or any folder window directly onto the toolbar, at any time. Here are a few possibilities, just to get your juices flowing:

- Install toolbar icons of the three or four programs you use the most (or a few documents you work on every day).

- Install toolbar icons for shared folders on the network. This arrangement saves several steps when you want to connect to them.

- Install toolbar icons of Web sites you visit often, so that you can jump directly to them when you sit down in front of your PC each morning.

You can drag these links around on the toolbar to put them into a different order, or remove a link by dragging it away—directly into the Recycle Bin, if you like. (They're only shortcuts; you're not actually deleting anything important.) To rename something here—a good idea, since horizontal space in this location is so precious—right-click it and choose Rename from the shortcut menu.

 Tip: When you're viewing a Web page, dragging a Web link from this toolbar into the address bar takes you to the page. But when you're viewing a *folder window*, dragging one of these Web links to the address bar creates an *Internet shortcut file* in the window. When double-clicked, this special document connects you to the Internet and opens the specified Web page.

The Taskbar

The permanent blue stripe across the bottom of your screen is the taskbar, one of the most prominent and important elements of the Windows interface (see Figure 3-7).

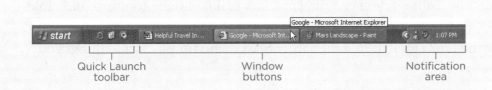

Figure 3-7. When you see nothing but microscopic icons, point without clicking to view an identifying tooltip.

The taskbar has several segments, each dedicated to an important function. Its right end, the *notification area,* contains little status icons that display the time, whether or not you're online, whether or not your laptop's plugged in, and so on. The main portion of the taskbar, of course, helps you keep your open windows and programs under control. You can even dress up your taskbar with additional little segments called toolbars, described on page 74.

This section covers each of these features in turn.

The Notification Area

In Windows XP, Microsoft has chosen a new name for the area formerly known as the tray (the group of tiny icons at the right end of the taskbar): the notification area. (Why use one syllable when eight will do?)

The purpose is much the same: to give you quick access to little status indicators and pop-up menus that control various functions of your PC. Many a software installer inserts its own little icon into this area: fax software, virus software, palmtop synchronization software, and so on.

To figure out what an icon represents, point to it without clicking so that a tooltip appears. To access the controls that accompany it, try both left-clicking and right-clicking the tiny icon. Often, each click produces a different pop-up menu filled with useful controls.

Despite the expansion of its name, you'll probably discover that this area is much smaller than it used to be. On a new PC, for example, you may find little more than the current time.

 Tip: By double-clicking the time display, you open the Date and Time Control Panel program. And if you point to the time without clicking, a tooltip appears to tell you the day of the week and today's date.

That's because Microsoft's XP anti-clutter campaign reached a fever pitch when it came to this component of the operating system. The designers of Windows had noticed that software companies large and small had been indiscriminately dumping little icons into this area, sometimes for prestige more than utility.

Turning Off Notification Area Auto-Hiding

In general, the temporary removal of notification-area icons you haven't used in a while is a noble ambition. Most of the time, you truly won't miss any invisible icons, and their absence will make the icons you do use stand out all the more.

Still, you can tell Windows to leave your tray alone—to leave every notification-area icon in full view all the time. To do so, right-click a blank area of the taskbar; from the drop-down menu, choose Properties. At the bottom of the resulting dialog box, turn off the "Hide inactive icons" checkbox, and click OK.

If that seems a little drastic, don't miss the Customize button just to the right of that checkbox. It opens a list of every tray icon that would normally

appear, if it weren't for Windows XP's efforts. Click in the Behavior column to produce a pop-up menu for each item. Choose the status you want for each individual tray icon: "Hide when inactive," "Always hide," or "Always show." Finally, click OK.

Therefore, Microsoft laid down two policies concerning this critical piece of screen real estate:

▶ Even Microsoft's own usual junk—the speaker icon for volume control, the display icon for changing screen resolution, the battery icon for laptops, and so on—is absent on a fresh XP installation. If you want to add these controls to the notification area, you must do it yourself, using the corresponding Control Panel programs as described in Chapter 10.

- If you don't use a Notification area icon for a couple of weeks, Windows XP takes the liberty of hiding it from you. But you can retake control—see Figure 3-8 for details. (And to make the Notification area stop being so darn tidy, see the box on page 70.)

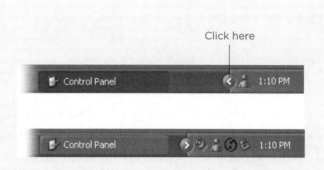

Figure 3-8. If you see a > button, Windows is telling you that it has hidden some of your notification-area icons. Click this button to expand the notification area, bringing all of the hidden icons into view (bottom).

Window Buttons

Every time you open a window, whether at the desktop or in one of your programs, the taskbar sprouts a button bearing that window's name and icon. Buttons make it easy to switch among open programs and windows: Just click one to bring its associated window into the foreground, even if it has been minimized.

The taskbar is the antidote for COWS (Cluttered Overlapping Window Syndrome). In fact, if you work with a lot of windows, you'll run smack into one of the biggest and most visible changes in Windows XP: taskbar button *groups*.

The new Windows taskbar does two things that no Windows taskbar has done before. First, when conditions become crowded, it automatically groups the names of open windows into a single menu that sprouts from the corresponding program button, as shown at bottom in Figure 3-9. Click the taskbar button bearing the program's name to produce a pop-up menu of the window names. Now you can jump directly to the one you want.

Figure 3-9. Left: Click a taskbar button with a tiny arrow to see the list of windows it's concealing.

Right: Right-click to operate on all of these windows at once.

Second, even when there is plenty of room, Windows XP aligns the buttons into horizontal groups *by program.* So you'll see all the Word-document buttons appear, followed by all the Excel-document buttons, and so on.

Despite these dramatic changes, most of the following time-honored basics still apply:

▶ To bring a window to the foreground, making it the active window, click its button on the taskbar. (If clicking a button doesn't bring a window forward, it's because Windows has combined several open windows into a single button. Just click the corresponding program's button as though it's a menu, and then choose the specific window you want from the resulting list, as shown in Figure 3-9.)

▶ To *hide* an active window that's before you on the screen, click its taskbar button—a great feature that a lot of PC fans miss. (To hide a background window, click its taskbar button *twice:* once to bring the window forward, again to hide it.)

▶ To minimize, maximize, restore, or close a window, even if you can't see it on the screen, right-click its button on the taskbar and choose the appropriate command from the shortcut menu. It's a real time-saver to close a window without first bringing it into the foreground. (You can still right-click a window's name when it appears in one of the consolidated taskbar menus described earlier.)

▶ To arrange all visible windows in an overlapping pattern, as shown in Figure 3-10, right-click a blank spot on the taskbar and choose Cascade Windows from the shortcut menu.

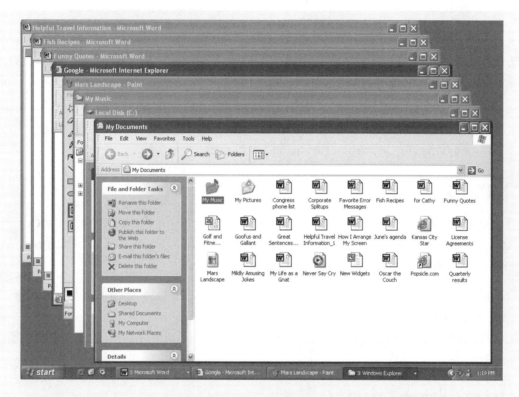

Figure 3-10. To see all open windows in a neat stack, right-click anywhere on the taskbar and choose Cascade. Then you can click any window's title bar to bring it to the foreground.

▶ To arrange all non-minimized windows in neat little boxes, each getting an equal rectangular chunk of your screen, right-click a blank spot on the taskbar and choose Tile Windows Vertically or Tile Windows Horizontally from the shortcut menu.

▶ To minimize all the windows in one fell swoop, right-click a blank spot on the taskbar and choose Show the Desktop from the shortcut menu—or just press the Windows logo key+D.

Note: When the taskbar is crowded with buttons, it may not be easy to find a blank spot to click. Usually there's a little gap near the right end. You can make it easier to find some blank space by enlarging the taskbar, as described in Figure 3-8.

▶ If you change your mind, the taskbar shortcut menu always includes an Undo command for the last taskbar command you invoked. (Its wording changes to reflect your most recent action—"Undo Minimize All," for example.)

▶ To close the windows from different programs all at once, Ctrl-click their taskbar buttons to select them. Then right-click the last one you clicked, and choose Close Group from the shortcut menu.

Taskbar Toolbars

Taskbar *toolbars* are separate, recessed-looking areas on the taskbar that offer special-function features. You can even build your own toolbar, for example, stocked with documents related to a single project.

To make a toolbar appear or disappear, right-click a blank spot on the taskbar and choose from the Toolbars shortcut menu (Figure 3-11). The ones with checkmarks are visible now; select one to make the toolbar (and checkmark) disappear.

Quick Launch Toolbar

The Quick Launch toolbar, once you've made it appear, is fantastically useful. In fact, in sheer convenience, it puts the Start menu to shame. It contains icons for functions that Microsoft assumes you'll use most often. They include:

▶ **Show Desktop,** a one-click way to minimize (hide) *all* the windows on your screen to make your desktop visible. Don't forget about this button the next time you need to burrow through some folders, put something in the Recycle Bin, or perform some other activity in your desktop folders. *Keyboard shortcut:* Windows logo key+D.

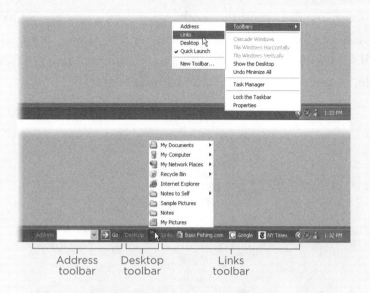

Figure 3-11. Top: Make toolbars appear by right-clicking a blank area on the taskbar, if you can find one.

Bottom: If you've added too many icons to the toolbar, a >> button appears at its right end. Click it to expose a list of the commands or icons that didn't fit.

▶ **Launch Internet Explorer Browser,** for one-click access to the Web browser included with Windows XP.

▶ **Windows Media Player,** for one-click access to the music and movie player included with Windows XP (see Chapter 6).

The buttons detailed above are only hints of this toolbar's power, however. What makes it great is how easy it is to add your *own* icons—particularly those you use frequently. There's no faster or easier way to open them (no matter what mass of cluttered windows is on your screen), since the taskbar displays your favorite icons at all times.

To add an icon to this toolbar, simply drag it there, as shown in Figure 3-12. To remove an icon, just drag it off the toolbar— directly onto the Recycle Bin, if you like. (You're not actually removing any software from your computer.) If you think you'll somehow survive without using Windows Media Player each day, for example, remove it from the Quick Launch toolbar.

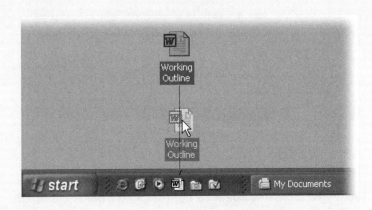

Figure 3-12. You can add almost any kind of icon (an application, document file, disk, folder, Control Panel, or whatever) to the Quick Launch toolbar just by dragging it there (top); a thick vertical bar shows you where it'll appear. The only challenge is to find the folder that houses the icon you want to add.

CHAPTER 4:
ORGANIZING YOUR STUFF

▶ Creating a Folder

▶ The Folders of Windows XP

▶ Life with Icons

▶ Copying and Moving Folders and Files

▶ The Recycle Bin

▶ Shortcut Icons

▶ Burning CDs from the Desktop

EVERY DISK, FOLDER, FILE, application, printer, and networked computer is represented on your screen by an icon. To avoid spraying your screen with thousands of overlapping icons seething like snakes in a pit, Windows organizes icons into folders, puts those folders into *other* folders, and so on.

This folder-in-a-folder-in-a-folder scheme works beautifully at reducing screen clutter, but it means that you've got some hunting to do whenever you want to open a particular icon. Helping you navigate and manage your files, folders, and disks with less stress and greater speed was one of the primary design goals of Windows—and of this chapter.

Creating a Folder

To create a new folder to hold your icons, right-click where you want the folder to appear (on the desktop, or in any desktop window except My Computer), and choose New → Folder from the shortcut menu. The new folder appears with its temporary "New Folder" name highlighted. Type a new name for the folder and then press Enter.

Note: Before Windows took over the universe, folders were called *directories*, and folders inside them were called *subdirectories*. Keep that in mind the next time you're reading an old user guide, magazine article, or computer book.

The Folders of Windows XP

The top-level, all-encompassing, mother-ship window of your PC is the My Computer window. From within this window, you have access to every disk, folder, and file on your computer. Its slogan may as well be: "If it's not in here, it's not on your PC."

To see it, choose Start → My Computer. You generally see several categories of icons (Figure 4-1):

▶ **Hard Disk Drives.** These icons, of course, represent your PC's hard drive (or drives, if you've installed or attached additional ones). Most people, most of the time, are most concerned with the Local Disk (C:), which represents the internal hard drive preinstalled in your computer. (You're welcome to rename this icon, by the way, just as you would any icon.)

▶ **Files Stored on This Computer.** This category appears only if your computer is a member of a *workgroup*, not if it's part of a domain network (see the box on page 80). These folders, which bear the names of people with accounts on the PC, store links to all files and preferences for each person.

Figure 4-1. The My Computer window, shown here on a corporate-network PC, is the starting point for any folder-digging you want to do. It shows the disk drives of your PC. If you double-click the icon of a removable-disk drive (like your CD-ROM drive, Zip drive, or Jaz drive), you receive only an error message unless there's actually a disk in the drive.

- **Devices with Removable Storage.** Here, Windows is talking about your floppy drive, CD or DVD drive, Zip drive, USB flash drive, and so on.

- **Scanners and Cameras.** This is where you see the icons for any digital cameras or scanners you've installed.

- **Other.** You may also see an icon for the Control Panel here.

FREQUENTLY ASKED QUESTION

The View from a Window

The My Computer window at home and the My Computer window on my PC at work don't look alike. What's up with that?

The difference is that your PC at work is probably on a network domain, and the one at home belongs to a smaller, less formal workgroup network (Chapter 13). As you'll discover over and over again, the Windows XP experience is slightly different depending on which kind of network you're on.

On a computer that's part of a domain, you see only two sections:

"Hard Disk Drives" and "Devices with Removable Storage" (Figure 4-1).

On a workgroup PC, you get a third section, called "Files Stored on This Computer." It lists the My Documents folders for each person who has an account on—and who has logged on to—this computer.

Why the difference? Because in a corporation, your files probably aren't even on your PC. They probably sit on some centralized server machine elsewhere on the network. So there probably aren't many "files stored on this computer."

What's in the Local Disk (C:) Window

You might be surprised to learn that your main hard drive window doesn't actually contain anything much that's useful to you, the PC's human companion. It's organized primarily for Windows' own benefit.

If you double-click the Local Disk C: icon in My Computer—that is, your primary hard drive's icon—a direly worded message lets you know that these files are hidden. "This folder contains files that keep your system working properly," it says. "You should not modify its contents." (Figure 4-2 shows a similar message.)

All of this important-sounding prose is aimed at the kind of person who, before the invention of this warning message, fearlessly or naively cruised through the important system files of their PCs, deleting and moving files until the computer was inoperable (and then calling Microsoft for tech support).

Truth is, the C: drive also contains a lot of stuff that *doesn't* belong to Windows—including your files. So when you're just looking (but not touching) the Windows system files, or when you want to burrow around in your own folders, it's perfectly OK to click the "Show the contents of this folder" link. Suddenly the C: drive's formerly invisible contents appear. They include these standard folders:

▶ **Documents and Settings.** This folder contains folders named for the different people who use this PC. In general, Limited account holders (page 324) aren't allowed to open anybody else's folder.

   If you're the sole proprietor of the machine, there's only one account folder here—and it's named for you, of course. If not, there's a folder here for each person who has an account on this PC.

▶ **Program Files.** This folder contains all of your applications—Word, Excel, Internet Explorer, your games, and so on. But that isn't the impression you get when you first open the folder (Figure 4-2).

   Fortunately, making them appear on your screen is easy enough: simply click the words "Show the contents of this folder." They appear just below the "These files are hidden" message, and also in the task pane. (The Local Disk (C:) drive window works the same way.)

Figure 4-2. Top: The C: drive and the Program Files folder start out looking empty.

Bottom: Here's what Microsoft Word actually looks like—75 little software crumbs in your Program Files → Microsoft Office → Office10 folder. Only one of these icons (the one called WINWORD) is the actual program. But don't try to move it, or any of its support files, out of this folder.

Tip: It's OK, however, and even encouraged, to drag a program icon onto your Start menu or Quick Launch toolbar, which leaves the program in the folder where it belongs while giving you a handy way to launch it.

▶ **Windows** (or **WINNT**, if you upgraded your machine from Windows 2000). Here's another folder that Microsoft wishes its customers would simply ignore. One exception: the Fonts folder contains the icons that represent the various typefaces installed on your machine. You're free to add or remove icons from this folder.

Your Account Folder

Everything that makes your Windows XP experience your own sits inside the Local Disk (C:) → Documents and Settings → [Your Name] folder. This is where Windows stores your preferences, documents, pictures and music, and so on.

In general, the only action you'll perform that involves this folder is periodically backing up the Local Disk (C:) → Documents and Settings → [Your Name] folder → My Documents folder.

Your account folder actually holds much more than this, but the rest of the folders are hidden, reserved for use by Windows itself. The hidden folders include: Application Data (which your programs may use to store user-specific settings and files), Local Settings (Internet Explorer's history list and cache file, for example), NetHood (shortcuts for the icons in your My Network Places window), My Recent Documents (document shortcuts, the ones that show up in the optional My Recent Documents submenu of the Start menu), and SendTo, which is described later in this chapter.

 Tip: Ordinarily, if your name is, say, Chris, you're not allowed to open the Frank's Documents folder; if you've been given a Limited XP account (page 324), then double-clicking it produces only an error message. That's the Windows XP security system at work.

But My Computer also contains a folder called Shared Documents. This folder is like the community bulletin board, in that everybody who uses this PC is free to deposit things, take things out, and read whatever resides there. See Chapter 12 for details.

Navigating My Computer

Most of the time, you can get where you're going on your computer using the commands, programs, and folders listed in the Start menu. But when you need to find something that isn't listed there—when you need to burrow manually through the labyrinth of folders on the machine—Windows offers two key methods of undertaking a folder quest.

First, you can open the My Computer window, as described at the beginning of this chapter. From there, you double-click one folder after another, burrowing ever deeper into the folders-within-folders.

As you navigate your folders, keep in mind the power of the Backspace key. Each time you press it, you jump to the parent window of the one you're now looking at—the one that contains the previous folder. For example, if you're perusing the My Pictures folder inside My Documents, pressing Backspace opens the My Documents window. (Backspace also works in most Web browsers, functioning as the Back button.)

Likewise, the Alt key, pressed with the right and left arrow keys, serves as a Back and Forward button. Use this powerful shortcut (instead of clicking the corresponding buttons on the Standard toolbar) to "walk" backward or forward through the list of windows most recently opened.

Navigating with Windows Explorer

The second method of navigating the folders on your PC is called Windows Explorer— for long-time Windows veterans, a familiar sight. (Note that some people use the term "Windows Explorer" to refer to everyday folder windows. In this book, the term refers exclusively to the split-window view shown in Figure 4-3.)

Using this method, you work in a single window that shows every folder on the machine at once. As a result, you're less likely to lose your bearings using Windows Explorer than burrowing through folder after folder, as described above.

You can jump into Explorer view using any of these methods:

▶ Shift–double-click any disk or folder icon.

▶ Right-click a disk or folder icon (even if it's in the Start menu) and choose Explore from the shortcut menu.

▶ Click Folders on the Standard toolbar.

▶ Choose View → Explorer Bar → Folders.

▶ Choose Start → All Programs → Accessories → Windows Explorer.

▶ Choose Start → Run, type *explorer*, and then press Enter.

No matter which method you use, the result is a window like the one shown in Figure 4-3.

As you can see, this hierarchical display splits the window into two panes. The left pane displays *only* disks and folders. The right pane displays the contents (folders *and* files) of any disk or folder you click. You can manipulate the icons on either side much as you would any other icons. For example, double-click one to open it, drag it to the Recycle Bin to delete it, or drag it into another folder in the folder list to move it elsewhere on your machine.

This arrangement makes it very easy to move files and folders around on your hard drive. First, make the right pane display the icon you want to move. Then, set up the left pane so that you can see the destination folder or disk—and drag the right-side icon from one side to the other.

Tip: When you click a folder icon (not its + button) on the left side of an Explorer window, Windows expands that folder's listing and instantly closes whichever folder you previously expanded.

If you really want to open two different "branches" (subfolders) of your folder tree simultaneously—to compare the contents of two folders simultaneously, for example—just click the little + symbols beside folder names instead of clicking the folder names. When you click the + buttons, Explorer leaves open the listings for the subfolders you've already opened.

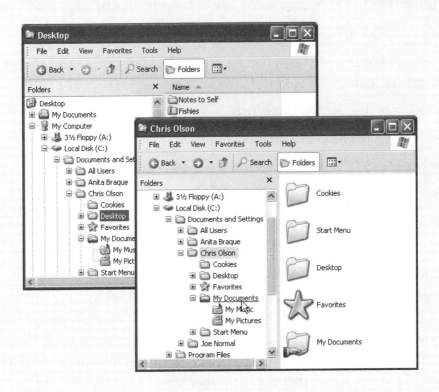

Figure 4-3. Front: Windows Explorer offers a treetop view of your computer's hierarchy. When you click a disk or folder in the left pane, the right pane displays its contents, including files and folders.

Back: If you turn off the new "simple folder view" display, the dotted vertical and horizontal lines in the left pane help you keep track of the hierarchical levels.

When the panel is too narrow

As shown in Figure 4-3, expanding a folder provides a new indented list of folders inside it. If you expand folders-within-folders to a sufficient level, the indentation may push the folder names so far to the right that you can't read them. You can remedy this problem with any of the following actions:

▶ Adjust the relative sizes of the window halves by dragging the vertical bar between them.

- Position your mouse pointer over a folder whose name is being chopped off. A tooltip balloon appears to display the full name of the folder.

- Use the horizontal scroll bar at the bottom of the left pane to shift the contents.

Viewing folder contents

To see what's in one of the disks or folders listed at the left side of the Explorer window, you can use either of these techniques:

- In the left pane, click a folder or disk; the contents appear in the right pane. To expand the listing for a disk or folder, double-click its name, double-click its icon, or single-click the + button beside it.

- Right-click a folder in the left pane and select Open from the shortcut menu. A new window opens, displaying the contents of the folder you clicked. (To open a *program or document* appearing in either side of the window, double-click it as usual.)

The right-side pane of the Explorer window behaves exactly like any folder window. Don't forget that you can change it to an icon view or list view, for example, using the View menu as usual.

Keyboard shortcuts

If you arrive home one day to discover that your mouse has been stolen, or if you just like using the keyboard, you'll enjoy the shortcuts that work in the Windows Explorer window, as shown in Table 4-1.

Table 4-1. Windows Explorer Keyboard Shortcuts

SHORTCUT	DESCRIPTION
Left arrow	Collapses the highlighted folder, or if it's already collapsed, highlights its "parent" folder. (The + key on your numeric keypad does the same thing.)
Right arrow	Expands a highlighted folder, or if it's already expanded, highlights the first folder inside it. (The – key on your numeric keypad does the same thing.)

Table 4-1. Windows Explorer Keyboard Shortcuts (continued)

SHORTCUT	DESCRIPTION
* (on number pad)	Displays *all* of the selected folder's subfolders.
F6 or Tab	Highlights the other half of the window.
Alt+left arrow	Highlights whichever folder you last highlighted.
Backspace	Highlights the "parent" disk or folder of whatever's highlighted.
Ctrl+Z	Undoes whatever you just did in this Explorer window.
Home, End	Highlights first or last icon in the folder list.
A, B, C, ...	Highlights the first visible file or folder in the left-pane hierarchy that matches the letter you typed. Type the same letter again to highlight the next matching icon.

You can also press the letter keys to highlight a folder or file that begins with that letter, or the up and down arrow keys to "walk" up and down the list.

Life with Icons

Both of the navigational schemes described so far in this chapter have only one goal in life: to help you manage your icons. You could spend your entire workday just mastering the techniques of naming, copying, moving, and deleting these icons—and plenty of people do.

Here's the crash course.

Renaming Your Icons

To rename a file, folder, printer, or disk icon, you need to open up its *renaming rectangle.* You can do so with any of the following methods:

▶ Highlight the icon and then press the F2 key at the top of your keyboard.

▶ Click carefully, just once, on a previously highlighted icon's name.

▶ Right-click the icon and choose Rename from the shortcut menu.

You can even rename your hard drive, so that you don't go your entire career with a drive named "Local Disk." Just rename its icon (in the My Computer window) as you would any other. You're not allowed to rename important system folders like Documents and Settings, Recycle Bin, Windows, WINNT, and System32, however.

In any case, once the renaming rectangle has appeared around the current name, simply type the new name you want, and then press Enter. Feel free to use all the standard text-editing tricks while you're typing: Press Backspace to fix a typo, press the left and right arrow keys to position the insertion point, and so on. When you're finished editing the name, press Enter to make it stick. (If another icon in the folder has the same name, Windows beeps and makes you choose another name.)

Tip: A folder or file name can be up to 255 characters long, including spaces and the *filename extension* (the three-letter suffix that identifies the file type). Because they're reserved for behind-the-scenes use, Windows doesn't let you use any of these symbols in a folder or filename: \ / : * ? " < > |

If you like, you can give more than one file or folder the same name, as long as they're not in the same folder. For example, you can have as many files named "Letter to Smith" as you wish, as long as each is in a different folder.

Windows XP comes factory-set not to show you filename extensions. That's why you sometimes might think you see two different files called, say, Quarterly Sales, both in the same folder.

The explanation is that one filename may end with .doc (a Word document), and the other may end with .xls (an Excel document). But because these suffixes are hidden (page 130), the files look like they have exactly the same name.

Warning: If you highlight a bunch of icons at once and then open the renaming rectangle for any one of them, you wind up renaming all of them. For example, if you've highlighted folders called Cats, Dogs, and Fish, renaming one of them *Animals* changes the original names to Animals (1), Animals (2), and Animals (3). Remain calm and press Ctrl+Z repeatedly until you've restored all the original names.

Icon Properties

As every Windows veteran knows, properties are a big deal in Windows. *Properties* are preference settings that you can change independently for every icon on your machine.

To view the Properties dialog box for an icon, choose from these techniques:

▶ Right-click the icon; choose Properties from the shortcut menu.

▶ While pressing Alt, double-click the icon.

▶ Highlight the icon; press Alt+Enter.

These settings aren't the same for every kind of icon, however. Here's what you can expect when opening the Properties dialog boxes of various icons (see Figure 4-4).

▶ **My Computer.** Here's where you can look up the specifications of your computer's processor, memory, and components (modem, monitor, mouse, and so on).

▶ **Disks.** This dialog box contains controls for sharing and security, as well as the disk's name (which you can change), how much of it is full, and a list of drives.

▶ **Data files.** The Properties for a plain old document depend on what kind of document it is. You always see a General tab containing all the obvious information about the document (location, size, modification date, and so on), but other tabs may also appear (especially for Microsoft Office files). You can even add your own customized properties using the Custom tab.

▶ **Folders.** These Properties are the same as found for data files, with the addition of the Sharing tab, which lets other people into the folder (either in person or from across the network).

▶ **Program Files.** Here's where you look up details about the program's version number, corporate parent, language, and so on.

▶ **Shortcuts.** You can read about these useful controls on page 87.

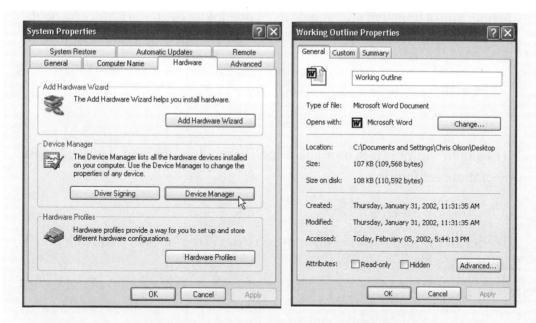

Figure 4-4. To view the information and settings for any icon, right-click it and choose Properties. What you see varies widely depending on the icon. For example, the properties for My Computer (left) include information on hardware hooked up to your PC, your system software, and so on. For a Word file (right), you get information on the document's size, location, and so on.

Copying and Moving Folders and Files

Windows XP offers two different techniques for moving files and folders from one place to another: dragging them, and using the Copy and Paste commands.

Whichever method you choose, you must start by showing Windows which icons you want to copy or move—by *highlighting* them.

Highlighting Icons

To highlight (that is, select) one icon, just click it once. But you don't have to move, copy, or delete one icon at a time; you can select a number of icons in the same folder or disk window. You may want to employ this technique, for example, when moving a bunch of documents from one folder to another, or copying them onto a backup disk en masse.

Tip: It's easiest to work with multiple icons in Details view (page 63), where every icon appears in a single column.

To highlight multiple files in preparation for moving, copying, or deleting, use one of these techniques:

To highlight all the icons

To select all the icons in a window, press Ctrl+A (the keyboard equivalent of the Edit → Select All command).

To highlight several icons

You can drag across file and folder names to highlight a group of consecutive icons. Start with your cursor above and to one side of the icons, then drag diagonally. As you drag, you create a temporary dotted-line rectangle. Any icon that falls within this rectangle darkens to indicate that it's been selected.

Alternatively, click the first icon you want to highlight and Shift-click the last file. All the files in between are automatically selected, along with the two icons you clicked. (These techniques work in any folder view: Details, Thumbnails, or whatever.)

Tip: If you include a particular icon in your diagonally dragged group by mistake, Ctrl-click it to remove it from the selected cluster.

To highlight only specific icons

Suppose you want to highlight only the first, third, and seventh icons in the list. Start by clicking icon No. 1, then Ctrl-click each of the others. (If you Ctrl-click a selected icon *again*, you deselect it. A good time to use this trick is when you highlight an icon by accident.)

The Ctrl key trick is especially handy if you want to select almost all the icons in a window. Press Ctrl+A to select everything in the folder, then Ctrl-click any unwanted subfolders to deselect them.

Copying by Dragging Icons

As you know, you can drag icons from one folder to another, from one drive to another, from a drive to a folder on another drive, and so on. (When you've selected several icons, drag any *one* of them and the others will go along for the ride.)

Here's what happens when you drag icons in the usual way (using the left mouse button):

- Dragging to another folder on the same disk *moves* the folder or file.
- Dragging from one disk to another *copies* the folder or file.
- Pressing the Ctrl key while dragging to another folder on the same disk *copies* the icon. (If you do so within a single window, Windows creates a duplicate of the file called "Copy of [filename].")
- Pressing Shift while dragging from one disk to another *moves* the folder or file (without leaving a copy behind).
- Pressing Alt while dragging an icon creates a shortcut of it.

 Tip: You can move or copy icons by dragging them either into an open window or directly onto a disk or folder icon. Press Esc to cancel a dragging operation at any time.

The right-mouse-button trick

Think you'll remember all of those possibilities every time you drag an icon? Probably not. Fortunately, you never have to. One of the most important tricks you can learn is to use the *right* mouse button as you drag. When you release the button, the menu shown in Figure 4-5 appears, so that you can either copy or move the icons.

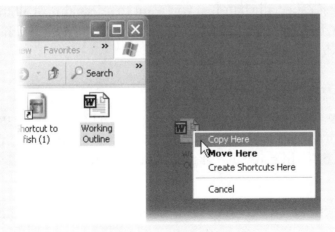

Figure 4-5. Thanks to this shortcut menu, right-dragging icons is much easier and safer than left-dragging when you want to move or copy something.

Dragging icons in Windows Explorer

You may find it easier to copy or move icons in Windows Explorer, since the two-pane display format makes it easier to see where your files are and where they're going. (See page 85 for a list of the ways to open the Explorer window.) Here's how to do it:

1. **Make the destination folder visible by clicking the + buttons next to your folder names, expanding your folder "tree" as necessary.**

   For example, to copy an icon into a certain folder, click the Local Disk (C:) icon to see its list of folders. If the destination is a folder *within* that folder, expand its parent folder as necessary.

2. **In the left pane, click the icon of the disk or folder that contains the icon you want to manipulate.**

   Its contents appear in the right pane.

3. **Locate the icon you want to move in the right pane, and drag it to the appropriate folder in the left pane (see Figure 4-6).**

Windows copies the icon.

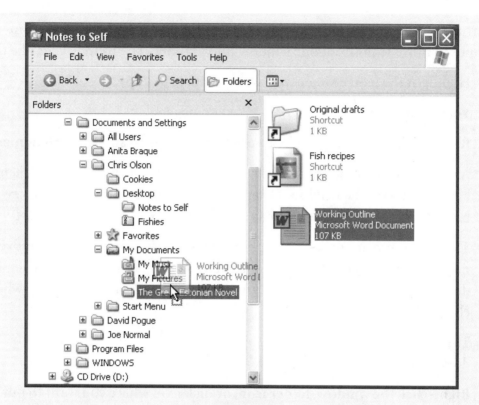

Figure 4-6. The file Working Outline, located in the "Notes to Self" folder on the desktop, is being dragged to the folder named The Great Estonian Novel (in the My Documents folder). As the cursor passes each folder in the left pane, the folder's name darkens to show that it's ready to receive the drag-and-dropped goodies. Let go of the mouse button when it's pointing to the correct folder or disk.

Copying by Using Copy and Paste

Dragging icons to copy or move them feels good because it's so direct. You actually see your arrow cursor pushing the icons into the new location.

But you also pay a price for this satisfying illusion. That is, you may have to spend a moment fiddling with your windows, or clicking in the Explorer hierarchy, so that you have a clear "line of drag" between the icon to be moved and the destination folder.

Fortunately, there's a better way: you can use the Cut, Copy, and Paste commands to move icons from one window into another. The routine goes like this:

1. **Highlight the icon or icons you want to move or copy.**

   You can use any of the tricks described on page 91.

2. **Right-click one of the icons. Choose Cut or Copy from the shortcut menu.**

   Alternatively, you can choose Edit → Cut or Edit → Copy, using the menu bar at the top of the window. (Eventually, you may want to learn the keyboard shortcuts for these commands: Ctrl+C for Copy, Ctrl+X for Cut.)

   The Cut command makes the highlighted icons show up dimmed; you've now stashed them on the invisible Windows Clipboard. (They don't actually disappear from their original nesting place until you paste them somewhere else.)

   The Copy command also places copies of the files on the Clipboard, but doesn't disturb the originals.

3. **Right-click the window, folder icon, or disk icon where you want to put the icons. Choose Paste from the shortcut menu.**

   Once again, you may prefer to use the appropriate menu bar option—Edit → Paste. *Keyboard equivalent:* Ctrl+V.

   Either way, you've successfully transferred the icons. If you pasted into an open window, you'll see the icons appear there. If you pasted onto a closed folder or disk icon, you need to open the icon's window to see the results. And if you pasted right back into the same window, you get a duplicate of the file called "Copy of [filename]."

If you find yourself copying or moving certain icons to certain folders or disks with regularity, it's time to exploit the File → Send To command (see Figure 4-7) that lurks in every folder window (and in the shortcut menu for almost every icon).

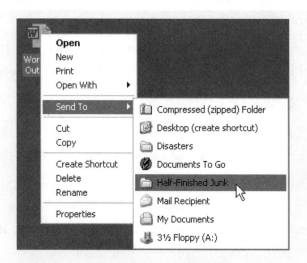

Figure 4-7. Clean up your clutter by filing icons inside folders. Right-click the icon, choose Send To from the shortcut menu, and choose the folder.

This command offers a quick way to copy and move highlighted icons to popular destinations. For example, you can teleport a copy of a highlighted file directly to a floppy disk by choosing File → Send To → 3 1/2 Floppy, or to a blank CD by choosing Send To → CD Burner. You're spared the tedium of choosing Copy, selecting the floppy drive, and choosing Paste.

Another useful command is Send To → Desktop (create shortcut), which dumps a shortcut icon onto your desktop background. Then there's the Send To → Mail Recipient, which bundles the highlighted icon as an email attachment that's ready to send.

The Recycle Bin

The Recycle Bin is your desktop trash basket. This is where files and folders go when they've outlived their usefulness, like a waiting room for data oblivion. Your files stay here until you *empty* the Recycle Bin—or until you rescue them by dragging them out again.

While you can certainly drag files or folders onto the Recycle Bin icon, it's usually faster to highlight them and then perform one of the following options:

▸ Press the Delete key.

▸ Choose File → Delete.

▸ Right-click a highlighted icon and choose Delete from the shortcut menu.

Windows XP asks if you're sure you want to send the item to the Recycle Bin. (You don't lose much by clicking Yes, since it's easy enough to change your mind, as explained in the following section.) Now the Recycle Bin icon looks like it's brimming over with paper.

 Tip: To turn off the "Are you sure?" message that appears when you send something Bin-ward, right-click the Recycle Bin. Then choose Properties from the shortcut menu, and turn off "Display delete confirmation dialog." Turning off the warning isn't much of a safety risk. After all, files aren't really being removed from your drive when you put them in the Recycle Bin.

You can put unwanted files and folders into the Recycle Bin from any folder window, from within Windows Explorer, or even from inside the Open File dialog box of many Windows applications (see Chapter 5).

Restoring Deleted Files and Folders

If you change your mind about sending something to the software graveyard, open the Recycle Bin by double-clicking it. A window like the one in Figure 4-8 opens.

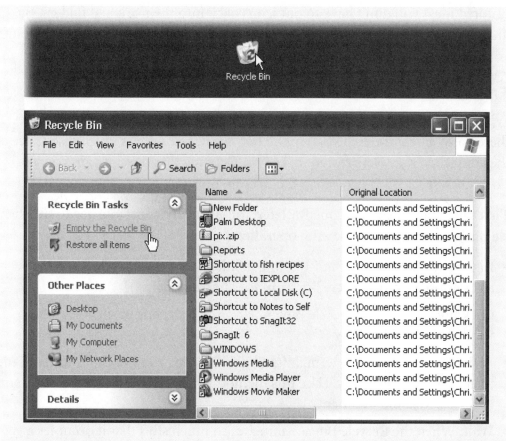

Figure 4-8. When you double-click the Recycle Bin (top), its window (bottom) displays information about each folder and file that it holds. To sort its contents in Details view, making it easier to find a deleted icon, click the gray column heading for the type of sort you need.

To restore a selected file or a folder—or a bunch of them—click the "Restore the selected items" link in the task pane, or choose File → Restore, or right-click any one of the selected icons and then choose Restore from the shortcut menu.

Restored means returned to the folder from whence it came—wherever it was on your hard drive when deleted. If you restore an icon whose original folder has been deleted in the meantime, Windows XP even recreates that folder to hold the restored file. (You don't have to put icons back into their original folders. By *dragging* them out of the Recycle Bin window, you can drop them into any folder you like.)

Emptying the Recycle Bin

While there's an advantage to the Recycle Bin (you get to undo your mistakes), there's also a downside: the files in the Recycle Bin occupy as much disk space as they did when they were stored in folders. Deleting files doesn't gain you additional disk space until you *empty* the Recycle Bin.

That's why most people, sooner or later, follow up an icon's journey to the Recycle Bin with one of these cleanup operations:

▶ Right-click the Recycle Bin icon, or a blank spot in the Recycle Bin window, and choose Empty Recycle Bin from the shortcut menu.

▶ Click the "Empty the Recycle Bin" link on the task pane in the Recycle Bin window.

▶ In the Recycle Bin window, highlight only the icons you want to eliminate, and then press the Delete key. (Use this method when you want to nuke only *some* of the Recycle Bin's contents.)

▶ Wait. When the Recycle Bin accumulates so much stuff that it occupies a significant percentage of your hard drive space, Windows empties it automatically, as described in the next section.

The first three procedures above produce an "Are you sure?" message. To avoid the hassle of emptying the Recycle Bin on a one-shot basis, press the Shift key while you delete a file. Doing so—and then clicking Yes in the confirmation box—deletes the file permanently, skipping its layover in the Recycle Bin.

 Tip: The Shift-key trick works for every method of deleting a file: pressing the Delete key, choosing Delete from the shortcut menu, and so on.

Shortcut Icons

A *shortcut* is a link to a file, folder, disk, or program (see Figure 4-9). You might think of it as a duplicate of the thing's icon—but not a duplicate of the thing itself. (A shortcut takes up almost no disk space.) When you double-click the shortcut icon, the original folder, disk, program, or document opens. You can also set up a keystroke for a shortcut icon, so that you can open any program or document just by pressing a certain key combination.

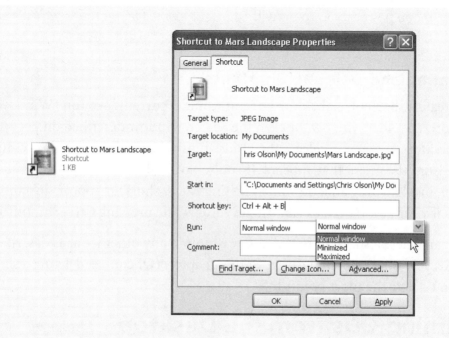

Figure 4-9. You can distinguish a desktop shortcut (left) from its original by the tiny arrow "badge" that identifies it as a shortcut. Its name probably also contains the word "shortcut," unless you've renamed it or an application has created its own shortcut on the desktop. The Properties dialog box for a shortcut (right) indicates which actual file or folder it "points" to.

Shortcuts provide quick access to the items you use most often. And because you can make as many shortcuts of a file as you want, and put them anywhere on your PC, you can effectively keep an important program or document in more than one folder. Just create a shortcut of each to leave on the desktop in plain sight, or drag their icons onto the Start button or the Quick Launch toolbar. In fact, everything listed in the Start → Programs menu is a shortcut—even the My Documents folder on the desktop is a shortcut (to the actual My Documents folder).

 Tip: Don't confuse the term *shortcut*, which refers to one of these duplicate-icon pointers, with *shortcut menu*, the context-sensitive menu that appears when you right-click almost anything in Windows. The shortcut menu has nothing to do with shortcut *icons*. Maybe that's why it's sometimes called the *context menu*.

Creating and Deleting Shortcuts

To create a shortcut, right-drag an icon from its current location (Windows Explorer, a folder window, or even the Search window described on page 41) to the desktop. When you release the mouse button, choose Create Shortcut(s) Here from the menu that appears. If you're not in the mood for using a shortcut menu, just left-drag an icon while pressing Alt. A shortcut appears instantly. (And if your keyboard lacks an Alt key, drag while pressing Ctrl+Shift instead.)

You can delete a shortcut in the same fashion as any other icon, as described in the Recycle Bin discussion earlier in this chapter. (Of course, deleting a shortcut doesn't delete the file it points to.)

Burning CDs from the Desktop

In the old days (two years ago), every PC came with a CD-ROM drive. Nowadays, most new PCs come with a CD *burner,* a drive that can record new CDs that contain your own stuff.

If your PC has such a drive—either a CD-R drive (CD *recordable,* which means you can record each disc only once) or a CD-RW drive (CD *rewriteable,* for which you can buy CD-RW discs that you can erase and rerecord as many times as you like), you're in for a treat. For the first time, Windows XP lets you burn

I'm burning a CD, and I get a message that I'm losing information. Why on earth would I want to click Yes?

When attempting to burn picture and music files onto a CD—not an uncommon task—you may be shown an error message that says, "This file has extra information attached to it that might be lost if you continue copying."

Windows is pointing out that some of the many informational tidbits it stores for pictures and music files (pixel dimensions of pictures, band names for music files, and so on) won't survive the transfer to a CD (whose more limited file format has only so much capacity for this kind of file trivia). This information won't be "lost" from the originals on your hard drive, of course—just in the CD copies.

Your best bet is to turn on "Repeat my answer each time this occurs" and then click Yes. (The alternative—clicking Skip so that Windows doesn't back up the file at all—is like throwing out the baby with the bathwater.)

your own CDs full of files and folders without having to buy a program like Roxio's Easy CD Creator.

That's because Windows XP *includes* Easy CD Creator (pieces of it, anyway). You now have a great feature for making backups, emailing people, or exchanging files with a Macintosh (the resulting CDs are cross-platform).

Tip: This entire section pertains to copying everyday computer files onto a CD. If you want to burn music CDs, don't use this method. Use Windows Media Player instead. (See page 154 for details.)

If your PC does, in fact, have a CD burner, start by inserting a blank CD. Windows offers to open a special CD-burning window, which will be the temporary waiting room for files that you want to copy to the CD (Figure 4-10, top left).

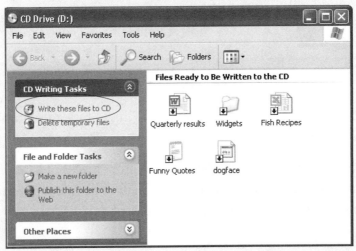

Figure 4-10. Top: When you insert a blank CD, this window appears, offering to open the writable CD folder that will hold shortcuts for the files you want to copy.

Bottom: The little down arrow next to each file means it hasn't been burned yet. Click "Write these files to CD" to start the burning process.

Tip: If you've turned off this feature, you can open the CD window yourself: open My Computer, and then double-click the CD icon.

Now tell Windows which files and folders you want copied onto it, using one of these three methods:

▶ Scurry about your hard drive, locating the files and folders you want on the CD. Drag their icons into the open CD window, or onto the CD icon in the My Computer window.

▶ Highlight the files and folders you want burned onto the CD. Choose File → Copy. Click in the CD's window, and then choose File → Paste to copy the material there.

▶ Explore your hard drive. Whenever you find a file or folder you'd like backed up, right-click it. From the shortcut menu, choose Send To → CD Drive.

In any case, Windows now copies the files and folders into a temporary, invisible holding-tank folder. (If you're scoring at home, this folder is in the Local Disk (C:) → Documents and Settings → [Your Name] → Local Settings → Application Data → Microsoft → CD Burning folder.) In other words, you need plenty of disk space before you begin burning a CD, at least double the size of the CD files themselves.

Remember that a standard CD can hold only about 700 MB of files. To ensure that your files and folders will fit, periodically highlight all the icons in the My Computer → CD window (choose Edit → Select All). Then inspect the Details box in the task pane to confirm that the Total File Size is within the legal limit.

At last, when everything looks ready to go, click the "Write these files to CD" link in the task pane (Figure 4-10, right), or choose File → "Write these files to CD."

The CD Writing Wizard guides you through the simple process of naming the new CD and burning the disc.

Hard-core Windows power users, of course, sneer at all this. Only with a commercial CD-burning program, they point out, can you burn MP3 music CDs, create *mixed-mode* CDs (containing both music and files), create Video CDs (low-quality video discs that play on DVD players), and so on.

Still, if you use your burner primarily for quick backups, long-term storage, or transferring big files to other computers, a little bit of free software goes a long way.

 Tip: When using a CD-RW disc (that is, one that you can erase and re-record), you can't change the disc's name once it's been recorded for the first time.

PART TWO: THE COMPONENTS OF WINDOWS XP

Chapter 5   Programs and Documents

Chapter 6   Pictures, Music, and Movies

CHAPTER 5:
PROGRAMS AND
DOCUMENTS

- ▶ Launching Programs
- ▶ Switching Programs
- ▶ Exiting Programs
- ▶ When Programs Die
- ▶ Saving Documents
- ▶ Closing Documents
- ▶ The Open Dialog Box
- ▶ Moving Data Between Documents
- ▶ Filename Extensions
- ▶ Installing Software
- ▶ Uninstalling Software

WHEN YOU GET RIGHT DOWN TO IT, an operating system like Windows is nothing more than a home base from which to launch *applications* (programs). And you, as a Windows person, are particularly fortunate, since more programs are available for Windows than any other operating system on earth.

But when you launch a program, you're no longer necessarily in the world Microsoft designed for you. Programs from other software companies work a bit differently, and there's a lot to learn about how Windows XP handles programs that were born before it was.

This chapter covers everything you need to know about installing, removing, launching, and managing programs; using programs to generate documents; and understanding how documents, programs, and Windows communicate with each other.

Launching Programs

Windows XP lets you launch (open) programs in many different ways:

▶ Choose a program's name from the Start → All Programs menu.

▶ Click a program's icon on the Quick Launch toolbar (page 74).

▶ Double-click an application's program-file icon in the My Computer → Local Disk (C:) → Program Files → application folder, or highlight the application's icon and then press Enter.

▶ Let Windows launch the program for you at startup (page 34).

▶ Open a document using any of the above techniques; its "parent" program opens automatically. For example, if you used Microsoft Word to write a file called *Last Will and Testament.doc*, double-clicking the document's icon launches Word and automatically opens that file.

What happens next depends on the program you're using (and whether or not you opened a document). Most present you with a new, blank, untitled document.

Some, such as FileMaker and Microsoft PowerPoint, welcome you instead with a question: do you want to open an existing document or create a new one? And a few oddball programs, like Adobe Photoshop, don't open any window at all when first launched. The appearance of tool palettes is the only evidence that you've even opened a program.

Switching Programs

In these days where PCs with 256 MB, 512 MB, or even gigabytes of RAM are common, it's the rare PC user who doesn't regularly run several programs *simultaneously*.

The key to juggling open programs is the taskbar, which lists all open programs (Figure 5-1). The taskbar also offers controls for arranging all the windows on your screen, closing them via the shortcut menu, and so on.

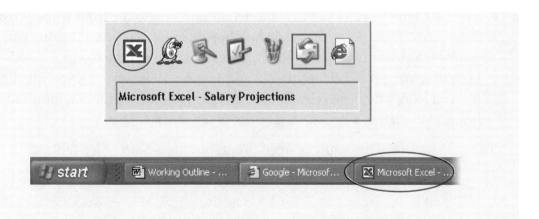

Figure 5-1. Top: Press Alt+Tab to highlight successive icons in the list. When you release the Alt key, the program whose icon you've highlighted (Excel, in this case) jumps to the front.

Bottom: The taskbar lets you know which programs are running; the darkest button tells you which program is active.

To bring a different program to the front, you can use any of these four tricks:

▶ **Use the Taskbar.** Clicking a button on the taskbar makes the corresponding program pop to the front, along with any of its floating toolbars, palettes, and so on.

If you see a parenthetical number on a taskbar button, however, then button *grouping* is under way (page 71). In that case, clicking the taskbar button *doesn't* bring the program's windows forward. You must actually click a selection in the taskbar button's menu of open windows.

▶ **Click the window.** You can also switch to another program by clicking the part of its window that's visible in the background.

▶ **The relaunch technique.** Repeat the technique you used to initially launch the program (choose its name from the Start → All Programs menu, press its keystroke, and so on).

▶ **Alt+Tab.** Finally, you can bring a different program to the front without using the mouse. If you press Tab while holding down the Alt key, a floating palette displays the icons of all running programs, as shown at the top in Figure 5-1. Each time you press Tab again (still keeping the Alt key down), you highlight the next icon; when you release the keys, the highlighted program jumps to the front, as though in a high-tech game of Duck Duck Goose.

To move *backward* through the open programs, press *Shift*+Alt+Tab.

 Tip: For quick access to the desktop, clear the screen by clicking the Desktop button on the Quick Launch toolbar (its icon looks like an old desk blotter)—or just press the Windows logo key+D. Pressing that keystroke again brings all the windows back to the screen exactly as they were.

Multiple Document Interface

The world of Windows programs is divided into two camps. First, there are *single-document interface* (SDI) programs, where the entire program runs in a single window. By closing that window, you also exit the application. (WordPad, Notepad, Internet Explorer, and Palm Desktop work this way.)

Second, there are *multiple-document interface* (MDI) programs, where the application itself is a mother ship, a shell, that can contain lots of different document windows. Word, Excel, and PowerPoint work like this. As shown here, you may see two sets of upper-right window controls, one just beneath the other. The top one belongs to the application; the one below it belongs to the document. Here, if you close a document window, you don't also quit the program.

To help you navigate your various open windows, MDI programs usually offer commands that arrange all open windows to fit neatly on the screen, each occupying an even fraction of the screen space. (These commands work much like the Tile and Cascade commands in desktop windows.) In Microsoft Word, for example, the Windows menu offers a command called Arrange All.

Getting to know which way a program deals with windows is important for a couple of reasons. First, it explains why the taskbar sometimes displays only one button for an entire program (such as Word), but sometimes displays a button for each open window in a program (such as Internet Explorer). Second, it explains why closing a window sometimes exits the application (when it's a single-document interface program) and sometimes doesn't (when it's an MDI program).

M	N	O
4Q Sales		
West	2345	6435
North	345	234
South	5233	4634

Exiting Programs

When you exit, or quit, an application, the memory it was using is returned to the Windows pot for use by other programs.

If you use a particular program several times a day, like a word processor or calendar program, you'll save time in the long run by keeping it open all day long. (You can always minimize its window to get it out of the way when you're not using it.)

But if you're done using a program for the day, exit it, especially if it's a memory-hungry one like, say, Photoshop. Do so using one of these techniques:

▶ Choose File → Exit.

▶ Click the program window's Close box, or double-click its Control-menu icon (at the upper-left corner of the window).

▶ Right-click the program's taskbar button and choose Close from the shortcut menu.

▶ Press Alt+F4 to close the window you're in. (If it's a program that disappears entirely when its last document window closes, you're home.)

▶ Press Alt+F, then X.

If you haven't yet saved the changes you've made to your document, the program offers the chance to do so before it shuts down all the way. Finally, after this step, program's windows, menus, and toolbars disappear, and you fall "down a layer" into the window that was behind it.

When Programs Die

Windows XP itself may be a revolution in stability (at least if you're used to Windows Me), but that doesn't mean that *programs* never crash or freeze. They crash, all right—it's just that in XP, you rarely have to restart the computer as a result.

When something goes horribly wrong with a program, your primary interest is usually exiting it in order to get on with your life. But when a program locks up (the cursor moves, but menus and tool palettes don't respond) or when a dialog box tells you that a program has "failed to respond," exiting may not be so easy. After all, how do you choose File → Exit if the File menu itself doesn't open?

As in past versions of Windows, the solution is to invoke the "three-fingered salute": Ctrl+Alt+Delete. What happens next depends on whether or not your PC is part of a domain network (page 23):

▶ **Part of a domain.** Ctrl+Alt+Delete summons the Windows Security dialog box. Click the Task Manager button. The Applications tab on the resulting dialog box, shown in Figure 5-2, provides a list of every open program. Furthermore, the Status column should make clear what you already know: that one of your programs is ignoring you.

▶ **Part of a workgroup (or not networked).** You save a step. Ctrl+Alt+Delete brings you directly to the Windows Task Manager dialog box (Figure 5-2).

Figure 5-2. As if you didn't know, one of these programs is "not responding." Highlight its name and then click End Task (indicated by the cursor) to slap it out of its misery. As described in the box on page 116, you also get a chance to tell Microsoft it messed up.

Tip: You can also run Task Manager by right-clicking the taskbar and then selecting Task Manager from the shortcut menu. Doing this bypasses the Windows Security dialog box and brings you directly to Windows Task Manager, with the Applications tab selected. Or just press Shift+Ctrl+Alt+Delete.

UP TO SPEED

Sending an Error Report to Microsoft

Whenever Windows XP discovers that you have terminated one program or another in some eccentric way—for example, by using the Task Manager (see Figure 5-2)—a dialog box that says, "Please tell Microsoft about this problem" appears.

If you click the Send Error Report button, your PC connects to the Internet and sends an email report back to Microsoft, the mother ship, providing the company with the technical details about whatever was going on at the moment of the freeze, crash, or premature termination. (To see exactly what information you're about to send, click the "click here" link.)

Microsoft swears up and down that it doesn't do anything with this information except to collate it into gigantic electronic databases, which it then analyzes using special software tools. The idea, of course, is to find trends that emerge from studying hundreds of thousands of such reports. "Oh, my goodness, it looks like people who own both Speak-it Pro 5 and Beekeeper Plus who right-click a document that's currently being printed experience a system lockup," an engineer might announce one day. By analyzing the system glitches of its customers en masse, the company hopes to pinpoint problems and devise software patches with much greater efficiency than before.

If you're worried about privacy, click Don't Send (or press Enter) each time this happens. (On the other hand, if you're truly concerned about privacy and Windows XP, this particular feature is probably the least of your worries.)

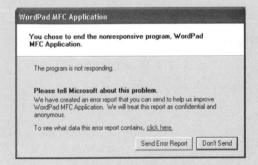

Shutting down the troublesome program is fairly easy; just click its name and then click the End Task button. (If yet another dialog box appears, telling you that "This program is not responding," click the End Now button.)

When you jettison a recalcitrant program this way, Windows XP generally shuts down the troublemaker gracefully, even offering you the chance to save unsaved changes to your documents.

If even this treatment fails to close the program, you might have to slam the door the hard way. Click the Processes tab, click the name of the program that's giving you grief, and then click the End Process button. (The Processes list includes dozens of programs, including many that Windows XP runs behind the scenes. Finding the abbreviated short name of the program may be the hardest part of this process.) You lose any unsaved changes to your documents using this method—but at least the frozen program is finally closed.

Saving Documents

In a few programs, such as the Calculator or Solitaire, you spend your time working (or playing) in the lone application window. When you close the window, no trace of your work remains.

Most programs, however, are designed to create *documents*—files that you can re-open for further editing, send to other people, back up on another disk, and so on. That's why these programs offer File → Save and File → Open commands, which let you preserve the work you've done, saving it onto the hard drive as a new file icon so that you can return to it later.

The Save File Dialog Box

When you choose File → Save for the first time, the computer shows you the dialog box shown in Figure 5-3, in which you're supposed to type a file name, choose a folder location, and specify the format for the file you're saving. Using the controls in this dialog box, you can specify exactly where you want to file your newly created document.

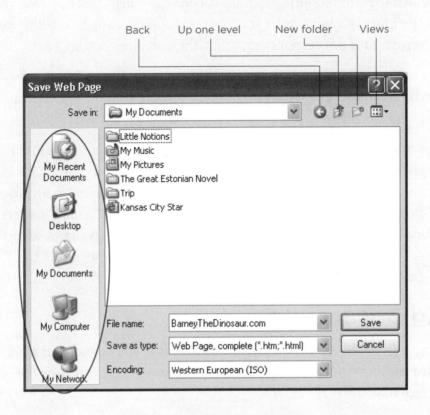

Figure 5-3. The buttons at the left side of the Save dialog box (circled) provide quick access to the folders where you're most likely to stash newly created documents: the My Documents folder, the desktop itself, and so on. If you click Save now, you'll be saving your BarneyTheDinosaur.com file in My Documents.

Saving into My Documents

The first time you use the File → Save command to save a file, Windows proposes your My Documents folder as the new home of the document you've just created. Now, you're free to navigate to some other folder location, as described in the next section. But the My Documents folder will suggest itself as the new-document receptacle every time.

Tip: Many programs let you specify a different folder as the proposed location for saved (and reopened) files. In Microsoft Word, for example, click the Tools → Options → File Locations tab to change the default folders for the documents you create, where your clip art is stored, and so on.

What's the benefit of saving your files into the My Documents folder? First, using the My Documents folder ensures that your file won't fall accidentally into some deeply nested folder where you'll never see it again (a common occurrence among first-time computer users). Instead, the newly minted document will be waiting for you in the My Documents folder, which itself is very difficult to lose.

Second, it's now very easy to make a backup copy of your important documents, since they're all in a single folder (which you can drag onto a backup disk in one swift move).

There's a third advantage, too: whenever you use a program's File → Open command, Windows once again displays the contents of the My Documents folder. In other words, the Documents folder saves you time both when *creating* a new file and when *retrieving* it.

Tip: If the Documents folder becomes cluttered, feel free to make sub-folders inside it to hold your various projects. You could even create a different folder in My Documents for each program.

Navigating in the Save Dialog Box

If the My Documents method doesn't strike your fancy, use the Save As dialog box's various controls to navigate your way into any folder. That's the purpose of the "Save in:" drop-down list at the top of the dialog box (Figure 5-3). It lists, and lets you jump to, any disk or folder on your PC—or the desktop level, if that's a more familiar landscape.

To save a new document onto, say, a Zip disk or floppy, choose the drive's name from this drop-down list before clicking the Save button. To save it into a *folder*

Dialog Box Basics

To the delight of the powerful Computer Keyboard lobby, you can manipulate almost every element of a Windows XP dialog box by pressing keys on the keyboard. If you're among those who feel that using the mouse takes longer to do something, you're in luck.

The rule for navigating a dialog box is simple: Press Tab to jump from one set of options to another, or Shift+Tab to move backward. If the dialog box has multiple tabs, like the one shown here, press Ctrl+Tab to "click" the next tab, or Ctrl+Shift+Tab to "click" the previous one.

Each time you press Tab, the PC's focus shifts to a different control or set of controls. Windows reveals which element has the focus using text highlighting (if it's a text box or drop-down menu) or a dotted-line outline (if it's a button). In the illustration shown at right, the "Different odd and even" checkbox has the focus.

Once you've highlighted a button or checkbox, simply press the Space bar to "click" it. If you've opened a drop-down list or set of mutually exclusive option buttons, or *radio buttons*, press

the up or down arrow key. (Tip: once you've highlighted a drop-down list's name, you can also press the F4 key to open it.)

Each dialog box also contains larger, rectangular buttons at the bottom (OK and Cancel, for example). Efficiency fans should remember that tapping the Enter key is always the equivalent of clicking the default button—the one with the darkened or thickened outline (the OK button in the illustration here). And pressing Esc almost always means Cancel (or "Close this box").

Finally, remember that you can jump to a particular control or area of the dialog box by pressing the Alt key along with the corresponding underlined letter key.

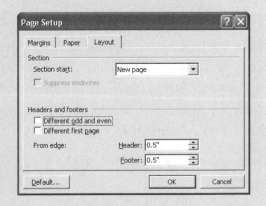

within a disk, simply double-click the successive nested folders until you reach the one you want.

Use the toolbar icons to help you navigate, like this:

▶ **Back** shows you the contents of the last folder you browsed. Click its tiny black down-triangle button to see a drop-down list of folders you've opened recently within this program.

▶ **Up One Level** moves you up one level in your folder hierarchy (from seeing the My Documents contents to the hard drive's contents, for example). *Keyboard shortcut:* the Backspace key.

▶ **Create New Folder** creates a new folder in the current list of files and folders. Windows asks you to name it.

▶ **Views** changes the way file listings look in this dialog box. Each time you click the icon, you get a different view: List, Details, Thumbnails, and so on. (To choose one of these views by name, use the drop-down list rather than clicking the icon repeatedly.)

The list of view options here depends on the program you're using. In general, they closely correspond to the View menu options described on page 59. But in some programs, including Microsoft Office programs, you may receive a few additional options—a choice of Large Icons or Small Icons, for example, or a Properties view that divides the window in half, with the list of files and folders on the left, and the properties (file size, date modified, and so on) of the highlighted icon on the right.

In some programs (such as Microsoft Office), you may find a few additional buttons across the top of the Save As dialog box, including:

▶ **Search the Web** closes the Save As dialog box, opens your browser, connects to the Internet, and prepares to search the Internet. (Next assignment: to figure out *why* you'd want to search the Web at the moment of saving your document.)

▶ **Delete** flings a highlighted file or folder into the Recycle Bin.

- **Tools** is a drop-down menu that offers some very useful commands, including **Delete** and **Rename**, that let you manage your files right from within this dialog box. **Add to Favorites** creates a shortcut of the highlighted disk, server, folder, or file in your Favorites folder, so that you don't have to burrow through your folders every time you want access; instead, you can just click the Favorites folder icon, which also appears in the Save As dialog boxes of Office programs, to see everything you've stashed there. The **Properties** command lets you see an icon's description and stats.

- **Map Network Drive** lets you assign a drive letter (like *G:*) to a folder that's on another PC of your network. Having that folder appear on your screen as just another disk makes it much easier to find, open, and manage.

Navigating the List by Keyboard

When the Save As dialog box first appears, the "File name" text box is automatically selected so that you can type a name for the newly created document.

But as noted in the box on page 87, a Windows dialog box is elaborately rigged for keyboard control. In addition to the standard Tab/Space bar controls, a few special keys work only within the list of files and folders. Start by pressing Shift+Tab (to shift Windows' attention from the "File name" text box to the list of files and folders) and then:

- Press various letter keys to highlight the corresponding file and folder icons. To highlight the Program Files folder, for example, you could type *PR*. (If you type too slowly, your key presses will be interpreted as separate initiatives—highlighting first the People folder and then the Rodents folder, for example.)

- Press the Page Up or Page Down keys to scroll the list up or down. Press Home or End to highlight the top or bottom item in the list.

- Press the arrow keys (up or down) to highlight successive icons in the list.

- When a folder (or file) is highlighted, you can open it by pressing the Enter key (or double-clicking its icon, or clicking the Open button).

Playing Favorites

Most people think of Favorites as Internet Explorer's version of "bookmarks"—a list of Web sites that you've designated as worth returning to. But Windows XP lets you designate anything as a favorite—a folder you open often, a document you consult every day, a program, and so on.

You can designate a particular icon as a Favorite in any of several ways. For example, in the Save As or Open dialog box of Microsoft Office programs, you can use the Add to Favorites command.

In a desktop window (Windows Explorer, for example), you can highlight an icon and then choose Favorites → Add to Favorites.

Later, when you want to open a Favorite icon, you can do so using an equally generous assortment of methods: choose from the Start → Favorites menu, choose File → Open in any program and click the Favorites folder or icon, choose from the Favorites menu of any desktop window, and so on.

The File Format Drop-Down Menu

The Save As dialog box in many programs offers a menu of file formats (usually referred to as the file *type*) below the "File name" text box. Use this drop-down menu when preparing a document for use by somebody whose computer doesn't have the same software.

For example, if you've typed something in Microsoft Word, you can use this menu to generate a Web page document or a Rich Text Format document that you can open with almost any standard word processor or page-layout program.

Closing Documents

You close a document window just as you'd close any window: by clicking the close box (marked by an X) in the upper-right corner of the window, by double-clicking the Control-menu icon just to the left of the File menu, or by pressing

Alt+F4. If you've done any work to the document since the last time you saved it, Windows offers a "Save changes?" dialog box as a reminder.

As described on page 113, sometimes closing the window also exits the application, and sometimes the application remains running, even with no document windows open. And in a few *really* bizarre cases, it's possible to exit an application (such as Outlook Express) while a document window (an email message) remains open on the screen, lingering and abandoned!

The Open Dialog Box

To reopen a document you've already saved and named, you can pursue any of these avenues:

▶ Open your My Documents folder (or whichever folder contains the saved file). Double-click the file's icon.

▶ If you've opened the document recently, choose its name from the Start → My Recent Documents menu.

▶ If you're already in the program that created the document, choose File → Open—or check the bottom of the File menu. Many programs add a list of recently opened files to the File menu, so that you can choose their names to reopen them.

▶ Type (or browse for) the document's path and name into a folder window's Address toolbar.

The Open dialog box looks almost identical to the Save As dialog box. The big change: the navigational drop-down list at the top of the window now says "Look in" instead of "Save in."

Once again, you start out by perusing the contents of your My Documents folder. Here, you may find that beginning your navigation by choosing Look In → My Computer offers a useful overview of your PC when you're searching for a particular file. Here, too, you can open a folder or disk by double-clicking its name in the list, or by pressing the keystrokes described in the previous section. And once again, you can press Backspace to back *out* of a folder that you've opened.

When you've finally located the file you want to open, double-click it or highlight it (from the keyboard, if you like), and then press Enter.

In general, most people don't encounter the Open dialog box nearly as often as the Save As dialog box. That's because Windows offers many more convenient ways to *open* a file (double-clicking its icon, choosing its name from the Start → My Documents command, and so on), but only a single way to *save* a new file.

Moving Data Between Documents

You can't paste a picture into your Web browser, and you can't paste MIDI music information into your word processor. But you can put graphics into your word processor, paste movies into your database, insert text into Photoshop, and combine a surprising variety of seemingly dissimilar kinds of data. And you can transfer text from Web pages, email messages, and word processing documents to other email and word processing files; in fact, that's one of the most frequently performed tasks in all of computing.

Cut, Copy, and Paste

You can cut and copy highlighted material in any of three ways. First, you can use the Cut and Copy commands in the Edit menu; second, you can press Ctrl+X (for Cut) or Ctrl+C (for Copy); and third, you can right-click the highlighted material and choose Cut or Copy from the shortcut menu, as shown in Figure 5-4.

When you do so, the PC memorizes the highlighted material, socking it away on an invisible storage pad called the Clipboard. If you choose Copy, nothing visible happens; if you choose Cut, the highlighted material disappears from the original document. At this point, you must take it on faith that the Cut or Copy command actually worked.

Pasting copied or cut material, once again, is something you can do either from a menu (choose Edit → Paste), by right-clicking and choosing Paste from the shortcut menu, or from the keyboard (press Ctrl+V).

The most recently cut or copied material remains on your Clipboard even after you paste, making it possible to paste the same blob repeatedly. Such a trick can

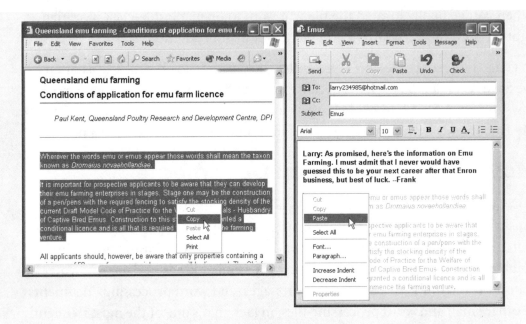

Figure 5-4. Suppose you want to email some text on a Web page to a friend. Start by dragging through it and then choosing Copy from the shortcut menu (or choosing Edit → Copy (left)). Now switch to your email program and paste it into an outgoing message (right).

be useful when, for example, you've designed a business card in your drawing program and want to duplicate it enough times to fill a letter-sized printout. On the other hand, whenever you next copy or cut something, whatever was previously on the Clipboard is lost forever.

 Tip: Folks who use a PC every day eventually learn to quickly trigger the Cut, Copy, and Paste commands from the keyboard—without even thinking.

Drag-and-Drop

As useful and popular as it is, the Copy/Paste routine doesn't win any awards for speed; after all, it requires four steps. In many cases, you can replace that routine with the far more direct (and enjoyable) drag-and-drop method. Figure 5-5 illustrates how it works.

Few people ever expected O'Keen to triumph over the Beast; he was tired, sweaty, and missing three of his four limbs. But slowly, gradually, he began to focus, pointing his one remaining index finger toward the lumbering animal. "You had my wife for lunch," O'Keen muttered between clenched teeth. "Now I'm going to have yours." And his bunion was acting up again

Few people ever expected O'Keen to triumph over the Beast; he was tired, sweaty, and missing three of his four limbs. And his bunion was acting up again. But slowly, gradually, he began to focus, pointing his one remaining index finger toward the lumbering animal. "You had my wife for lunch," O'Keen muttered between clenched teeth. "Now I'm going to have yours."

Figure 5-5. Click in the middle of some highlighted text (left) and drag it into another place within the document (right), or into a different window or program.

Note: To drag highlighted material offscreen, drag the cursor until it approaches the top or bottom edge of the window. The document scrolls automatically; as you approach the destination, jerk the mouse away from the edge of the window to stop the scrolling.

Several of the built-in Windows XP programs work with the drag-and-drop technique, including WordPad and Outlook Express. Most popular commercial programs offer the drag-and-drop feature, too, including email programs and word processors, America Online, Microsoft Office programs, and so on.

As illustrated in Figure 5-5, drag-and-drop is ideal for transferring material between windows or between programs. It's especially useful when you've already copied something valuable to your Clipboard, since drag-and-drop doesn't involve (and doesn't erase) the Clipboard.

Its most popular use, however, is rearranging the text in a single document. In, say, Word or WordPad, you can rearrange entire sections, paragraphs, sentences, or even individual letters, just by dragging them—a terrific editing technique.

Note: Using drag-and-drop to move highlighted text within a document also deletes the text from its original location. By pressing Ctrl as you drag, however, you make a copy of the highlighted text.

Text-Selection Fundamentals

Before doing almost anything to text in a word processor, like making it bold, changing its typeface, or moving it to a new spot in your document, you have to highlight the text you want to affect. For millions of people, this entails dragging the cursor extremely carefully, perfectly horizontally, across the desired text. And if they want to capture an entire paragraph or section, they click at the beginning, drag very carefully diagonally, and release the mouse button when they reach the end of the passage.

That's all fine, but because selecting text is the cornerstone of every editing operation in a word processor, it's worth learning some of the faster and more precise ways of going about it. For example, double-clicking a word highlights it, instantly and neatly. In fact, by keeping the mouse button pressed on the second click, you can now drag horizontally to highlight text in crisp one-word chunks—a great way to highlight text more quickly and precisely. These

tricks work anywhere you can type. In most programs, including Microsoft's, additional shortcuts await. For example, triple-clicking anywhere within a paragraph highlights the entire paragraph. (Once again, if you keep the button pressed at the end of this maneuver, you can then drag to highlight your document in one-paragraph increments.)

In many programs, including Word and WordPad, you can highlight exactly one sentence by clicking within it while pressing Ctrl.

Finally, here's a universal trick that lets you highlight a large blob of text, even one that's too big to fit on the current screen. Start by clicking to position the insertion point cursor at the very beginning of the text you want to capture. Now scroll, if necessary, so that the ending point of the passage is visible. Shift-click there. Windows instantly highlights everything that was in between your click and your Shift-click.

Drag-and-drop to the desktop

Figure 5-6 demonstrates how to drag text or graphics out of your document windows and directly onto the desktop. There, your dragged material becomes an icon—a *Scrap file*.

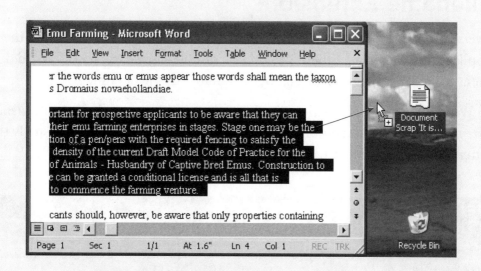

Figure 5-6. A Scrap file will appear when you drag material out of the document window and onto the desktop. Its icon depends on the kind of material contained within, as shown here at left.

When you drag a clipping from your desktop *back* into an application window, the material in that clipping reappears. Drag-and-drop, in other words, is a convenient and powerful feature; it lets you treat your desktop itself as a giant, computer-wide pasteboard—an area where you can temporarily stash pieces of text or graphics as you work.

You can drag a Scrap file onto a document's taskbar button, too. Don't release the mouse button yet. In a moment, the corresponding document window appears, so that you can continue your dragging operation until the cursor points to where you want the Scrap file to appear. Now release the mouse; the Scrap material appears in the document.

 Tip: Like any icon, you can rename a Scrap file to remind yourself what's in it. But if you forget, simply double-click it to open it in its original program.

Filename Extensions

Every operating system needs a mechanism to associate documents with the applications that created them. When you double-click a Microsoft Word document icon, for example, Word launches and opens the document.

In Windows, every document comes complete with a normally invisible *filename extension* (or just *file extension*)—a period followed by a suffix that's usually three letters long. Here are some common examples:

WHEN YOU DOUBLE-CLICK THIS ICON...	...THIS PROGRAM OPENS IT
Fishingtrip.*doc*	Microsoft Word
Quarterly results.*xls*	Microsoft Excel
HomePage.*htm*	Internet Explorer
Agenda.*wpd*	Corel WordPerfect
A Home Movie.*avi*	Windows Media Player
Animation.*dir*	Macromedia Director

Displaying Filename Extensions

It's possible to live a long and happy life without knowing much about these extensions. Indeed, because file extensions don't feel very user-friendly, Microsoft designed Windows to *hide* the suffixes on most icons (see Figure 5-7). If you're new to Windows, and haven't poked around inside the folders on your hard drive much, you may never even have seen them.

Some people appreciate the way Windows hides the extensions, because the screen becomes less cluttered and less technical-looking. Others make a good argument for the Windows 3.1 days, when every icon appeared with its suffix.

For example, in a single Desktop window, suppose one day you discover that three icons all seem to have exactly the same name: PieThrower. Only by making filename extensions appear would you discover the answer to the mystery: that

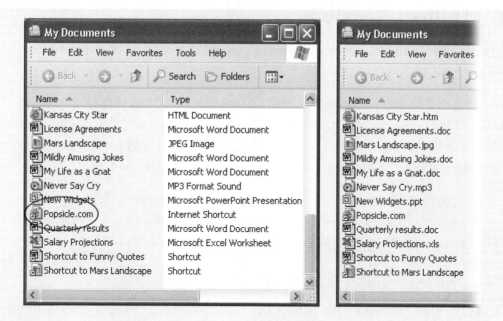

Figure 5-7. Normally, Windows only shows you filename extensions it doesn't recognize (see Popsicle.com, circled at left). To make Windows show all extensions, all the time (right), turn off the "Hide extensions" feature, as described below.

is, one of them might be called PieThrower.ini, another is an Internet-based software updater called PieThrower.upd, and the third is the actual PieThrower program, PieThrower.exe.

One way to make sense of such situations is simply to look at the window in Details view (right-click in the window and choose View → Details from the shortcut menu).

But that's too easy. To fully breathe in Windows technology, you can instruct Windows to reveal the file suffixes on *all* icons. To do so, choose Tools → Folder Options from any folder window's menu bar. In the Folder Options dialog box, click the View tab. Turn off "Hide extensions for known file types," and then click OK: the filename extensions for all icons appear.

Installing Software

Today, almost all new software comes to your PC from one of two sources: a CD or the Internet.

Modern software usually comes with an installer program that's designed to transfer the software files to the correct places on your hard drive. The installer also adds the new program's name to the Start → All Programs menu, and tells Windows about the kinds of files (file extensions) it can open.

 Tip: You don't actually have to install any software to work in Windows. Your Windows XP PC has a bunch of free, preinstalled programs for everyday tasks, like typing words and creating pictures.

The Pre-Installation Checklist

You can often get away with blindly installing some new program without heeding the checklist below. But for the healthiest PC and the least time on hold with tech support, answer these questions before you install anything:

▶ **Are you an administrator?** Windows XP derives part of its security and stability by handling new software installations with suspicion. For example, you can't install most programs unless you have an *administrator account* (see page 324).

▶ **Does it run in Windows XP?** Windows XP is compatible with far more programs than Windows 2000 was—but far fewer than, say, Windows 98 or Windows Me.

If the software or its Web site specifically says it's compatible with Windows XP, great. Install away. Otherwise, consult the Microsoft Web site, which includes a list—not a complete one, but a long one—of all XP-compatible programs. (The easiest way to get there is to choose Start → Help and Support, then click the "Find compatible hardware and software for Windows XP" link.)

▶ **Is the coast clear?** Exit all your open programs. (One quick way: right-click the buttons on the taskbar, one at a time, and choose Close from the shortcut menu.) You should also turn off your virus-scanning software, which may take the arrival of your new software the wrong way.

Installing Software from a CD

Most commercial software these days comes on a CD. On each one is a program called Setup, which, on most installation CDs, runs automatically when you insert the disk into the machine. You're witnessing the *AutoPlay* feature at work.

If AutoPlay is working, a few seconds after you insert the CD into your drive, the hourglass cursor appears. A few seconds later, the Welcome screen for your new software appears, and you may be asked to answer a few onscreen questions (for example, to specify the folder into which you want the new program installed). Along the way, the program may ask you to type in a serial number, which is usually on a sticker on the CD envelope or the registration card.

If the last installer window has a Finish button, click it. The installation program transfers the software files to your hard drive. When it's all over, you may be asked to restart the machine. In any case, open the Start menu; a yellow "New programs have been installed" balloon appears next to the All Programs button. If you click there, the program's name appears highlighted in orange, and your Start → All Programs menu is now ready for action.

Installing software using Add or Remove Programs

Windows XP offers a second, more universal installation method: the greatly improved, but still ingeniously named, Add or Remove Programs program. To see it, open Start → Control Panel → Add or Remove Programs.

A dialog box opens showing every program on your PC—well, at least those that were installed using a standard Windows installer. Click the name of one to expand its "panel," a thick gray bar that shows you how much disk space the program takes, when you last used it, and so on. (This dialog box comes up again when you uninstall programs; see page 137.)

 Tip: Some programs include a "Click here for support information" link, which produces a little window revealing the name, Web site, and sometimes the phone number of the software company responsible for the software in question.

Use Add or Remove Programs whenever the usual auto-starting CD installation routine doesn't apply—for example, when the CD hasn't been programmed for AutoPlay, when the installer comes on floppy disks (remember those?), or when the installer is somewhere else on your office network.

To make it work, insert the floppy disk or CD that contains the software you want to install. Then click the Add New Programs button at the left side of the window. Finally, click the CD or Floppy button to make Windows look around for the Setup program on the disk or CD you've inserted. If the technology gods are smiling, the installation process now begins, exactly as described above.

Installing Downloaded Software

The files you download from the Internet (see Figure 5-8) usually aren't ready-to-use, double-clickable applications. Instead, almost all of them arrive on your PC in the form of a compressed file, with all the software pieces crammed together into a single, easily downloaded icon. The first step in savoring your downloaded delights is restoring this compressed file to its natural state.

Not that it's much work. Most Zip files unzip themselves. If you get one that doesn't, just double-click it. After unzipping the software, you'll usually find, among the resulting pieces, an installer, just like the ones described in the previous section.

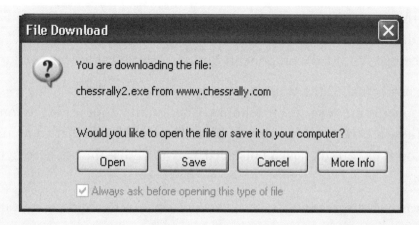

Figure 5-8. You can find lots of free programs (and payment-optional shareware) at sites like www.download.com and www.computingcentral.msn.com. When you download software, click Save in this dialog box and put the installer file in, say, a Downloads folder you've created.

Installing Preloaded Software

As you probably know, Microsoft doesn't actually sell PCs (yet). Therefore, you bought your machine from a different company, which probably installed Windows on it before you took delivery.

Many PC companies sweeten the pot by preinstalling other programs, such as Quicken, Microsoft Works, Microsoft Office, more games, educational software, and so on. The great thing about preloaded programs is that they don't need installing. Just double-click their desktop icons, or choose their names from the Start → All Programs menu, and you're off and working.

Installing Windows Components

The Windows XP installer may have dumped over a gigabyte of software onto your hard drive, but it was only warming up. Plenty of second-tier programs and features are left behind on the CD—stuff that Microsoft didn't want to burden you with right off the bat, but included on the CD just in case.

To see the master list of software components that you have and haven't yet installed, choose Start → Control Panel → Add or Remove Programs." Click the Add/Remove Windows Components button at the left side of the window.

You've just launched the Windows Components Wizard—basically a list of all the optional Windows software chunks. Checkmarks appear next to some of them; these are the ones you already have. The checkboxes that aren't turned on are the options you still haven't installed. As you peruse the list, keep in mind the following:

▶ To learn what something is, click its name once. A description appears below the list.

▶ Turn on the checkboxes for software bits you want to install. Clear the check-boxes of elements you already have, but that you'd like Windows to delete in order to create more free space on your hard drive.

▶ To the right of the name of each software chunk, you can see how much disk space it uses when it's installed. Keep an eye on the "Space available on disk" statistic at the bottom of the dialog box to make sure you don't overwhelm your hard drive.

▶ Windows may ask you to insert your Windows CD.

As you click the name of a software component, the Details button may spring to life, "waking up" from its faded look. When you click it, another list of elements appears—the ones that make up the software category.

Uninstalling Software

When you've had enough of a certain program, and want to reclaim the disk space it occupies, don't just delete its folder. The typical application installer tosses its software components like birdseed all over your hard drive; therefore, only some of it is actually in the program's folder.

Instead, ditch software you no longer need using the Add or Remove Programs program described above. Click the Change or Remove Programs button at the top left, and then proceed as shown in Figure 5-9.

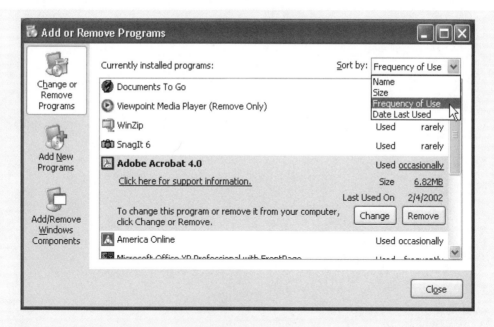

Figure 5-9. To vaporize a program, click its name to reveal its gray, highlighted panel, as shown here, and then click the Remove button. You can use the "Sort by" drop-down menu to sort the list by Frequency of Use or Date Last Used. (Note, though, that Windows doesn't keep perfect track of all types of programs, especially those that run in the background, so these statistics are likely to be unreliable.)

Warning: If you do the Add or Remove Programs thing, sooner or later you'll get this scary message that one of the deleted program's files is also needed by other programs, and asking if you want to delete it. Don't. Leaving it behind does no harm, but deleting it may cripple one of your other applications.

CHAPTER 6:
PICTURES, MUSIC, AND
MOVIES

▶ Digital Photos in XP

▶ Scanning

▶ Windows Media Player

WINDOWS XP IS THE MOST ADVANCED version yet when it comes to playing and displaying multimedia files—photos, sounds, and movies. New features make it easier than ever for your PC to control your digital camera or scanner, play movies and sounds, and play radio stations from all over the world as you work on your PC (thanks to your Internet connection).

In this chapter, you'll find guides to all of these features.

Digital Photos in XP

The new stability of XP is nice, and the new task pane can save you time. But if you have a digital camera, few of the new features in Windows XP are quite as useful as its ability to manage your digital photos. Microsoft has bent over backward to simplify and streamline a process that was once a chain of pain: transferring photos from your camera to the PC, and then trying to figure out what to do with them.

Hooking Up Your Camera

If your digital camera is less than a few years old, it probably came with a USB cable designed to plug into your PC. Fortunately, if your PC is young enough to run Windows XP, it probably has a USB jack, too. (If your camera is *more* than a few years old, see the box on page 143 for more advice.)

Windows XP comes preloaded with drivers for hundreds of current camera models, generally sparing you the standard installation process described on page 132. That's why, for most people, the instructions for transferring photos from the camera to the PC are as follows:

1. **Connect the camera to the PC, using the USB cable.**

That's it—there is no step 2. Windows XP automatically opens the Camera and Scanner Wizard, a series of screens that guides you through the process of selecting and then transferring the photos you want.

The various screens of the Camera Wizard take you through the following steps:

- **Welcome screen.** If you're the kind of person who prefers to let others do your grunt work, just click Next.

  Note, however, this screen contains an "advanced users only" link. If you click it, Windows XP opens up a new folder window that shows you the contents of the camera's memory card, with an icon for each photo. At this point, you can copy these photos to your hard drive by dragging them. Use this technique if you want to file them into different folders, for example, rather than using the wizard to dump them all into a single place.

  > **Tip:** If hooking up the camera produces the dialog box shown at the top of Figure 6-1, then you've installed some photo-management software of your own (maybe some that came with the camera). In that case, you have a choice: either select that program to download and manage your photos, or click Cancel to let XP do the job as described in these pages. Then open your My Pictures folder (Start → My Pictures) and, at the left side of the window, click "Get pictures from camera or scanner."

- **Choose Pictures to Copy.** As shown in Figure 6-1, this is the fun part. You can look over slide-sized versions of the pictures currently on the camera and, by turning on the checkboxes above them, tell Windows which ones you want to copy to your hard drive.

  > **Tip:** To straighten a photo that's turned 90 degrees, click it and then click one of the two tiny Rotate buttons at the lower-left corner of the dialog box.

The various screens of the Camera Wizard take you through these steps:

- **Picture Name and Destination.** After you pick the photos you want to import, Windows asks you to name the batch. If you name this group *Robin's Party*, for example, Windows puts the downloaded photos into a My Pictures → Robin's Party folder. (That is, unless you intervene by clicking the Browse button to choose a different folder.)

Figure 6-1. Top: When you connect the camera, Windows may ask which editing program you want to open. Otherwise, the Scanner and Camera Wizard launches.

Middle: The Clear All and Select All buttons can save time when you want to include, or exclude, only a few pictures.

Bottom: Once the digital pictures are on your PC, the wizard offers some fun options.

This screen also offers one of the most useful options: a checkbox called "Delete pictures from my device after copying them." If you turn on this checkbox, then you'll find your memory card freshly erased after the photo transfer, ready for more picture taking.

▶ **Other Options.** When the transfer process is over, the next screen (Figure 6-1, bottom) offers you direct links to publishing the photos to a Web site, ordering prints by mail via the Web, or Nothing—which is almost always what you want to do here.

▶ **Completing the Scanner and Camera Wizard.** The final screen completes the process by offering you a link that opens the folder currently containing the pictures (on your hard drive). Click either the link or the Finish button, which does the same thing.

TROUBLESHOOTING MOMENT

When the Wizard Doesn't Show Up

If the wizard doesn't appear when you hook up your camera, you may be one of the unlucky ones whose camera driver didn't come installed with XP. Technically speaking, the Camera Wizard gets triggered only by cameras whose manufacturers promise WIA (Windows Image Acquisition) compatibility. Almost all cameras sold since the year 2000 are WIA-compatible.

If the wizard doesn't appear even though you have a compatible camera, you may have to install the driver yourself, using the CD-ROM that came with your camera, as described on page 133. If the camera is reasonably new, it should thereafter work just as described on these pages.

If your camera is too old for Windows XP's tastes, you won't be able to use any of the automated downloading features described in this chapter. You can still get your pictures onto the PC, however, either by using the software provided with the camera (or an updated version—check the camera maker's Web site) or by buying a card reader, an inexpensive external "disk drive" that accepts the memory card from your camera. Once inserted, Windows treats the memory card exactly as though it's a giant floppy disk. Opening the card (from within the My Computer window) lets you manually drag the photos to your hard drive.

Fun with Downloaded Pictures

Once you've transferred pictures to your hard drive, you can enjoy a long list of photo-manipulation features, new in Windows XP. These features put to shame the national photo-management system: shoving drugstore prints into a shoebox, which then goes into a closet.

Suppose you've opened a folder of freshly downloaded pictures. (As noted above, they're usually in a folder in your My Pictures folder, which itself is in your My Documents folder. Unless you've deliberately removed My Pictures from your Start menu, just choose its name from the Start menu to get going. Or you can put a shortcut icon for My Pictures right on your desktop.)

Here are some of the ways you can manage your pictures after their safe arrival on your PC.

Download more photos

When a camera or scanner is turned on and connected to the PC, the first link in the task pane of your My Pictures folder is, "Get pictures from camera or scanner." Click it to launch the Camera and Scanner Wizard all over again.

Look them over

Windows XP comes with two folder window views especially designed for digital photos: Thumbnail and Filmstrip (page 59). For now, it's enough to note that Filmstrip view (Figure 6-2) is ideal for reviewing a batch of freshly transferred pictures at the size that's big enough for you to recognize them.

Remember to press the F11 key to maximize the window and hide a lot of the ancillary toolbar junk that eats into your photo-displaying space. (Press F11 again to restore the window size when you're done.) Also remember to rotate the photos that were taken with the camera turned sideways, especially if you plan to use the slide show, Web page, or email features described in the following paragraphs.

Figure 6-2. In Filmstrip view, the enlarged image shows the currently selected photo. You can select a different one for enlargement by clicking another image icon (bottom row) or by clicking the Previous and Next buttons beneath the selected photo. Don't miss the special tasks listed in the task pane at the left side—or the options in the menu that appear when you right-click the central, enlarged image.

Start a slide show

When you click "View as a slide show" in the task pane, your screen goes dark, thunder rumbles somewhere, and your entire monitor fills with a gorgeous, self-advancing slide show of the pictures in the folder. If you then move the mouse, a tiny palette appears in the upper-right corner with control buttons that correspond to Play, Pause, Previous, Next, and Stop.

The beauty of a slide show like this is that everyone at your presentation (or, if this is your home computer, in your family) can see it at once. It beats the pants off the ritual of passing out individual 4×6 drugstore prints to each person.

To stop the slide show, press the Esc key on your keyboard (or click the X button in the floating palette that appears when you move your mouse).

Order prints online

If you click this link in the task pane, Windows XP presents a wizard that helps you select photos in your folder for uploading to an online photo processor, like Kodak, Shutterfly, or Fuji. You can specify how many copies you want of each print, and at what sizes (Figure 6-3). Once you've plugged in your credit card number, the prints arrive by mail in about a week.

Make a printout

This task-pane link, too, opens a wizard. This time, it guides you through a selection of photos in your folder to print, a selection of printers to use, and the layout of photos on each $8 \frac{1}{2} \times 11$ sheet (four 3×5 inch prints, 9 wallet-sized prints, and so on). Note that many of these layouts chop off parts of your pictures to make them fit the page; the layout previews will reveal exactly which parts of the image you'll lose.

Install new wallpaper

The "Set as desktop background" link (which appears whenever you've highlighted a picture) plasters the currently selected photo across the entire background of your screen, turning your PC into the world's most expensive picture frame. (To change or remove this background, use the Display program; see page 266 for instructions.)

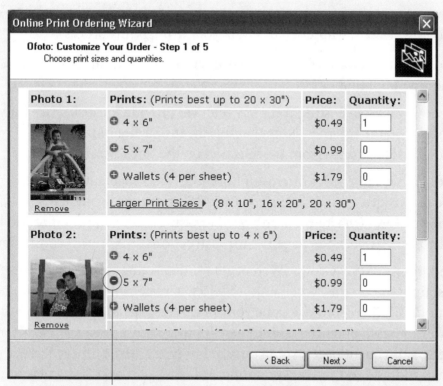

Low-resolution warning

Figure 6-3. The price for prints via the Web is usually 50 cents for 4×6 prints, and up to $20 for a 20×30 inch poster. Be especially careful when you see the red minus symbol shown here. It lets you know that the resolution of that photo is too low to make a good-quality print at that size. A 640×480 pixel shot, for example, will look grainy when printed at 5×7 inches.

Post the photos on the Web

In the old days, creating and posting Web pages was a task fit only for geeks. In Windows XP, however, anybody can create a gallery of photos that hangs on the Web for everyone in the world to see.

Start by clicking "Publish this file ([folder] if no file is selected) to the Web" in the task pane at the left side of your pictures' folder window. Yes, it's the Web Publishing Wizard, whose screens walk you through this process:

▶ Choosing the photos (from the assortment in the current folder) that you want to put online.

▶ Choosing a Web-hosting company that will provide the disk space for your pictures on the Internet. Note that this means paying money—*unless* you choose MSN Groups from the selection on the third wizard screen.

   Although it's free to let Microsoft host your Web page in this way, there are two downsides. First, it limits you to 3 MB of storage—and that's not very many pictures (maybe a dozen). Second, using MSN requires that you have a Microsoft *Passport*. See page 172 for instructions and privacy considerations.

▶ Choosing an MSN Group (Web page) for displaying your new photos. The first time you do this, you'll want to select "Create a new MSN Group to share your files." Microsoft will name your first Web page for you, tell you the URL (Web address), and offer to add the URL to your list of Favorites. When you create subsequent pages, you'll be asked to type a name for each, enter your email address, and type a description. Whether you're creating new or additional Web pages, the wizard then asks you to indicate whether or not you want the Internet at large to be able to find this page.

▶ The next wizard screen provides the URL (Web address) for your finished Web page gallery: [whatever name you provided for your Web page]. You can distribute this address to friends, family, or whomever you'd like to invite to view your masterpieces online.

▶ Another wizard screen tells you exactly where your Web-page document and graphics files have been stored online. Unless you're some kind of Web-savvy HTML guru, you probably won't care.

▶ Most digital cameras create enormous photo files, containing enough resolution for high-quality prints. Unfortunately, those files are much too large for use as Web-page graphics, which feature far lower resolution than printouts do. As a remedy, the wizard screen shown in Figure 6-4 offers to scale the photos down to reasonable dimensions, so that you won't tie up the modems of your potential audience all day.

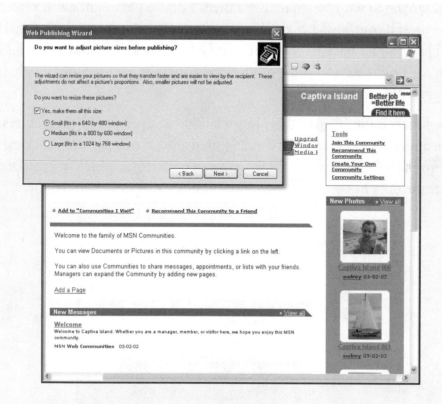

Figure 6-4. Top: The Web Publishing Wizard offers to scale down your graphics (the Web versions, not the originals) to reasonable dimensions.

Bottom: You're a published photographer! Click a photo to open it up full size and start a photo slide show.

At last, Windows uploads your reduced-size photos to the Internet, which can take some time. The final wizard screen offers you the chance to go online, opening your browser automatically to the new Web page.

Email photos

Photo files destined for *printing* are much too massive for *emailing*. A single digital photo can occupy 2 MB of disk space or more, which would take until Thanksgiving to send by email. Even then, a photo file might never reach your recipient. If it overflows her email account's storage limit (typically 5 or 10 MB), it will just bounce back to you. Then you'll be forced to sit and wait while it downloads right back to you—a fitting punishment for uploading such a big file to begin with!

The solution is the "E-mail this file" link in the task pane of your pictures folder, which appears whenever you've highlighted at least one picture. Clicking this link produces the dialog box shown in Figure 6-5 (top), which offers to smoothly reduce the dimensions of your pictures in the process of emailing them.

Figure 6-5. Top: If you just click OK, the selected photos will get emailed at 640 X 480 pixel resolution—just right for satisfactory viewing (and fairly speedy transferring) by email.

Bottom: Clicking the "Show more options" link offers you the opportunity to specify which reduced size you want.

Once you click OK, Windows automatically launches your email program and opens a new, outgoing email message, with the photo files (reduced in size, if that's what you specified) already attached. All you need to do is indicate the address, a subject line, and some comments (in the body of the message), if you like.

At this point, you can drag the reduced-size picture attachments directly out of the email and back to your desktop, or to a waiting folder, without ever addressing or sending the message. Doing so capitalizes on the photo-shrinking power of the "E-mail this file" feature—without actually emailing anything.

Create a photo screen saver

There's no "Create photo screen saver" link in the task pane of a photo folder, but Windows XP can still turn your favorite pictures into an automatic slide show whenever your computer isn't in use. Just right-click the desktop, choose Properties from the shortcut menu, click the Screen Saver tab in the resulting dialog box, and then choose My Pictures Slideshow from the "Screen saver" drop-down list.

The screen saver is composed of photos in your My Pictures folder. If you'd like to choose a different folder as fodder for the slide show, click the Settings button, and then click the Browse button. You'll be offered the chance to choose any folder on your hard drive.

From now on, whenever your PC has gone untouched for five minutes (or whatever interval you specify here), your pictures will fill the screen, complete with special transition effects between images, if you so choose.

 Tip: If you're the impatient sort, simply press the right and left arrow keys on your keyboard to summon the next or previous photo while the screen saver is playing.

View them bigger

If you double-click a picture or scan a file whose file type you haven't assigned to open in a particular graphics program, it opens up in a program called Windows Picture and Fax Viewer. WPFV, as Windows veterans don't call it, is a strange, phantom little program. It doesn't show up in your Start menu, and you can't find it by searching for it. You can open it only by double-clicking a graphic or by right-clicking a picture's icon and choosing Preview from the shortcut menu.

The result is a simple preview window (Figure 6-6). At the bottom edge, you'll find buttons that do exactly the kinds of things you've been reading about: show the previous or next image, start a slide show, rotate the graphic, print it, email it, and so on.

POWER USERS' CLINIC

Special Pictures for Special Folders

Filmstrip view, shown in Figure 6-2, isn't the only way to view pictures in Windows XP. Thumbnails view has charms of its own—including the ability to display folders like the ones illustrated here, complete with miniature

Captiva Island

Captiva Island2

photos on the folder icon to show you what's inside. If you open your My Pictures folder and set it to Thumbnails view, for example, you'll see that Windows XP has already dressed up the icons of any picture folders inside.

It's worth knowing that, if the collection of pictures inside one of these folders changes, their miniatures on the folder icon itself don't change—at least not until you right-click the folder icon and choose Refresh Thumbnail from the shortcut menu.

Zoom in   Zoom out

Figure 6-6. To learn what each button does, point to it without clicking. The Zoom In and Zoom Out buttons magnify or reduce the image on the screen, and the Delete button deletes the file from your hard drive (or, rather, flings it into the Recycle Bin).

Scanning

As far as Windows XP is concerned, a scanner is just another kind of digital camera. When an XP-compatible scanner is turned on and connected to the PC, for example, the Camera and Scanner Wizard starts up automatically. (If it doesn't, open your My Pictures folder. You'll see that the first link in the task pane is, "Get pictures from camera or scanner." Clicking launches—you guessed it—the Scanner and Camera Wizard.)

The options you see during the march of the wizard screens are very similar to the ones described in the previous pages. The chief difference is the Choose Scanning Preferences screen, where you're supposed to indicate what kind of scan you want to make (color, grayscale, or black and white) and what portion of the page you want scanned (by dragging the little square handles on the preview of the page).

To view and manipulate your scanned images, use the commands in the My Pictures task pane. You'd be nuts to order prints of something you've just scanned, however. Instead, you'll probably want to use the software provided by the manufacturer to open and edit your image files. Or, if you haven't installed such a program, you can just double-click the scanned document's icon to open it in the Windows Picture and Fax Viewer (page 152).

Windows Media Player

You can use Windows Media Player—one of the most useful freebie features of Windows XP—to play sounds, play digital movies, or tune in to Internet radio stations. It's the Grand Central Station for digital music and movies, as well as the junction for your hard drive, CD player, CD burner, MP3 player, and the Internet (from which you can download new music files and movie clips). If you don't have the latest version of Windows Media Player, you can download it for free from Microsoft's Web site.

The Lay of the Land

To fire up Windows Media Player, choose Start → Programs → Accessories → Entertainment → Windows Media Player.

The top edge, as you may have noticed, offers six primary tabs, which cover the essential functions of Media Player. They're described in more detail in the following pages, but here's a quick overview:

▶ **Now Playing.** Click this tab while music or video is playing from any source. This is where you can see a list of songs on the CD, a graphic equalizer, and a wild, psychedelic screen saver that pulses in time to the music.

- **Library.** This screen is like a Windows Explorer display—a folder tree on the left side, and the contents of a selected folder listed on the right—that lists every piece of music or video your copy of Media Player "knows about" on your hard drive. This is also where you can sort your songs into subsets called *playlists*.

- **Rip.** This screen is used to copy songs from one of your music CDs onto your hard drive, as described on page 156.

- **Burn.** After transferring some songs to your hard drive—from the Internet or your own music CD collection—you can then burn your own CDs. This screen is the loading dock.

- **Sync.** Here's where you line up music or video that you'd like transferred to a portable music or video player, if you have one that Media Player understands.

- **Guide.** This page is a rabbit hole into Alice in Marketingland. You wind up on a Microsoft Web site that tells (and sells) you everything about Media Player and the latest downloadable offerings from Microsoft and its partners.

Playing Music CDs

For its first trick, Media Player can simulate a $25 CD player, capable of playing your music CDs while you're working at your computer. To fire it up, just insert an audio CD into your computer's CD or DVD drive.

Unless you've fiddled with the settings, Media Player opens automatically and the CD begins to play. The screen even fills with a shimmering, laser-light show (called a *visualization*) that pulses along with the music. Ta-da! (If you see a message asking what to do with the CD, choose "Play Audio CD.")

 Note: If all the fancy dancing-to-the-music graphics are slowing down your machine as you try to work in other programs, you can always turn them off (choose View → Visualizations → No Visualizations). If you can't find the menu bar, see Figure 6-7.

And if you have more than one CD drive with a disc in it (or, say, one audio CD and one DVD), you can tell Media Player which disc you want to play by choosing from the little down-arrow menu next to the Now Playing tab.

Figure 6-7. Windows Media Player lets you do so many things to change the size, shape, and appearance of its window that it's easy to forget where the controls are. You can always bring the main menu bar back into view by clicking a button that looks like a down arrow (or sometimes a double-headed arrow) and choosing Show Menu Bar.

Copying CDs to Your Hard Drive

You can copy an album, or selected tracks, to your hard drive in the form of standalone music files that play when double-clicked (a process called *ripping*, much to the consternation of sleepless record executives who think that it's short for *ripping off*). Having CD songs on your hard drive is handy because:

▶ You can listen to your songs without having to hunt for the CDs they came from.

▶ You can listen to music even if you're using the CD-ROM drive for something else (like a CD-based game).

- You can build your own *playlists* (sets of favorite songs) consisting of cuts from different albums.

- You can compress the file in the process, so that each song takes up much less disk space.

- You can transfer the songs to a portable music player or burn them onto a homemade CD.

If you're sold on the idea, begin with a quick trip to the Tools → Options menu. Click the Rip Music tab, and then inspect your settings. For example, unless you intervene by clicking the Change button near the top, Windows will copy your song files into the My Documents → My Music folder.

Note, too, that Microsoft has designed Windows Media Player to generate files in the company's own proprietary format, something called Windows Media Audio (WMA) format (.wma). But many people prefer, and even require, MP3 files. For example, most recent CD players and portable music players (including the iPod) can play back MP3 files—but won't know what to do with WMA files.

If you'd prefer the more universally compatible MP3 files, use the Format pop-up menu to choose "mp3" (see Figure 6-8). And rejoice: until Media Player 10 came along, you had to pay $10 extra for the ability to create MP3 files.

 Tip: If you have a stack of CDs to rip, don't miss the two checkboxes here: "Rip CD when inserted" and "Eject CD when ripping is complete." Together, they turn your PC into an automated ripping machine, leaving nothing for you to do but feed it CDs and watch TV.

Finally, the slider in this dialog box lets you control the tradeoff, in the resulting sound files, between audio quality and file size. At 128 Kbps, for example, a three-minute MP3 file might consume about 2.8 megabytes. At 192 Kbps, the same file will sound much better, but it will eat up about 4.2 MB. And at a full 320 Kbps, the file will be roughly 7 MB.

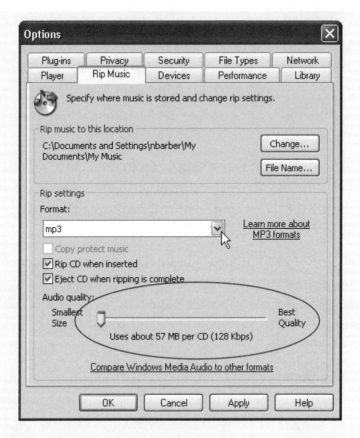

Figure 6-8. Music files occupy a lot of space on the hard drive. By adjusting the circled slider, you can specify how much Windows compresses the song files, with the understanding that you sacrifice sound quality as you make the file smaller. Experiment with the other settings to accommodate your ears and speakers.

These are important considerations if you're ripping for a portable MP3 player, like the iPod. For instance: if your music player contains a 20 GB hard drive, it can hold 142 hours of music you've ripped at 320 Kbps, or 357 hours at 128 Kbps.

For MP3 files, most people find the 192 Kbps setting (on the "Audio quality" slider) to produce great-sounding, relatively compact files. For WMA, 128 Kbps might be a good starting point. Needless to say, let your ears (and the capacity of your portable music player) be your guide.

Click OK, then begin:

1. **Insert the music CD. Click the Rip tab at the top of the Media Player window.**

    The list of songs on the CD appears. See the box below for information on ensuring that the album name and track names are correct.

2. **Turn off the checkbox of any track you don't want to copy.**

    You've waited all your life for this: at last, you have the power to eliminate any annoying songs and keep only the good ones.

    And while you're playing record-company executive, take a moment to drag the names of the songs up or down the list to rearrange them.

GEM IN THE ROUGH

Filling in Track Names

Precious few audio CDs come programmed to know their own names (and song names). Every day, millions of people insert music CDs into their computers and see the songs listed as nothing more than "Track 1," "Track 2," and so on—and the album itself goes by the catchy name Unknown Album.

If your PC is online when you insert a certain music CD—you lucky thing—you'll bypass that entire situation. Windows takes a quick glance at your CD, sends a query to allmusic.com (a massive database on the Web containing information on over 200,000 CDs), and downloads the track list and a picture of the album cover for your particular disc.

You can also type in the names of your songs manually. Once again, click "Copy from CD" at the left side of the screen to view the list of tracks. Now right-click the track and, from the shortcut menu, choose Edit. A little text box opens so that you can type in the track information manually.

No matter how the track names and album art get onto your PC, Windows XP saves this information in your music library (see "Copying CDs to Your Hard Drive" on page 156). Therefore, the next time you insert this CD, the Media Player will recognize it and display the track names and album information automatically.

3. **Click Rip Music.**

   You'll find this button in the narrow strip above the list of songs.

   Media Player may take this opportunity to present a Rip Options dialog box, whose purpose is to beg you, one last time, to choose one of Microsoft's WMA formats instead of MP3. Click "Keep my current format settings" and click OK.

   Windows begins to copy the songs onto your hard drive. The Copy Music button changes to Stop Copy, which you can click to interrupt the process.

Organizing Your Music Library

Every CD transferred to your hard drive winds up with an entry in your Library menu, identified in Figure 6-9. Make that several entries, actually, as this Explorer-like tree view lets you see your collection sorted by composer, album, year released, or whatever. Whenever you want to play back some music, just double-click its name in this list—there's no need to hunt around in your shoe-boxes for the original CD the songs came from.

But that's just the beginning of Media Player's organizational tools. Transferring CD songs to your hard drive isn't the only way to log your files in the Media Player database. You can also add sound and video files to this master list using any of these methods:

▶ Use the Tools → Search for Media Files command (or press F3).

▶ Drag sound or video files directly from your desktop or folder windows into the Media Player window.

▶ Choose File → Add to Library (or click the Add to Library button at the bottom of the Library screen). From the submenu, choose Add Currently Playing Item, Add Folder, Add URL (for files on the Web), or whatever.

▶ The Internet is crawling with Web sites that sell downloadable music files that you can make part of your music library. At the top-right corner of the Media

Figure 6-9. Click All Music (left panel) to bring up the complete list in the middle panel. Drag each song or CD name into the New Playlist list (right panel) to create a brand-new list of songs.

Player window, a drop-down menu lists them (Napster, Musicmatch, MSN Music, Wal-Mart Music Downloads, and so on). When you choose a music store's name, the Media Player window ducks into a phone booth and becomes a Web browser, filled with the corresponding company's wares. Anything you buy gets gulped right into your Library, ready for burning to a CD or syncing with an audio player.

Once you've created a well-stocked fridge of music, you can call up a particular song by typing into the Search box (at the top of the Library list), by navigating the folder tree (at the left side of the Media Library list), or by using the playlist list (in the My Playlists category of the Library list).

Playlists

As noted earlier, each CD that you transfer to your hard drive becomes a *playlist* in Windows Media Player: a group of songs, listed in the folder tree at the left side, that you can play back with a single click. Media Player automatically turns your CDs into playlists, but you can also create your own, mixing and matching songs from different albums for different purposes (which you might name Downer Tunes, Makeout Music, or whatever).

To create a new playlist, make sure you've selected the Library tab. Then click New Playlist (upper-right of the Media Player window). From the drop-down list, choose New List → Playlist.

The Playlist panel, at the right side of your screen, is empty (Figure 6-9). It says, "Drag items here to build a list of items for your playlist." Once you've created a playlist, click that New Playlist button/menu thing above it once again. This time, choose Save Playlist As from the drop-down menu, type a name for your playlist, and thrill to the appearance of a new icon in the My Playlists "category" of your library list (left panel).

Deleting things

Whenever you want to delete a song, a playlist, or almost anything else, simply right-click it. You'll find the Delete command in the shortcut menu.

Burning Your Own CDs.

The beauty of a CD burner is that it finally frees you from the stifling restrictions put on your musical tastes by the record companies. You can create your own "best of" CDs that play in any CD player—and that contain only your favorite songs in your favorite order (see Figure 6-10).

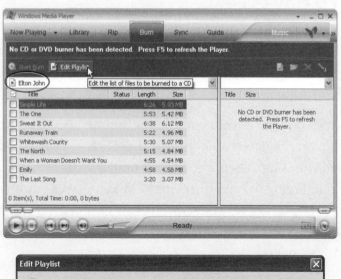

Figure 6-10. The easiest way to create a CD in Media Player is to assemble a custom playlist as described on page 162. Then go to the Burn tab (top) and choose the playlist's name from the drop-down menu (circled). You can click Edit Playlist (indicated by the cursor) to make further changes to the list in a separate window (bottom). Click OK to return to the burn window, and then click Start Burn (to the left of Edit Playlist). Your PC spits out the newly minted CD when it's done.

Playing DVD Movies

If your PC has a drive that's capable of playing DVDs *and* a piece of software called a DVD decoder, you're in for a treat. Media Player can play rented or purchased Hollywood movies on DVD as though it was born to do so—a new feature in Windows XP.

Watching movies on your screen couldn't be simpler: just insert the DVD. Windows XP automatically detects that it's a video DVD—as opposed to, say, one that's just filled with files. Then, depending on the settings you made in the dialog box shown in Figure 6-7, it either opens Media Player automatically, opens your add-on DVD-playing software, or gives you the choice. (If not, no problem: open Media Player yourself and then choose Play → DVD, VCD or CD Audio → [your DVD drive's name].)

Media Player starts out playing your movie in a relatively small window. But you didn't come this far, and pay this much, just to watch movies on a mere *slice of* your screen.

Your first act, therefore, should be to enlarge the picture to fill the screen. Pressing Alt+Enter is the easiest way, but you can also choose View → Full Screen or click the Full Screen button (see Figure 6-11).

After you enlarge the screen, playback controls appear for a few seconds at the lower-left corner of the screen, permitting you to speed backward or forward through the movie, and then fade away so as not to obscure Arnold Schwarzenegger's face. To pause the movie, jump around in it, or advance one frame at a time, just twitch the mouse to make the controls (and the playlist of DVD chapters) reappear.

Figure 6-11. Once the DVD is playing, you control the playback using the standard Media Player controls at the bottom left.

Alternatively, you can right-click anywhere on the "movie screen" itself to reveal a menu of disc-navigation features.

PART THREE: WINDOWS ONLINE

Chapter 7   Getting on the Web

Chapter 8   Outlook Express 6

CHAPTER 7:
GETTING ON THE WEB

▶ How to Get Online

▶ Establishing a New Dial-Up Internet
Account

▶ Manually Plugging in Internet Settings

▶ Dialing Up to the Internet

▶ Surfing the Web

▶ Internet Explorer

PLENTY OF PEOPLE BUY A PC to crunch numbers, scan photos, or cultivate their kids' hand-eye coordination. But for millions of people, Reason One for using a PC is to access the Internet. This chapter covers getting online and surfing the Web. The next chapter covers that other thing you can do on the Internet—email.

To join the Internet party already in progress, you need three components: a connection (like a modem, cable modem, DSL, or corporate network), an Internet account, and Internet software (like a Web browser). Windows XP comes with a browser—Microsoft Internet Explorer (but this chapter also mentions some alternatives).

How to Get Online

Most people connect to the Internet using a *modem*, a device that connects your PC to a standard voice phone line. Almost every modern computer comes with a dial-up modem built right in. All you have to do is sign up for an Internet account, and you can be online in minutes. (For more detail on choosing a service, see the box on page 176.)

Cable and DSL

Nearly half of all Internet fans have abandoned their dial-up modem in favor of much faster gear like a cable modem or a DSL connection. Actually, neither cable "modems" nor DSL connections are modems in the true sense of the word. The word "modem" is an abbreviation of *modulator-dem*odulator, which refers to the way the device converts data into bursts of sound. Still, people have to call them *something*, so "cable modem" and "DSL modem" are the common terms.

Whatever you call them, these systems offer several gigantic advantages over dial-up modems. For example:

▶ **Speed.** These modems operate at 5 to 50 times the speed of a traditional dial-up modem. For example, you might wait 5 minutes to download a 2 MB file with a standard modem—a job that would take about 10 *seconds* with a cable modem. And complex Web pages that take almost a minute to appear in your browser with a standard modem will pop up almost immediately with a cable modem or DSL.

- **No dialing.** These fancier connection methods hook you up to the Internet permanently, full time, so that you don't waste time connecting or disconnecting—ever. You're *always* online.

- **No weekends lost to setup.** Best of all, there's no need to do any of the setup yourself. A representative from the phone company or cable company comes to your home or office to install the modem *and* configures Windows XP to use it. If you sign up for a cable modem, the cable TV company pays you a visit, supplies the modem, installs a network card into your PC, and sets up the software for you.

- **Possible savings.** As of this writing, cable modems and DSL services cost about $30 to $50 a month. Sounds pricey, but it *includes* the Internet account for which you'd ordinarily pay $20 if you signed up for a traditional ISP. And you may be able to save even more money by canceling a second phone line you were using for a dial-up modem.

Virtually all cable TV companies offer cable modem service. Unfortunately, you may not be able to get DSL if the phone company doesn't have a central office within about three miles of your home. It's also worth noting that cable modems and DSL modems aren't *always* blazing fast. The cable modem can slow down as more people in your area use their cable modems simultaneously. And DSL modems may be slower the farther away you are from the telephone company.

 Note: DSL stands for *digital subscriber line*, and unlike a cable modem, it doesn't require the installation of any special cables or wiring. DSL works by taking advantage of unused signal capacity on your existing telephone line—the very same line your plain-old phone number uses.

Wireless Networks

If you have a broadband connection like a cable modem or DSL, you're in heaven, but not on the penthouse floor of heaven. These days, the ultimate bliss is connecting without wires, from anywhere in your house or building—or, if you're a laptop warrior, someone *else's* house or building, like Starbucks, McDonald's, airport lounges, hotel lobbies, and anywhere else that an Internet "hot spot" has been set up.

Those are places where somebody has set up an *802.11 access point* (or base station), which is a glorified antenna for their cable modem or DSL box. Any computer that's been equipped with a corresponding wireless networking card (as most new laptops are these days) can hop online, at high speed, with only a couple of clicks.

Say you open up your laptop in a hotel lobby, which just happens to be a hot spot. You'll see a little balloon pop up over your notification area, in the lower-right of your screen: "Wireless networks detected." That's Windows' dull way of saying, "You've found a hot spot!" To start making the wireless connection, click the balloon.

Next, you get to read about the network you've found. To get online, click the network's name and then click Connect. (The message onscreen warns you that hackers with network-sniffing software could, in theory, intercept your wireless transmissions—always a concern with public wireless networks.) If a yellow padlock appears, you can't use the network without a password.

You can wander around your house and yard with a laptop and pull the same stunt. For the basics of setting up your own wireless network, see page 344.

Establishing a New Dial-Up Internet Account

If you'd like to sign up for Microsoft's Internet service, called MSN (and by the way, Microsoft would *love* you to sign up for MSN), or a traditional ISP, you're ready for the New Connection Wizard.

1. **Choose Start → All Programs → Accessories → Communications → New Connection Wizard.**

   If you managed to mouse across that labyrinth of menus, the New Connection Wizard appears (Figure 7-1).

2. **Click Next. On the next screen, click Connect to the Internet, and then click the Next button.**

   Now you reach an important juncture: the Getting Ready screen (third from top in Figure 7-1).

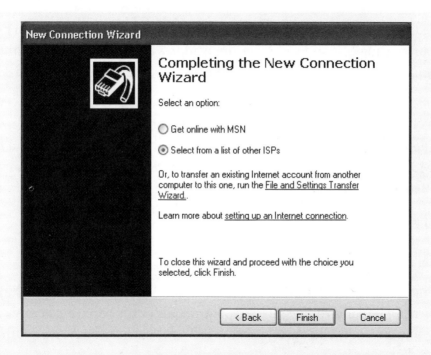

Figure 7-1. To sign up for a standard Internet account, launch the New Connection Wizard as described on page 172 and keep clicking the first choice on each wizard screen. At the last step, you'll have to choose between signing up for Microsoft's own Internet service, called MSN, or an independent one like EarthLink or AT&T.

3. **Click "Choose from a list of Internet service providers (ISPs)." Click Next.**

   Here's where you tell the wizard whether you want to sign up for the pricier, but sanitized, world of MSN, or a standard Internet service provider.

4. **Click either "Get online with MSN" or "Select from a list of other ISPs," and then click Finish.**

   If you choose MSN, the graphic design scheme of the wizard changes—suddenly you're in pastel land. This, of course, is the MSN Signup Wizard. Over the next few minutes, you'll be guided through the process of signing up for a new account. You'll be asked for your name, address, birthday, occupation, credit card number, and so on. You'll also be offered the chance to preserve your existing Microsoft-service email address (anything ending with *@hotmail.com* or *@msn.com*). (During the process, the computer will dial a toll-free number to connect with MSN.)

   If you choose "Select from a list of other ISPs," the wizard disappears, and Windows deposits you into a folder window containing two shortcuts: "Get online with MSN" (which opens the same wizard described in the previous paragraph) and "Refer me to more Internet Service Providers." Use the latter shortcut to sign up for traditional Internet accounts, as shown in Figure 7-2.

   Whether you choose MSN or a more traditional ISP, however, both sign-up wizards share a few things in common:

   ▸ Along the way, the wizard dials a second time. This time, it's contacting the Internet company you've selected. The details of the service plan now appear on your screen. If you agree with the ISP's rules, click the Accept button, and then click Next.

   ▸ You'll also be asked to invent an email address for yourself. The ending part of the address is determined by your choice of ISP—*@earthlink.net*, for example, or *@msn.com*. The first part is up to you, but keep in mind that names like *Bob* and *Tiffany* were snapped up some time in the Reagan era. Therefore, if the email name you type isn't unique, you'll be asked to try a different one.

Figure 7-2. In the U.S., the Internet Connection Wizard starts by calling a toll-free number to retrieve a list of Internet service providers that have deals with Microsoft in "your area" (in general, this means "in your country"). Click one, and then read the details of its deal in the scrolling right-side window. After settling on one, click the Next button to begin the sign-up process (providing your name, address, credit card number, and so on).

▶ When you're shown a list of phone numbers, choose one that's local. If there are no local numbers listed, and you'd rather not pay long distance charges every time you connect to the Internet, consider canceling this entire sign-up operation and spending some time researching smaller, regional ISPs.

ISP vs. Online Service

If you decide to connect to the Net using a dial-up modem, your next task is to get an Internet account. You can get one in either of two ways: by signing up for an *online service*, such as America Online or MSN, or through a direct Internet account with an *Internet service provider* (or ISP, as insiders and magazines inevitably call them).

National ISPs like EarthLink and AT&T have local telephone numbers in every U.S. state and many other countries. If you don't travel much, you may not need such broad coverage. Instead, you may be able to save money by signing up for a local or regional ISP. Either way, dialing the Internet is a local call for most people.

The Internet is filled with Web sites that list, describe, and recommend ISPs. To find such directories, visit Google and search for ISP listings. Of course, until you've actually got your Internet account working, you'll have to do this research on a PC that is online, like the free terminals available at most public libraries.

Online services like AOL give you all Internet functions in one program, including email and Web surfing, and provide a few members-only features like games and chat rooms. When using an ISP, on the other hand, you have to fire up a different application for each function: Internet Explorer for surfing the Web, Outlook Express for email, and so on.

Because online services are slightly easier to use than ISP accounts, some hostile, insecure people look down on MSN and America Online members. You've been warned.

The Connection Icon

When it's all over, Windows XP stores your ISP information, your name, your password, and so on, into a single icon called a *connection*. To see the one you've just created, choose Start → All Programs → Accessories → Communications → Network Connections. There are dozens of ways to get online, and one way is to double-click this special icon.

Doing so produces the dialog box shown in Figure 7-3 at left. This box will soon become extremely familiar, since it appears every time your computer attempts to access the Internet for any reason.

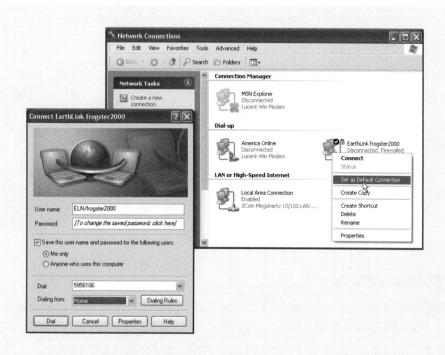

Figure 7-3. Right: This particularly well-endowed individual has four different ways to get to the Internet: MSN Explorer, America Online, Local Area Connection, and EarthLink Frogster 2000.

Left: Double-clicking one of these icons (in this case, EarthLink), produces this dialog box, where you can click Dial to go online. If you use the same Internet connection most of the time, right-click the icon and choose "Set as Default Connection."

Once you've set up your connection, skip ahead to "Connecting to the Internet." You're now ready to explore the Net.

Manually Plugging in Internet Settings

Although the New Connection Wizard does an admirable job of trying to simplify the hairy process of accessing the Internet, it's not always appropriate. Here are a few cases when you may want to arrange your settings manually:

▶ You already have an Internet account.

▶ You have a cable modem or DSL connection.

▶ The New Connection Wizard didn't find any ISPs with local phone numbers for you, but you've heard about a local service—offered by your local PC user group, for example—that sounds just right.

▶ Your PC is connected to a network through which your company provides Internet service.

In each of these cases, you can still use the New Connection Wizard; however, a good deal more typing is required.

Via Dial-up Modem

If you connect to the Internet via telephone jack, like most of the world, choose Start → All Programs → Accessories → Communications → New Connection Wizard. Make sure that your computer is plugged into a phone jack.

Click Next, "Connect to the Internet," Next, "Setup my Internet connection manually," and Next. Now click "Connect using a dial-up modem," and then Next.

On the following several screens, you'll be asked to type in a few pieces of information that only your ISP can provide: the local phone number that connects your PC to the Internet, your user name, and your password. (You can call your ISP for this information, or consult the literature delivered by postal mail when you signed up for an ISP account.)

You'll also be offered these three important checkboxes:

▶ **Use this account name and password when anyone connects to the Internet from this computer.** This option refers to the Windows XP user accounts feature described in Chapter 12, in which various people who share the same computer keep their worlds of information and settings separate by signing in each time they use the machine. It's asking you: "Is this the Internet account you want this PC to use no matter who's logged in at the moment?"

▶ **Make this the default Internet connection.** Some people have more than one way to access the Internet. Maybe you connect your laptop to a cable modem when you're at home but dial out using the modem when you're on the road. Turn on this checkbox if the account you're setting up is the one you want it to use most often.

> **Tip:** You can always change your mind. In the Network Connections window, right-click the connection icon and choose Cancel as Default Connection from the shortcut menu.

▶ **Turn on Internet Connection Firewall for this Connection.** Windows XP offers a certain degree of protection from incoming hacker attacks in the form of a personal firewall. Turn this off only if you've equipped your PC with other firewall software.

When it's all over, you'll find that you've given birth to a *connection icon*, as shown at right in Figure 7-3. Once you've correctly typed in all of the necessary information, you should be ready to surf.

> **Tip:** If you carry a laptop from city to city—each of which requires a different local Internet number—you may want to create more than one connection icon by plugging in a different local access number each time.

Via Cable Modem, Network, or DSL

As noted earlier in this chapter, you're usually spared the hassle of setting up these so-called broadband accounts. The installation person generally handles it for you.

XP's ESP Connection

Whenever you try to get online, Windows XP automatically hunts for a working connection—wired or wireless. That's a blessing for laptops: when you're at the office plugged into an Ethernet cable, you can use its stability and speed. When you're in some hotel-lobby hot spot, and your laptop can't find the Ethernet cable, it automatically hops onto the wireless network, if possible.

And how does the dial-up modem enter into all this? That's up to you. Open Internet Options in your Control Panel, click the Connections tab, and turn on, for example, "Dial whenever a network connection is not present" or "Never dial a connection."

Dialing Up to the Internet

If you enjoy a full-time Internet connection like a cable modem, DSL, or some wireless variation thereof, you're constantly online. Skip to the section on surfing the Web.

If you have a dial-up modem, however, you should now have a connection icon in your Network Connections window.

Manual Connections

Double-click the connection's icon in the Network Connections window. The Connect To dialog box appears, as shown at left in Figure 7-3. Just press Enter, or click Dial, to go online.

But that's just the beginning. If you crave variety, here are a few other ways of opening the connection:

▶ Right-click your connection icon, and then choose Connect from the shortcut menu.

- Create a desktop shortcut for your connection icon (the icon in the Network Connections window) by right-dragging it out of the window and onto the desktop. When you release the mouse button, choose Create Shortcut(s) Here from the shortcut menu. Now just double-click the shortcut whenever you feel the urge to surf.

- Drag your connection icon shortcut onto the Quick Launch toolbar (page 74), so that you can now get to the Internet with just one click.

The Notification Area Icon

While you're connected to your ISP, Windows XP puts an icon in the notification area reminding you that you're online. You can watch the icon light up as data zooms back and forth across the connection. And if you point to it without clicking, you'll see a yellow tooltip showing your speed and how much data has been transmitted. (If this little taskbar icon isn't visible, take a moment to turn it back on, as directed in Figure 7-4. You'll find it to be an important administrative center for going online and offline.)

Automatic Dialing

It's important to understand that when your PC dials, it simply opens up a connection to the Internet. But aside from tying up the phone line, your PC doesn't actually *do* anything until you then launch an Internet program, such as an email program or a Web browser. By itself, making your PC dial the Internet is no more useful than dialing a phone number and then not saying anything.

Therefore, using the Internet is generally a two-step procedure: First, open the connection; second, open a program.

Fortunately, Windows offers a method of combining these two steps. You can make the dialing/connecting process begin automatically whenever you launch an Internet program. This way, you're saved the trouble of fussing with the connection icon every time you want to go online.

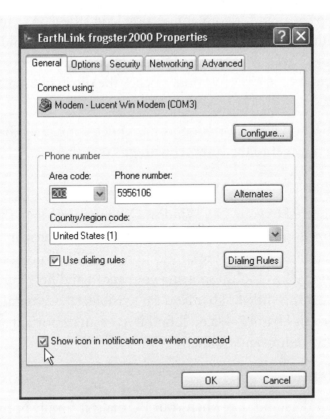

Figure 7-4. To make the notification area icon appear, right-click the icon for your connection. From the shortcut menu, choose Properties. The Properties dialog box opens to the General tab. At the bottom of this tab, turn on "Show icon in notification area when connected."

To turn on this option, just open your Web browser and try to Web surf. When the PC discovers that it's not, in fact, online, it will display the Dial-up Connection dialog box at left in Figure 7-5. Turn on the "Connect automatically" checkbox, and then click Connect.

From now on, whenever you use a feature that requires an Internet connection, your PC dials automatically. (Examples: specifying a Web address in a window's Address bar, clicking the Send and Receive button in your email program, clicking a link in the Windows Help system, and so on.)

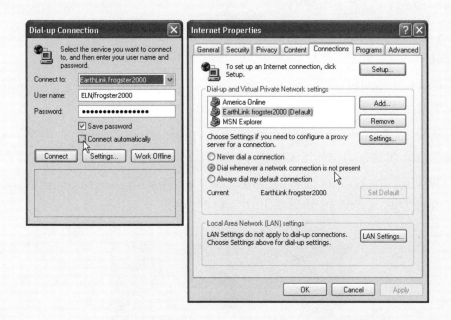

Figure 7-5. Left: "Connect automatically" (indicated by cursor) makes your PC dial whenever any of your programs tries to go online.

Right: If you can't seem to get online despite taking this step, open the Internet Options Control Panel. Click the Connections tab. Make sure that "Never dial a connection" isn't selected; choose one of the other options.

Disconnecting

The trouble with the standard dial-up Internet connection is that, unless you intervene, it will never hang up. It will continue to tie up your phone line until the other family members hunt it down, hours later, furious and brandishing wire cutters.

Therefore, it's worth taking a moment to configure your system so that it won't stay online forever.

Disconnecting manually

When you're finished using the Internet, end the phone call by performing one of the following steps:

▶ Right-click the little connection icon on your taskbar. Choose Disconnect from the shortcut menu (Figure 7-6, top).

▶ Double-click the little connection icon on the taskbar. Click the Disconnect button in the Status dialog box that appears (Figure 7-6, bottom), or press Alt+D.

▶ Right-click the connection icon in your Network Connections window. Choose Disconnect from the shortcut menu.

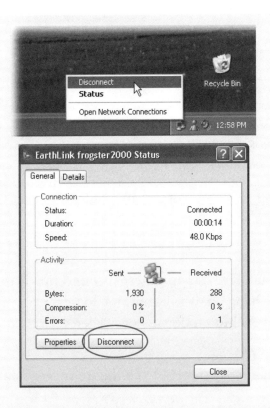

Figure 7-6. Top: The quickest way to hang up is to use the notification-area icon. Right-click it and choose Disconnect from the shortcut menu that appears.

Bottom: You can also double-click the icon to view statistics on your session so far, and to produce a Disconnect button for hanging up.

Laptop's Lament: Away from the Cable Modem

When I'm home, I connect my laptop to my cable modem. But when I'm on the road, of course, I have to use my dial-up ISP. Is there any way to automate the switching between these two connection methods?

If there weren't, do you think your question would have even appeared in this book?

The feature you're looking for is Internet Options in the Control Panel (page 270). Open it, click the Connections tab, and then turn on "Dial whenever a network connection is not present."

From now on, your laptop will use its dial-up modem only when it realizes that it isn't connected to your cable modem.

Disconnecting automatically

You can also set up your PC to hang up the phone automatically several minutes after your last activity online.

To find the necessary controls, right-click your connection icon (page 176); then, from the shortcut menu, choose Properties. In the resulting dialog box, click the Options tab. Near the middle of the box, you'll see a drop-down list called "Idle time before hanging up." You can set it to 1 minute, 10 minutes, 2 hours, or whatever.

Surfing the Web

The most popular Internet service has got to be the World Wide Web. In fact, the Web is becoming synonymous with the Internet in popular usage (though purists will still correct you if you use the two terms interchangeably).

Most Windows XP users wind up using Internet Explorer, which is built right into the operating system, for Web surfing. But other browsers do exist, including the free Mozilla Firefox (*www.mozilla.org*), described in the box on page 199.

Internet Explorer

Internet Explorer (or IE, as it's often abbreviated) is the most famous Web browser on earth, thanks to several years of Justice-department scrutiny and newspaper headlines. Windows XP comes with IE version 6, which you can open in a number of ways:

▶ Choosing its name from the Start menu (either the left column or the All Programs menu).

▶ Clicking its shortcut on the Quick Launch toolbar.

▶ Choosing a Web site's name from your Start → Favorites menu (that is, if you've put favorites there).

▶ Typing a Web address—sometimes called its *URL* (*Uniform Resource Locator*) into a window's Address bar. A Web page URL usually begins with the prefix *http://*, but you can leave that part off when typing into the Address bar.

▶ Clicking a blue, underlined link on a Windows Help screen.

As you can see in Figure 7-7, the Internet Explorer window is filled with tools that are designed to facilitate a smooth trip around the World Wide Web.

Browsing Basics and Toolbars

Navigating the Web requires little more than clicking buttons or those underlined blue phrases, as shown in Figure 7-7.

When you click an underlined *link* (or *hyperlink*), you're transported from one Web page to another. One may be the home page of General Motors; another may contain critical information about a bill in Congress; another might have baby pictures posted by a parent in Omaha. Several hundred million Web pages await your visit.

Standard buttons bar Address bar Links bar Logo

Explorer bar Form Graphic links Text links

Figure 7-7. The Internet Explorer window offers tools and features that let you navigate the Web easily. Some of these various toolbars and status indicators are pointed out in this figure. Chief among them: the Address bar, which displays the address (URL) of the Web page you're currently seeing, and the standard set of buttons, which let you control the Web-page loading process.

Around the edges of any Web page, as well as within it, you'll encounter standard Internet features. For example:

▶ **Explorer logo.** When this globe is spinning, your PC is still downloading (receiving) the information and graphics on the Web page. In other words, you're not seeing everything yet.

▶ **Button and picture links.** Clicking a picture or a button generally takes you to a new Web page.

- **Text links.** Clicking a link takes you to a different Web page (or a different place on the same Web page).

 Tip: Web designers don't *always* indicate text links with underlines, which can make them hard to spot. Try moving your cursor over some text. If the arrow changes to a pointing-finger cursor, you've found yourself a link.

- **Graphics worth saving.** When you see a picture you'd like to keep, right-click it and choose Save Picture As from the shortcut menu. After you name the picture and then click the Save button, the result is a new graphics file on your hard drive containing the picture you saved. (You can also choose Set as Background, which makes the picture part of your desktop image itself.)

- **Scroll bars.** Use the scroll bar to move up and down the page—or to save mousing, press the Space bar each time you want to see more. Press Shift+Space bar to scroll *up*. (The Space bar has its traditional, space-making function only when the insertion point is blinking in a text box or the Address bar.)

  You can also press your up and down arrow keys to scroll. Page Up and Page Down scroll in full-screen increments, while Home and End whisk you to the top or bottom of the current Web page. If you have a mouse with a scroll wheel on the top, you can use the roller wheel to scroll the page, too.

Internet Explorer Toolbars

Many of Internet Explorer's most useful controls come parked on toolbars exactly like those described on page 64. You summon or hide these toolbars the same way, too: by choosing their names from the View → Toolbars submenu. Here's what you'll find on each.

The Standard Buttons toolbar

This toolbar, identified in Figure 7-7, contains the buttons that most people use for browsing most of the time. Some of them lack text labels, but all offer screen tip labels:

- **Back button, Forward button.** Click the Back button to revisit the page you were just on. (*Keyboard shortcut:* Backspace, or Alt+left arrow.)

  Once you've clicked Back, you can then click the Forward button (or press Alt+right arrow) to return to the page you were on *before* you clicked the Back button. Click the tiny black triangle for a drop-down list of *all* the Web pages you've visited during this online session.

- **Stop button.** Click to interrupt the downloading of a Web page you've just requested (by mistake, for example). (*Keyboard shortcut:* Esc.)

- **Refresh.** Click if a page doesn't look or work quite right, or if you want to see the updated version of a Web page (such as a stock ticker) that changes constantly. This button forces Internet Explorer to redownload the Web page and reinterpret its text and graphics.

- **Home button.** Click to bring up the Web page you've designated as your home page.

 Tip: Drag the tiny *grab bar* at the left end of a toolbar up or down to rearrange the bars' vertical stacking order. You can even drop this grab bar halfway across another toolbar, thus placing two toolbars side-by-side on the same horizontal strip.

The Address bar

When you type a new Web page address (URL) into this strip and press Enter, the corresponding Web site appears. (If only an error message results, then you may have mistyped the address, or the Web page may have been moved or dismantled—a relatively frequent occurrence.)

Because typing out Internet addresses is so central to the Internet experience and such a typo-prone hassle, the Address bar is rich with features that minimize keystrokes. For example:

- You don't have to click in the Address bar before typing; just press Alt+D.

- You don't have to type out the whole Internet address. You can omit the *http:// www* and *.com* portions by pressing Ctrl+Enter—which makes Internet

Explorer fill in those standard address bits for you. To visit Amazon.com, for example, a speed freak might press Alt+D to highlight the Address bar, type *amazon*, and then press Ctrl+Enter.

▶ Even without the Ctrl+Enter trick, you can still omit the *http://* from any Web address, since Internet Explorer adds it automatically. (Most of the time, you can omit the *www*, too. To jump to today's Dilbert cartoon, type *dilbert.com* and then press Enter.)

▶ When you begin to type into the Address bar, the AutoComplete feature compares what you're typing against a list of Web sites you've recently visited. IE displays a drop-down list of Web addresses that seem to match what you're typing. To spare yourself the tedium of typing out the whole thing, just click the correct complete address with your mouse, or use the down arrow key to reach the desired listing and then press Enter. The complete address you selected then pops into the Address bar.

Tip: To make Windows *forget* one of the Web sites you've visited recently, highlight it in the drop-down AutoComplete list and then press your Delete key. Or, to make Windows forget *all* of the sites you've seen, choose Tools → Internet Options, click the General tab, and then click the Clear History button.

▶ Press F4 (or use the drop-down list at the right end of the Address bar) to view a list of URLs you've visited during this browsing session. (The list drops down from the Address bar.) Once again, you can click the one you want—or press the up or down arrow keys to highlight one, and the Enter key to select it.

You can also type a plain English phrase into the Address bar. When you press Enter, IE does a Web search for that term and opens up the first Web page that seems to contain what you're looking for. At the same time, the Search pane appears at the left side of the browser window, offering a list of other Web sites that seem to match your query.

AutoComplete

Having your browser remember the names and passwords for your various Web sites is a great time-saver, even though it doesn't work on all Web sites. Internet Explorer can also remember your address, phone number, and other information you type into Web page forms. Turn on this feature by choosing Tools → Internet Options, clicking the Content tab, clicking AutoComplete, and turning on the appropriate check-boxes. Or you can just wait for Internet

Explorer to invite you to turn it on, via a little dialog box that appears when you first type something into such a form.

When you want Internet Explorer to "forget" your passwords—for security reasons, for example—choose Tools → Internet Options, click the Content tab, click the AutoComplete button, and then click Clear Forms and Clear Passwords.

The Links toolbar

The Favorites menu (page 197) is one way to maintain a list of Web sites you visit frequently. But opening a Web page listed in that menu requires two mouse clicks—an exorbitant expenditure of energy. The Links toolbar, on the other hand, lets you summon a few, very select, *very* favorite Web pages with only one *click*.

Figure 7-8 illustrates how to add buttons to, and remove them from, this toolbar. It's also worth noting that you can rearrange these buttons simply by dragging them horizontally. You can also drag a link from a Web page onto your Links toolbar. But you can also drag it directly to the desktop, where it turns into a special Internet shortcut icon. To launch your browser and visit the associated Web page, just double-click this icon whenever you like.

Figure 7-8. Once you've got a juicy Web page on the screen, you can turn it into a Links icon just by dragging the tiny Explorer-page icon from the Address bar directly onto the Links bar, as shown here. (You can also drag any link, like a blue underlined phrase, from a Web page onto the toolbar.) To remove a button, right-click it and choose Delete from the shortcut menu.

 Tip: Better yet, stash a few of these icons in your Start menu or Quick Launch toolbar for even easier access. (If you open your My Computer → C: drive → Documents and Settings → [Your Name] → Favorites folder, you'll see these shortcut icons for all your favorite links. Feel free to drag them to the desktop, Quick Launch toolbar, Links toolbar, or wherever you like.)

Status Bar

The status bar at the bottom of the window tells you what Internet Explorer is doing (such as "Opening page..." or "Done"). When you point to a link without clicking, the status bar also tells you which URL will open if you click it.

If you consult this information only rarely, you may prefer to hide this bar, thus increasing the amount of space actually devoted to showing you Web pages. To do so, choose View → Status Bar. (A checkmark appears next to its name in the View menu to indicate that the status bar is showing.)

Explorer Bar

From time to time, the *Explorer bar* appears at the left side of your browser window. Choosing commands from the View → Explorer Bar menu triggers a number of helpful lists: Search, Favorites, History, and so on.

Ways to Find Something on the Web

There's no tidy card catalog of every Web page. Because Web pages appear and disappear hourly by the hundreds of thousands, such an exercise would be futile.

The best you can do is to use a *search engine*: a Web site that searches *other* Web sites. Good search sites, like *www.google.com*, consist of little more than a text box where you can type in your desired subject. Then, when you click the Search button (or press Enter), you're shown a list of Web site links that contain the information you want.

Other popular search pages include *www.yahoo.com*, *www.altavista.com*, *www.infoseek.com*, and *www.hotbot.com*. Using the Search panel of the Explorer bar, you can even search several of these simultaneously. That's handy, because no single search engine "knows about" every Web page on earth.

UP TO SPEED

More Web Pages Worth Knowing

The Web can be an overwhelming, life-changing marketplace of ideas and commerce. Here are some examples of Web pages that have saved people money, changed their ways of thinking, and made history:

www.zap2it.com or *www.tvguide.com*

Free TV listings for your exact area or cable company.

www.shopper.com, www.shopping.com, www.mysimon.com

Comparison-shopping sites that produce a list of Web sites that sell the particular book, computer gadget, or other product you're looking for. A little research can save you a lot of money.

www.efax.com

A free service that gives you a private fax number. When someone sends a fax to your number, it's automatically sent by email.

http://terraserver.microsoft.com

Satellite photographs of everywhere (your tax dollars at work). Find your house!

www.yourdictionary.com

A web of online dictionaries.

www.homefair.com/homefiar/cmr/salcalc.html

The International Salary Calculator.

Note: If you value your time, you'll install the Google toolbar, a free, delicious IE enhancer available at *http://toolbar.google.com*. It blocks pop-ups, fills in forms for you, and, best of all, lets you search Google from any Web page.

Tips for Better Surfing

Internet Explorer is filled with shortcuts and tricks for better speed and more pleasant surfing, as described in the following sections.

Full-screen browsing

All of the toolbars and other screen doodads give you plenty of surfing control, but also occupy huge chunks of your screen space. The Web is supposed to be a *visual* experience; this encroachment of your monitor's real estate isn't necessarily a good thing.

But if you press F11 (or choose View → Full Screen), all is forgiven. The browser window explodes to the very borders of your monitor, hiding the Explorer bar, status bar, stacked toolbars, and all. The Web page you're viewing fills your screen, edge to edge—a glorious, liberating experience. Whatever toolbars you had open collapse into a single strip at the very top edge of the screen, their text labels hidden to save space.

You can return to the usual crowded, toolbar-mad arrangement by pressing F11 again—but you'll be tempted never to do so.

Bigger text, smaller text

You can adjust the point size of a Web page's text using the View → Text Size commands (and then pressing F5 to refresh the screen, if necessary). When your eyes are tired, you might like to make the text bigger. When you visit a Web site designed for Macintosh computers (whose text tends to look too large on PC screens), you might want a smaller size.

Tip: If you have a scroll-wheel mouse, you can also enlarge or reduce the type on the page by pressing the Ctrl key as you turn the mouse's wheel. (This works in Microsoft Office programs, too.)

Enlarge or shrink online photos

Internet Explorer has always offered a number of great features when it comes to graphics found online. Right-clicking an image, for example, produces a shortcut menu that offers commands like Save Picture As, E-mail Picture, Print Picture, Set as Background (that is, wallpaper), and Set as Desktop Item (that is, an Active Desktop item, as described on page 266). There was only one problem: most people never knew these features existed.

In Internet Explorer 6, therefore, Microsoft tries to make it more obvious that this browser has some smarts with regards to pictures. Whenever your cursor moves over a graphic, a small *image toolbar* appears, as shown in Figure 7-9. And if it's a big picture—too big to fit in your browser window—Internet Explorer automatically shrinks it so that it does fit.

Faster browsing without graphics

Of course, graphics are part of what makes the Web so compelling. But they're also responsible for making Web pages take so long to arrive on the screen. Without them, Web pages appear almost instantaneously. You still get fully laid-out Web pages; you still see all the text and headlines. But wherever a picture would normally be, you see an empty rectangle containing a generic "graphic goes here" logo, usually with a caption explaining what that graphic would have been.

To turn off graphics, choose Tools → Internet Options, which opens the Internet Options dialog box. Click the Advanced tab, scroll halfway down the list of checkboxes, and turn off "Show pictures." Now try visiting a few Web pages; you'll feel a substantial speed boost.

And if you wind up on a Web page that's nothing without its pictures, you can choose to summon an individual picture. Just right-click its box and choose Show Picture from the shortcut menu.

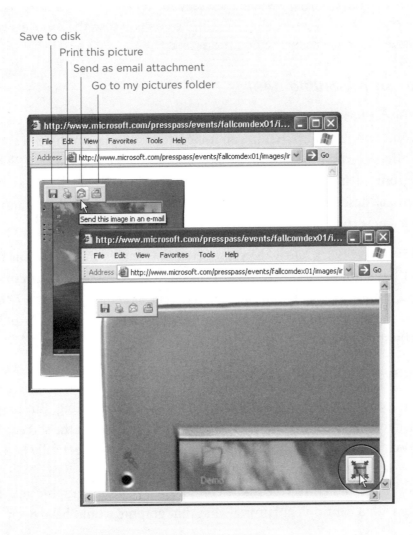

Figure 7-9. Top left: Internet Explorer automatically displays its image toolbar whenever your cursor points to a graphic. One click on its icons can save a graphic, print it, email it, or open your My Pictures folder to manage your collection.

Bottom right: If you click the Expand button (found at lower right), you see the graphic at its regularly scheduled size, which may be much too big for your browser window. Click the Shrink button (circled) to make Internet Explorer do its shrink-to-fit favor for you once again.

Favorites: "Bookmarking" favorite Web sites

When you find a Web page you might like to visit again, press Ctrl+D. That's the keyboard shortcut for Favorites → Add to Favorites—but it's better, because it doesn't make you slog through a dialog box. The Web page's name appears instantly at the bottom of your Favorites menu. The next time you want to visit that page, just choose its name.

You can rearrange the commands in your Favorites menu easily enough: just drag them up and down the open menu (something that doesn't occur to most Web fans.)

If your Favorites *pane* is open at the left side of the window, you can rearrange them there, too, just by dragging with the Alt key pressed.

For more dramatic management tasks—to edit, rename, or delete your favorites, for example—see Figure 7-10.

Viewing Web pages offline

You don't have to be connected to the Net to read a favorite Web page. Using the Offline feature, you can make Internet Explorer *store* a certain Web page on your hard drive so that you can peruse it later—on your laptop during your commute, for example.

The short way is to choose File → Save As. For greatest simplicity, choose "Web Archive, single file (*.mht)" from the "Save as Type" drop-down list. (The other options here save the Web page as multiple files on your hard drive—a handy feature if you intend to edit them, but less convenient if you just want to read them later.) Name the file and click the Save button. You've just preserved the Web page as a file on your hard drive, which you can open later by double-clicking it or by choosing File → Open from within Internet Explorer.

That sweet, simple technique isn't quite what Microsoft has in mind when it refers to Offline Browsing, however. The following more elaborate feature adds

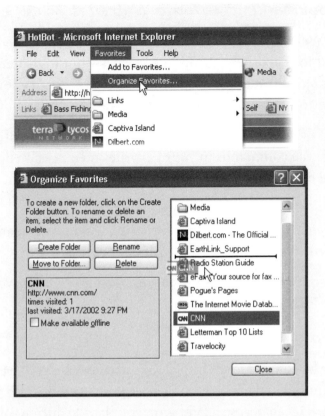

Figure 7-10. Top: To edit the Favorites menu, choose Favorites → Organize Favorites.

Bottom: When the Organize Favorites window opens, you can drag names up or down to rearrange the list, as shown with the CNN link. Or click one and then use the buttons at left to rename, delete, or file it in a folder.

more options, such as automatic *updating* of the page you've saved and the ability to click *links* on that same page.

To store a Web page in this way, follow these steps:

1. **Add the Web page to your Favorites menu or Links toolbar, as described earlier.**

   Before saving a Web page for offline viewing, you must first designate it as a Link or Favorite.

2. **Right-click the Web page's name in the Favorites menu or on the Links toolbar; from the shortcut menu, choose "Make available offline."**

   The Offline Favorite Wizard appears.

3. **Answer the questions posed by the wizard, clicking Next after each answer.**

   You'll be asked, for example, whether or not you want IE to store pages that are *linked* to the page you're saving—and how many "levels deep" you want this page-to-linked-page storage to proceed. In other words, if you're storing a World News page, you'll probably find nothing but headlines on its home page. When you're sitting on the train to work with your laptop, you'll appreciate the ability to click the headlines to open the attached article pages, which are one link "deep."

ALTERNATIVE REALITIES

Outfoxing the Crowd

Just because Internet Explorer comes free on your Windows PC doesn't mean it's the best browser for your PC. An increasing number of PC fans have found a browser they like even better—and it doesn't cost a penny more.

Firefox, created by the fine folks at Mozilla, suffers from far fewer security holes and exploitable issues than Internet Explorer. Firefox also offers a sleek interface and nifty features like pop-up blocking, tabbed browsing, and a built-in Google search box. (And if you type a search term into the address bar, Firefox automatically runs a Google "I'm Feeling Lucky" search.)

Despite the cool features, Firefox is speedier than IE and takes up little room on your hard drive.

For a nice set of answers to frequently asked questions about Firefox, see *www.mozilla.org/support/firefox/faq*. To download the program, head over to *www.mozilla.org/products/firefox*.

On the other hand, be careful. Links to links exponentially increase the amount of disk space IE uses. Increasing the "Download pages ___ links deep from this page" number too high could fill your hard drive with hundreds of Web pages and thousands of graphics you never intended to download.

The wizard also asks how often you want this stored page updated when you *are* connected to the Internet. (If you decline to specify a schedule, you can always update the stored page manually by choosing Tools → Synchronize.)

4. **When you want a page you've stored offline, choose File → Work Offline. Then use the Favorites menu or Links toolbar to choose the page you want.**

It springs instantly to the screen—no Internet connection required.

Ditching Pop-Ups and Pop-Unders

The ad banners at the top of every Web page are annoying enough—but nowadays, they're just the beginning. The world's smarmiest advertisers have begun inundating us with *pop-up* and *pop-under* ads: nasty little windows that appear in front of the browser window, or, worse, behind it, waiting to jump out the moment you close your browser. They're often deceptive, masquerading as error messages or dialog boxes...and they'll do absolutely anything to get you to click inside them.

With Service Pack 2, Microsoft finally got around to adding a basic pop-up blocker right in IE. You won't have to browse for very long before you see the "Pop-up blocked" message in the yellow Information bar.

Note that IE blocks only pop-ups that are spawned *automatically*, not those that appear when you click something (like a seating diagram on a concert-tickets site). And it doesn't block pop-ups from your local network, or from Web sites you've designated as Trusted (choose Tools → Internet Options → Security, click "Trusted sites," and then click Sites).

CHAPTER 8:
OUTLOOK EXPRESS 6

▶ **Setting Up Outlook Express**

▶ **Sending Email**

▶ **Reading Email**

EMAIL IS A FAST, CHEAP, convenient communication medium; these days, it's almost embarrassing to admit that you don't have an email address. To spare you that humiliation, Windows XP includes Outlook Express 6, a program that lets you receive and send email messages. (Incidentally, don't confuse Outlook Express with Outlook, a far bigger and more complex corporate email program that's sold as part of the Microsoft Office software suite.)

To use Outlook Express, you need several technical pieces of information: an email address, an email server address, and an Internet address for sending email. Your Internet service provider or your network administrator is supposed to provide all of these ingredients.

 Tip: Outlook Express doesn't work with online services like America Online or SBC/Yahoo. Instead, you're supposed to check and send your email using the software you got when you signed up for these services.

Setting Up Outlook Express

This section assumes that you used the New Connection Wizard in the previous chapter (page 172) to establish your Internet account, which means that your settings are probably already in place. If you didn't, the Internet Connection Wizard appears the first time you use Outlook Express to help you plug in the necessary Internet addresses and codes that tell the program where to find your email.

If you want to add a second email account for someone else who uses your PC (assuming you're not using the User Accounts feature described in Chapter 12), choose Tools → Accounts in Outlook Express. In the resulting dialog box on the Mail tab, click Add → Mail; the Internet Connection Wizard will reappear.

Sending Email

When you arrive at the main Outlook Express screen for the first time, you've got mail; the Inbox contains a message for you. The message is a welcome from

Microsoft, but it wasn't actually transmitted over the Internet; it's a starter message just to tease you. Fortunately, all your future mail will come via the Internet.

In order to receive and send new mail, you must use the Send & Receive command. You can trigger it in any of several ways:

▶ Click the Send/Recv button on the toolbar. (It's identified in Figure 8-1, which depicts Outlook Express after you've been living in it for a while.)

▶ Choose Tools → Send and Receive → Send and Receive All.

▶ Press Ctrl+M.

 Tip: You can have Outlook Express check your email accounts automatically on schedule. Just choose Tools → Options. On the General tab, you'll see the "Check for new messages every ___ minutes" checkbox, which you can change to your liking.

Now Outlook Express contacts the mail servers listed in the account list, retrieving new messages and downloading any files attached to those messages. It also sends any outgoing messages and their attachments.

In the list on the right side of your screen, the names of new messages show up in bold type; folders containing new messages show up in bold type, too (in the Folders list at the left side of the screen). The bold number in parentheses after the word "Inbox" represents how many messages you haven't read yet.

Mail folders in Outlook Express

Outlook Express organizes your email into *folders* at the left side of the screen. To see what's in a folder, click it once:

▶ **Inbox** holds mail you've received.

▶ **Outbox** holds mail you've written but haven't sent yet.

▶ **Sent Items** holds copies of messages you've sent.

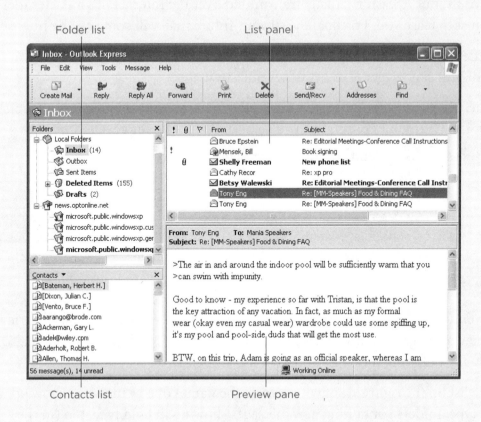

Figure 8-1. The four panes of Outlook Express. Click a folder in the upper-left pane to see its contents in the upper-right pane. When you click the name of a message in the upper-right pane, the message itself appears in the lower-right pane.

Lower left: your list of MSN Messenger Service "buddies."

▸ **Deleted Items** holds mail you've deleted. It works a lot like the Recycle Bin, in that messages placed there don't actually disappear. Instead, they remain in the Deleted Items folder, awaiting rescue on the day you retrieve them. To empty this folder, right-click it and choose "Empty Deleted Items' Folder" from the shortcut menu (or just choose Edit → Empty Deleted Items' Folder).

Tip: To make the folder empty itself every time you exit Outlook Express, choose Tools → Options, click the Maintenance tab, and turn on "Empty messages from the Deleted Items' folder on exit."

▶ **Drafts** holds messages you've started but haven't finished—and don't want to send just yet.

You can also add to this list, creating folders for your own organizational pleasure—Family Mail, Work Mail, or whatever. See page 217 for more detail on email folders.

Composing and sending messages

To send email to a recipient, click the Create Mail icon on the toolbar (or press Ctrl+N, or choose Message → New Mail). The New Message form, shown in Figure 8-2, opens so you can begin creating the message.

Another way to start writing a message to someone, new in Outlook 6, is by finding that person's name in the Contacts list at the lower-left side of the screen. (Scroll directly to a name by typing the first couple of letters.)

Then right-click the name and choose Send E-Mail from the drop-down list. A blank, outgoing piece of mail appears, already addressed to the person whose name you clicked.

Composing the message requires several steps:

1. **Type the email address of the recipient into the "To:" field.**

   If you want to send a message to more than one person, separate their email addresses using semicolons, like this: *bob@earthlink.net; billg@microsoft.com; steve@apple.com.*

   There's no need to type out all those complicated email addresses, either. As you begin typing the person's plain-English name, the program attempts to guess who you mean (if it's somebody in your address book)—and fills in the email address automatically. If it guesses the correct name, great; press Tab to

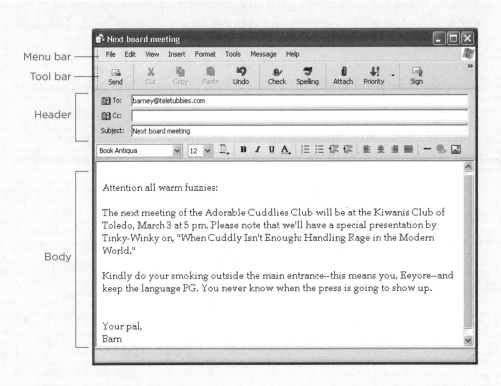

Menu bar

Tool bar

Header

Body

Figure 8-2. A message has two sections: the header, which holds information about the message; and the body, which contains the message itself. In addition, the Outlook Express window has a menu bar and a toolbar, which you can use to access other available features for composing and sending messages.

move on to the next text box. If it guesses wrong, just keep typing; the program quickly retracts its suggestion and watches what you type next. (You can also double-click somebody's name in your address book.)

As in most Windows dialog boxes, you can jump from blank to blank in this window (from the "To:" field to the "CC:" field, for example) by pressing the Tab key.

2. **To send a copy of the message to other recipients, enter the additional email address(es) in the "CC:" field.**

CC stands for *carbon copy*. There's very little difference between putting all your addressees on the "To:" line (separated by semicolons) and putting them on the "CC:" line; the only difference is that your name in the "CC:" line implies, "I sent you a copy because I thought you'd want to know about this correspondence, but I'm not expecting you to reply." (See the box below.)

UP TO SPEED

Blind Carbon Copies

A blind carbon copy is a secret copy. This feature lets you send a copy of a message to somebody secretly, without any of the other recipients knowing. The names in the "To:" and "CC:" fields appear at the top of the message for all recipients to see, but nobody can see the names you typed into the BCC: box. To view this box, choose View → All Headers.

You can use the "BCC:" field to quietly signal a third party that a message has been sent. For example, if you send your co-worker a message that says, "Chris, it bothers me that you've been cheating the customers," you could BCC your boss or supervisor to clue her in without getting into trouble with Chris.

The BCC box is useful in other ways, too. Many people send email messages (containing jokes, for example) to a long list of recipients. You, the recipient, must scroll through a very long list of names the sender placed in the "To:" or "CC:" field.

But if the sender used the "BCC:" field to hold all the recipients' email addresses, you, the recipient, won't see any names but your own at the top of the email. (Unfortunately, spammers—the miserable cretins who send you junk mail—have also learned this trick.)

Once again, use the address book to quickly type in these names, and be sure to separate email addresses with semicolons. Press Tab when you're finished.

3. **Type the topic of the message in the "Subject:" field.**

   Some people, especially those in the business world, get bombarded with email. That's why it's courteous to put some thought into the Subject line (use "Change in plans for next week" instead of "Hi," for example).

   Press the Tab key to move your cursor into the large message-body area.

4. **Choose a format (HTML or plain text), if you like.**

   When it comes to formatting a message's body text, you have two choices: *plain text* or *HTML* (Hypertext Markup Language).

   Plain text means that you can't format your text with bold type, color, specified font sizes, and so on. HTML, on the other hand, is the language used to create Web pages, and it lets you use formatting commands (such as font sizes, colors, and bold or italic text). But there's a catch: some email programs can't read HTML-formatted email, and HTML mail is much larger, and therefore slower to download, than plain-text messages. (For that reason, it really irritates many computer pros.)

   So which should you choose? Plain text tends to feel a little more professional, never irritating anybody—and you're guaranteed that the recipient will see exactly what was sent. If you send an HTML message to someone whose email program can't handle HTML, all is not lost—your message appears in a friendly, plain-text format at the top, and then again at the bottom, cluttered with HTML codes.

   To specify which format Outlook Express *proposes* for all new messages (plain text or HTML), choose Tools → Options. Click the Send tab. Then, in the section labeled Mail Sending Format, choose either the HTML or Plain Text button, and then click OK.

No matter which setting you specify there, however, you can always switch a particular message to the opposite format. Just choose Format → Rich Text (HTML), or Format → Plain Text.

If you choose the HTML option, clicking in the message area activates the HTML toolbar (Figure 8-3), whose various buttons control the formatting, font, size, color, paragraph indentation, line spacing, and other word processor–like formatting controls.

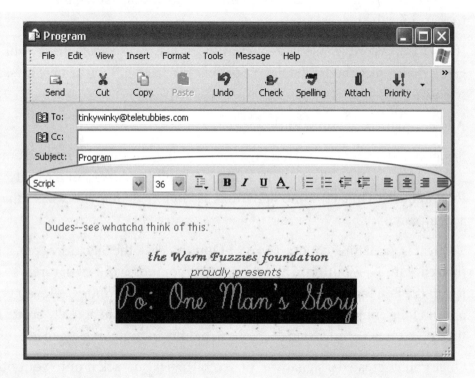

Figure 8-3. HTML-based email lets you exercise some control over the layout of your email messages, including text colors, font selection, and text alignment. The HTML toolbar (circled) looks and acts like a toolbar that you might find in a word processing program. With it, you can turn plain-Jane email into an HTML-formatted wonderland.

Tip: Less is more. If you go hog wild formatting your email, the message may be difficult to read. Furthermore, since most *junk* email is formatted using HTML codes, using HTML formatting may route your message into some people's Junk Mail folders.

5. **Enter the message in the message box (the bottom half of the message window).**

   You can use all standard editing techniques, including Cut, Copy, and Paste, to rearrange the text as you write it.

   If Microsoft Word is installed on your PC, you can also spell check your outgoing mail—just choose Tools → Spelling (or press F7) in the new message window.

6. **Add a signature, if you wish.**

   Signatures are bits of text that get stamped at the bottom of outgoing email messages. They typically contain a name, a mailing address, or a Monty Python quote. (In fact, some signatures are longer than the messages they accompany.)

   To create a signature, choose Tools → Options, click the Signatures tab, and then click the New button. The easiest way to compose your signature is to type it into the Edit Signatures text box at the bottom of the window. (If you poke around long enough in this box, you'll realize that you can actually create multiple signatures— and assign each one to a different outgoing email account.)

   Once you've created a signature (or several), you can tack it onto your outgoing mail for all messages (by turning on "Add signatures to all outgoing messages" at the top of this box) or on a message-by-message basis (by choosing Insert → Signature in the New Message window).

7. **Click the Send button.**

   Alternatively, press Alt+S, or choose File → Send Message. Your PC connects to the Internet and sends the message.

If you'd rather have Outlook Express place each message you write in the Outbox folder, choose Tools → Options, and click the Send tab. Turn off "Send messages immediately."

If you leave this option on, as soon as you click the Send button, Outlook Express tries to send the message, even if that means triggering your modem to dial. But if you turn this option off, then clicking the Send button simply places a newly written message into the Outbox, where it waits patiently until you choose Tools → Send and Receive (or click Send/Recv on the toolbar, or press Ctrl+M). Then, all outgoing mail is sent in one batch, at the same time Outlook Express is checking for incoming messages.

The Address Book

Accumulating names in an address book eliminates the need to enter complete email addresses whenever you want to send a message. Click the Addresses button on the toolbar; then, to begin adding names and email addresses, click New.

 Tip: Outlook Express offers a convenient time-saving feature: the Tools → Add Sender to Address Book command, which stores the email address of the person whose message is on the screen. (Alternatively, you can right-click an email address in the message and choose "Add to Address Book" from the shortcut menu.)

Attaching Files to Messages

Sending little text messages is fine, but it's not much help when you want to send somebody a photograph, a sound recording, a Word or Excel document, and so on.

Fortunately, attaching such files to email messages is one of the world's most popular email features.

To attach a file to a message, use either of two methods:

▶ **The long way.** Click the Attach button on the New Message dialog box toolbar. When the Insert Attachment dialog box opens, navigate the folders on your drive to locate the file and select it. (In the resulting navigation window, Ctrl-click multiple files to attach them all at once.)

When you click the Attach button, the name of the attached file appears in the message in the Attach text box. (In fact, you can repeat this process to send several attached files with the same message.) When you send the message, the file tags along.

Tip: If you have a high-speed connection like a cable modem, have pity on your recipients if they don't. A big picture or movie file might take you only seconds to send, but tie up your correspondent's modem for hours. If you intend to send a photo, for example, use the technique described on page 150, and take advantage of XP's offer to scale down the image to emailable size before sending it.

▶ **The short way.** If you can see the icon of the file you want to attach—in its folder window behind the Outlook Express window—then attach it by *dragging* its icon directly into the message window. That's a handy technique when you're attaching many different files.

To remove a file from an outgoing message before you've sent it, right-click its icon and choose Remove from the shortcut menu—or just left-click it and then press the Delete key.

Reading Email

Just seeing a list of the *names* of new messages in Outlook Express is like getting wrapped presents; the best part is yet to come. There are two ways to read a message: using the preview pane, and opening the message into its own window:

▶ To **preview** a message, click its name in the list pane; the body of the message appears in the preview pane below. Don't forget that you can adjust the relative sizes of the list and preview panes by dragging the gray border between them up or down.

▶ To **open** a message into a window of its own, double-click its name in the list pane. An open message has its own toolbar, along with Previous and Next message buttons.

Regardless of your viewing preference, any attached pictures, sounds, or movies *also* appear in the body of the message; what's more, these sounds and movies can be played in the email message itself.

Once you've read a message, you can view the next one in the list either by pressing Ctrl+right arrow (for the next message) or Ctrl+U (for the next *unread* message), or by clicking its name in the list pane. If you're using preview mode, and haven't opened a message into its own window, you can also press the up or down arrow key to move from one message to the next. (For more tips on selecting messages in this list, see the box on page 214.)

 Tip: To mark a message that you've read as an unread message, so that its name remains bolded, right-click its name in the list pane and choose Mark as Unread from the shortcut menu.

Here's another time-saver: to hide all the messages you've already read, just choose View → Current View → Hide Read Messages. Now, only unread messages are visible in the selected folder. To bring the hidden messages back, choose View → Current View → Show All Messages.

How to Process a Message

Once you've read a message and savored the feeling of awe brought on by the miracle of instantaneous electronic communication, you can process the message in any of several ways.

Deleting messages

Sometimes it's junk mail, sometimes you're just done with it; either way, it's a snap to delete a message. Just click the Delete button on the toolbar, press the

Delete key, or choose Edit → Delete. (You can also delete a batch of messages simultaneously by highlighting the entire group and then using the same button, menu command, or keystroke.)

Outlook Express doesn't truly vaporize messages in the Deleted Items folder until you "empty the trash." You can empty it in any of several ways:

▶ Right-click the Deleted Items folder. Choose "Empty Deleted Items' Folder" from the shortcut menu.

▶ Click a message, or a folder, within the Deleted Items Folder list and then click the Delete button on the toolbar (or press the Delete key). You'll be asked to confirm its permanent deletion.

▶ Set up Outlook Express to delete messages automatically when you quit the program. To do so, choose Tools → Options. On the Maintenance tab, turn on "Empty messages from the Deleted Items' folder on exit." Click OK.

UP TO SPEED

Selecting Messages

In order to process a group of messages simultaneously—to delete, move, or forward them, for example—you must first master the art of multiple message selection.

To select two or more messages that appear consecutively in your message list, click the first message, then Shift-click the last. Known as a contiguous selection, this trick selects every message between the two that you clicked.

To select two or more messages that aren't adjacent in the list (that is, skipping a few messages between selected ones), Ctrl-click the messages you want. Only the messages you click get selected—no filling in of messages in between, this time.

After using either technique, you can also deselect messages you've managed to highlight—just Ctrl-click them again.

Replying to messages

To reply to a message, click the Reply button in the toolbar, or choose Message →
Reply to Sender, or press Ctrl+R. Outlook Express creates a new, outgoing email
message, preaddressed to the sender's return address.

To save additional time, Outlook Express pastes the entire original message at
the bottom of your reply (complete with the > brackets that serve as Internet
quoting marks); that's to help your correspondent figure out what you're talking
about. (To turn off this feature, choose Tools → Options, click the Send tab, and
turn off "Include message in reply.") Outlook Express even tacks *Re:* ("regarding") onto the front of the subject line.

Your cursor appears at the top of the message box; now begin typing your reply.
You can also add recipients, remove recipients, edit the subject line or the message, and so on.

Tip: Use the Enter key to create blank lines within the bracketed original
message in order to place your own text within it. Using this method, you
can splice your own comments into the paragraphs of the original message, replying point by point. The brackets preceding each line of the
original message help your correspondent keep straight what's yours and
what's hers.

Note, by the way, that there is more than one kind of reply, each represented by a
different icon on the toolbar:

▶ A **standard reply** goes to the sender of the message (click the Reply button). If
that sender is a mailing list (see the box on page 216), then the message gets
sent to the *entire* mailing list, which has gotten more than one unsuspecting
novice PC fan into trouble.

▶ The **Reply To All** button addresses a message to all recipients of the original
message, including any CC recipients. This is the button to use if you're partic-
ipating in a group discussion of some topic. For example, six people can
simultaneously carry on an email correspondence, always sending each
response to the other five in the group.

About Mailing Lists

During your email experiments, you're likely to come across something called a mailing list—a discussion group conducted via email. By searching Yahoo!, Google Groups, or other Web directories, you can find mailing lists covering just about every conceivable topic.

You can send a message to all members of such a group by sending a message to a single address—the list's address. The list is actually maintained on a special mail server. Everything sent to the list gets sent to the server, which forwards the message to all of the individual list members. That's why you have to be careful when you think you're replying to one person in the discussion group; if you reply to the list and not to a specific person, you'll be sending your reply to every address on the list—sometimes with disastrous consequences.

Forwarding messages

Instead of replying to the person who sent you a message, you may sometimes want to *forward* the message—pass it on—to a third person.

To do so, click the Forward button in the toolbar, choose Message → Forward, or press Ctrl+F. A new message opens, looking a lot like the one that appears when you reply. Once again, before forwarding the message, you have the option of editing the subject line or the message itself. (For example, you may wish to precede the original message with a comment of your own, along the lines of: "Frank: I thought you'd be interested in this joke about Congress.")

All that remains is for you to specify who receives the forwarded message. Just address it as you would any outgoing piece of mail.

Printing messages

Sometimes there's no substitute for a printout of an email message—an area where Outlook Express shines. Just click the Print button in the toolbar, and choose File → Print or press Ctrl+P. The standard Windows Print dialog box pops up, so that you can specify how many copies you want, what range of pages, and so on. Finally, click the Print button to begin printing.

Filing messages

Outlook Express lets you create new folders in the Folders list; by dragging messages from your Inbox onto one of these folder icons, you can file away your messages into appropriate storage cubbies. You might create one folder for important messages, another for order confirmations when shopping on the Web, still another for friends and family, and so on. In fact, you can even create folders *inside* these folders, a feature beloved by the hopelessly organized.

To create a new folder, choose File → Folder → New, or right-click the Local Folders icon (in the folder list), and choose New Folder from the shortcut menu (Figure 8-4, left). Either way, a Create Folder window appears, providing a place to name the new folder (Figure 8-4, right).

To rename an existing folder, right-click it and choose Rename from the shortcut menu.

To move a message into a folder, proceed like this:

▶ Drag it out of the list pane and onto the folder icon. You can use any part of a message's "row" in the list as a handle. You can also drag messages en masse onto a folder.

▶ Control-click a message (or one of several that you've highlighted). From the resulting shortcut menu, choose Move to Folder. In a dialog box, the folder list appears; select the one you want, then press Enter or click OK.

For more pointers on the folder shuffle, see the box on page 218.

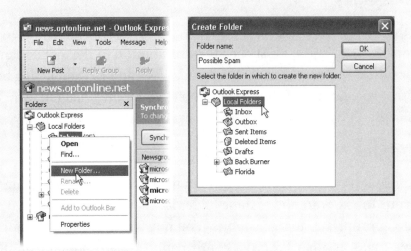

Figure 8-4. Before you click OK, be sure to click the name of the existing folder that you want to contain your new one. Most of the time, you'll probably want to click the Local Folders icon before creating the new folder.

When you click a + button in the Folder list, you see all folders contained within that folder, exactly as in Windows Explorer. You can drag folders inside other folders, nesting them to create a nice hierarchical folder structure. To drag a nested folder back into the main list, drag it to the Local Folders icon.

You can also drag messages between folders; just drag one from the message list onto the desired folder at the left side of the screen.

This can be a useful trick when applied to a message in your Outbox. If you decide to postpone sending it, drag it into any other folder; Outlook Express won't send it until you drag it back into the Outbox.

Flagging messages

Sometimes, you'll receive an email message that prompts you to take some sort of action, but you may not have the time (or the fortitude) to face the task at the moment. ("Hi there…it's me, your accountant. Would you mind rounding up your expenses for 1993 through 2001 and sending me a list by email?")

That's why Outlook Express provides the Flag commands, which let you *flag* a message, positioning a little red flag in the corresponding column next to a message's name. These little red flags are simply visual indicators that you place for your own convenience, meaning whatever you want them to mean. You can bring all flagged messages to the top of the list by choosing View → Sort By → Flag.

To flag a message in this way, select the message (or several messages) and choose Message → Flag Message. (Use the same command again to clear a flag from a message.)

Opening Attachments

Just as you can attach files to a message, people can also send files to you. You know when a message has an attachment because a paper clip icon appears next to its name in the Inbox.

Outlook Express doesn't store downloaded files as normal file icons on your hard drive. All your messages *and* all the attached files are part of one big, specially encoded mail file. To extract an attached file from this mass of software, use one of the following methods:

▶ Click the attachment icon (Figure 8-5). A shortcut menu appears, from which you can either choose the name of the attachment to open the file directly (in Word, Excel, or whatever), or Save Attachments to save it to the disk.

▶ If you've double-clicked the message so that it appears in its own window, then drag the attachment icon out of the message window and onto any visible portion of your desktop, as shown in Figure 8-5.

► Again, if you've opened the message into its own window, you can double-click the attachment's icon in the message. Once again, you'll be asked whether you want to open the file or save it to the disk.

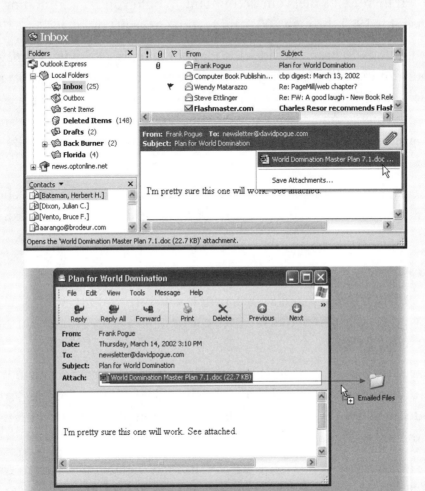

Figure 8-5. Top: One way to rescue an attachment from an email message is to click the paper clip icon and choose Save Attachments.

Bottom: Dragging an attachment's icon onto your desktop takes the file out of the Outlook Express world and into your standard Windows world, where you can file it, trash it, open it, or manipulate it as you would any file.

Not Everyone Has the Same Software

People send me documents in Microsoft Word, but I use WordPerfect. I write back and tell them to paste the text into the email message itself, but they don't like to do that. Do I have to buy tons of software I don't want just to open attachments?

No. There's often a way to open attachments even if you don't own the program used to create them. Microsoft Word documents, for instance, automatically open in Word-Pad if you don't have Microsoft Word on your system.

Word processors and spreadsheet programs can usually import documents created by other applications, complete with formatting. To try this approach, open the email message that contains the attachment. Then right-click the icon for the attachment. From the shortcut menu, choose Save As and save the file in a folder (the My Documents folder is a good choice).

Finally, launch your own equivalent application (word processor, spread-sheet program, or whatever), and then choose File → Open or File → Import. Locate the file you moved into your My Documents folder. You'll be pleased at how often this trick opens a document that was created by a program that you don't have...using a program that you do.

Whenever you open an attachment directly from within the email (rather than saving it to the disk first), use the File → Save As command to save the file into a folder. Otherwise, you won't be able to open the file again except from within Outlook Express—and any changes you make to that document will appear only when you open it from within Outlook Express, too.

 Tip: If the Save As shortcut menu is dimmed, or if you see a "This attachment has been blocked" message, it's because Outlook Express is protecting you from an attachment it believes might contain a virus.

Message Rules

Once you know how to create folders, the next step in managing your email is to set up a series of *message rules*. Message rules are filters that can file, answer, or delete an incoming message *automatically* based on its subject, address, or size. Message rules require you to think like the distant relative of a programmer, but the mental effort can reward you many times over. In fact, message rules can turn Outlook Express into a surprisingly smart and efficient secretary.

Setting up message rules

Now that you're thoroughly intrigued about the magic of message rules, here's how to set one up:

1. **Choose Tools → Message Rules → Mail.**

   The New Mail Rule dialog box appears, as shown in Figure 8-6, top.

2. **Use the top options to specify how Outlook Express should select messages to process.**

   For example, if you'd like Outlook Express to watch out for messages from a particular person, you would choose, "Where the From line contains people."

   To flag messages containing *loan, $$$$, XXXX, !!!!,* and so on, choose, "Where the Subject line contains specific words."

   If you turn on more than one checkbox, you can set up another condition for your message rule. For example, you can set up the first criterion to find messages *from* your uncle, and a second that watches for subject lines that contain "humor." Now, only jokes sent by your uncle will get placed in, say, Deleted Items.

   (If you've set up more than one criterion, you'll see the underlined word *and* at the bottom of the dialog box. It indicates that the message rule should apply only if *all* of the conditions are true. Click the *and* to produce a little

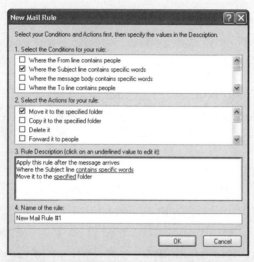

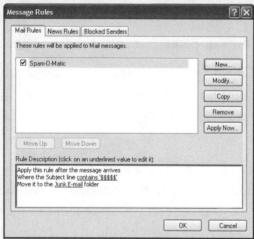

Figure 8-6. Top: Building a message rule entails specifying which messages you want Outlook Express to look for (1) and what to do with them (2). By clicking the underlined words (3), you specify what criteria to look for in a box that pops up. In 4, you give the rule a name.

Bottom: All message rules you've created appear in the Message Rules dialog box. Select a rule to read what it does (in the lower box).

dialog box, where you have the option to apply the rule if *any* of the conditions are met.)

3. **Using the second set of checkboxes, specify what you want to happen to messages that match the criteria.**

   If, in step 2, you told your rule to watch for junk mail containing *$$$$* in the Subject line, here's where you can tell Outlook Express to delete the message or move it into, say, a Spam folder.

   With a little imagination, you'll see how these checkboxes can perform absolutely amazing functions with your incoming email. Outlook Express can delete, move, or print messages; forward or redirect them to somebody; automatically reply to certain messages; and even avoid downloading files bigger than a certain number of kilobytes (ideal for laptop lovers on slow hotel room connections).

4. **Specify which words or people you want the message rule to watch out for.**

   In the bottom of the dialog box, you can click any of the underlined phrases to specify which people, which specific words, which file sizes you want Outlook Express to watch out for—a person's name, or *XXX*, in the previous examples.

   If you click *contains people*, for example, a dialog box appears in which you can access your address book to select certain individuals whose messages you want handled by this rule. If you click *contains specific words*, you can type in the words you want a certain rule to watch out for (in the Subject line, for example; see Figure 8-6, top). And so on.

5. **In the very bottom text box, name your mail rule. Click OK.**

   Now the Message Rules dialog box appears (Figure 8-6, bottom). Here, you can manage the rules you've created, choose a sequence for them (those at the top get applied first), and apply them to existing messages (by clicking Apply Now).

Canning Spam

Help! I'm awash in junk email! How do I get out of this mess?

Spam is a much hated form of advertising that involves sending unsolicited emails to thousands of people. While there's no instant cure for spam, you can take certain steps to protect yourself from it:

1. Use one email account for online shopping, Web site and software registration, and newsgroup posting; use a second one for person-to-person email.

   Spammers have automated software robots that scour every public Internet message and Web page, automatically locating and recording email addresses they find. These are the primary sources of spam, so at least you're now restricting the junk mail to one secondary mail account.

2. Whenever you receive a piece of junk mail, choose Message → Block Sender from the Outlook Express toolbar. Outlook Express will no longer accept email from that sender.

3. When filling out forms or registering products online, always look for checkboxes requesting permission for the company to send you email or share your email address with its "partners." Just say no.

4. When posting messages in a newsgroup, insert the letters NOSPAM somewhere into the email address you've specified in the News Account dialog box. Anyone replying to you via email must manually remove the NOSPAM from your email address, which is a slight hassle; meanwhile, the spammers' software robots (which aren't very bright) will lift a bogus email address from newsgroup posts.

5. Create message rules to filter out messages containing typical advertising words such as casino, Rolex, herbal, and so forth. (You'll find instructions in this chapter.)

6. Buy an anti-spam program like SpamAssassin or IHateSpam.

Tip: Outlook Express applies rules as they appear—from top to bottom—in the Message Rules window; if a rule doesn't seem to be working properly, an earlier rule may be intercepting and processing the message before the "broken" rule even sees it. To fix this, try moving the rule up or down in the list by selecting it and clicking the Move Up or Move Down buttons.

Two sneaky message-rule tricks

You can use message rules for many different purposes. But here are two of the best:

▶ **Create a spam filter.** When a spammer sends junk email, he usually puts your address on the "BCC:" (blind carbon copy) line, to prevent you from seeing who else received the message. This characteristic makes it easy to screen out such mail, and create a message rule that looks for messages where the "To:" or "CC:" line contains *your* address—and files them into the Inbox as usual.

But then create another message rule for "For all messages" that puts messages into a folder that you've created—called, for example, Possible Spam. Because the second rule doesn't kick in until *after* the first one has done its duty, the second rule affects only messages in which your name appeared on the "BCC:" line (which is almost always spam). Once a week, it's wise to look through the Possible Spam folder in case a legitimate message found its way there.

▶ **The email answering machine.** If you're going on vacation, turn on "For all messages" in step 2, and then "Reply with message" in step 3. In other words, you can turn Outlook Express into an email answering machine that automatically sends a canned "I'm away until the 15th" message to everyone who writes you.

 Tip: Be sure to unsubscribe from, or turn off, any email mailing lists before you turn on "For all messages"; otherwise, you'll incur the wrath of the other Internet citizens by littering their email discussion groups with copies of your auto-reply message.

PART FOUR: BEYOND THE BASICS

Chapter 9   Printers and Other Hardware

Chapter 10 The Control Panel

Chapter 11 Help, Maintenance, and Backups

CHAPTER 9:
PRINTERS AND OTHER
HARDWARE

▶ Installing a Printer

▶ Printing

▶ Controlling Printouts

▶ Printer Troubleshooting

▶ Hardware

▶ Connecting New Gadgets

▶ The Device Manager

TECHNOLOGISTS GOT PRETTY EXCITED about "the paperless office" in the eighties, but the PC explosion had exactly the opposite effect: thanks to the proliferation of inexpensive, high-quality PC printers, we generate far more printouts than ever.

Installing a Printer

A printer is designed to follow computer instructions called *printer codes* from your PC. These codes tell the printer what fonts to use, how to set margins, which paper tray to use, and so on.

But the codes aren't identical for every printer. Therefore, every printer requires a piece of software—the printer driver—that tells the printer how to interpret what it "hears" from your computer.

Windows XP comes with hundreds of printer drivers built right in; your printer also came with a set of drivers on a CD or floppy. You can often find more recent driver software for your printer on the manufacturer's Web site or from a central driver repository like *www.download.com*.

Existing Printers

Did you upgrade your PC to Windows XP from an earlier version—one that worked fine with your printer? In that case, Windows XP automatically notices and inherits your existing settings. If it's a fairly recent printer with a fairly recent driver, it'll probably work fine with Windows XP.

But if the printer is especially elderly, the printer software may be incompatible with Windows XP. In that case, your first activity after dinner should be to search the printer company's Web site for an updated version, or use the Add Printer Wizard, as described on page 232.

If you just bought a new computer or a new printer, however, you'll have to hook it up yourself and install its software. In general, there's not much to it.

Note: Only people with Administrator accounts can install a new printer to a Windows XP machine (see Chapter 12).

USB Printers

If you're like most people at home these days, you use an inkjet printer that connects to your PC's USB (Universal Serial Bus) port. As a technology, USB has lots of advantages: USB gadgets are easy to connect and disconnect, are very fast, conserve space, can be plugged and unplugged while the PC is running, and so on.

Just the act of connecting a USB printer to your PC, for example, inspires Windows XP to dig into its own bag of included driver modules to install the correct one (Figure 9-1).

Figure 9-1. You got lucky. Windows recognizes your printer, has the appropriate driver, and has put the software into place. Let the printing begin.

Network Printers

If you work in an office where numerous people on the network share a single laser printer, the printer usually isn't connected directly to your computer. Instead, it's elsewhere on the network; the Ethernet cable coming out of your PC connects you to it indirectly.

In general, there's very little involved in ensuring that your PC "sees" this printer. Its icon simply shows up in the Start → Control Panel → Printers and Faxes folder. (If you don't see it, run the Add Printer Wizard. On its second screen, you'll be offered the chance to look for "A network printer, or printer attached to another computer." That's the one you want.)

If the technology gods are smiling, you can just connect the printer, turn on your Windows XP machine, and delight in the "Found new hardware" message that appears on your taskbar. You're ready to print.

But if Windows doesn't "know about" the printer model you've hooked up, it can't install its drivers automatically. In that case, the Add Printer Wizard appears (Figure 9-2)—or you can always open it. (Choose Start → Control Panel → Printers and Faxes; click the Add Printer link.) Click Next to walk through the questions until you've correctly identified your printer and installed the appropriate software.

Here are the guidelines for using the next screen:

▶ Try the "Automatically detect and install my Plug and Play printer" checkbox first (see Figure 9-2 at bottom). If it doesn't succeed in locating your printer and installing the software, run the wizard again, this time turning that option off.

▶ If the "Automatically detect" option didn't work, you'll be asked to specify which PC port your printer's connected to. You'll then be asked to indicate, from a gigantic scrolling list of every printer Microsoft has ever heard of, your exact brand and model (Figure 9-3).

At this point, you must lead Windows by the nose to the printer's driver software. On the Add Printer Wizard screen, select your printer from the list of printers. If Windows doesn't list your printer there, or if its manufacturer supplied the Windows XP driver on a disk, click the Have Disk button, and then navigate to the CD, floppy disk, or downloaded Internet installation file that contains the driver.

Either way, subsequent wizard screens will invite you to type a short name for your printer, in order to make it available to other computers on the network

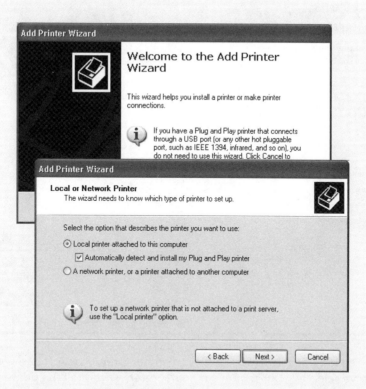

Figure 9-2. Top: Use the Add Printer Wizard only if your printer doesn't connect to your USB or FireWire (IEEE 1394) port.

Bottom: In this window, try the "Automatically detect and install my Plug and Play printer" option first, as shown here. If Windows can't automatically detect the brand and model of the printer you've attached, return to this screen and turn off this option. You'll wind up in the dialog box shown in Figure 9-3.

(yes, Windows can even share, for example, a USB inkjet, even though it's not technically a network printer), to print a test page, and so on. (If the test page doesn't print out correctly, Windows XP launches its printer troubleshooter—a specialized wizard that offers you one troubleshooting suggestion after another until either you or Windows quits in frustration.)

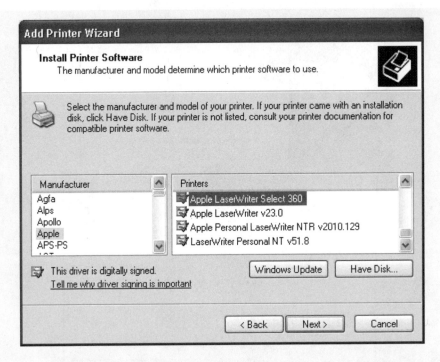

Figure 9-3. The left pane lists every printer manufacturer Microsoft has ever heard of. Once you've selected your printer's manufacturer, a list of all the printer models from that manufacturer (that Windows XP knows about) appears in the right pane. Click the Have Disk button if your printer's driver software is on a disk supplied by the manufacturer.

The Printer Icon

If your driver-installation efforts are ultimately successful, you're rewarded by the appearance of an icon that represents your printer.

This icon appears in the Printers and Faxes window—an important window that you'll be reading about over and over again in this chapter. Exactly how you arrive there depends on how you've set up Windows XP:

▶ If you've set up your Start menu to display a submenu for the Control Panel, just choose Start → Control Panel → Printers and Faxes.

▶ If you view your Control Panel in Classic view (Chapter 10), choose Start → Control Panel, and then open the Printers and Faxes icon.

▶ If you view your Control Panel in Category view, choose Start → Control Panel, click the Printers and Other Hardware link, and finally click the "View installed printers or fax printers" link.

▶ The Printers and Faxes window should be listed in your Start menu, which saves you some burrowing if you use this feature a lot. If it's not there, for some reason, right-click the Start button. From the shortcut menu, choose Properties. On the Start Menu tab, click Customize, then click the Advanced tab. Scroll down in the list of checkboxes, and finally turn on "Printers and Faxes." Click OK twice.

In any case, the Printers and Faxes window now contains an icon bearing the name you gave it during the installation (Figure 9-4). This printer icon comes in handy in several different situations, as the rest of this section clarifies.

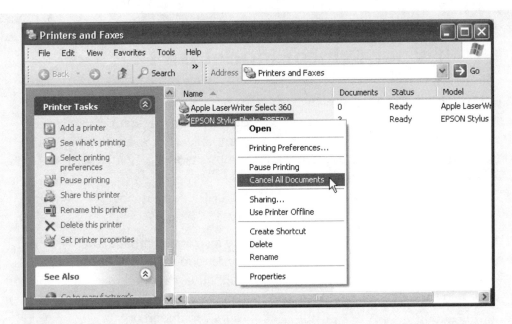

Figure 9-4. To view all the printers hooked up to your PC, choose Start → Control Panel → Printers and Faxes. When you click a printer icon, a long list of useful options appears in the task pane. Many of them also appear when you right-click a printer icon.

Printing

Fortunately, the setup described so far in this chapter is a one-time-only task. Once it's over, printing is little more than a one-click operation.

Printing from Applications

After you've created a document you want to see on paper, choose File → Print (or press Ctrl+P). The Print dialog box appears, as shown in Figure 9-5.

This box, too, changes depending on the program you're using—the Print dialog box in Microsoft Word looks a lot more intimidating than the WordPad version—but here are the basics:

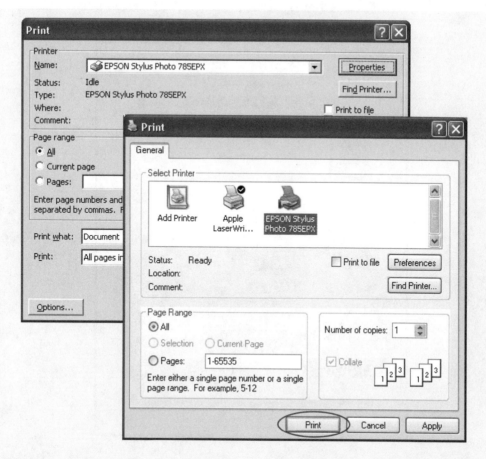

Figure 9-5. The options in the Print dialog box are different on each printer model and each application, so your Print dialog box may look slightly different. For example, here are the Print dialog boxes from Microsoft Word (left) and WordPad (right). Just click OK or Print (or press Enter) to send the document to the printer.

▶ **Select Printer.** If your PC is connected to several printers, or if you've created several differently configured icons for the same printer, choose the one you want from this drop-down list or scrolling panel of printer icons.

▶ **Preferences/Properties.** Clicking this button opens a version of the printer's Properties dialog box, as shown in Figure 9-6.

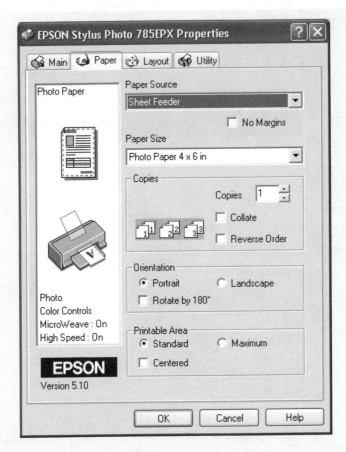

Figure 9-6. When you choose Properties from the Print dialog box, you can specify the paper size you're using, whether you want to print sideways on the page (Landscape), what kind of photo paper you're using, and so on. Here, you're making changes only for a particular printout; you're not changing any settings for the printer itself. (The specific features of this dialog box depend on the program you're using.)

▶ **Page range.** These controls specify which pages of the document you want to print. If you want to print only some of the pages, click the Pages option and type in the page numbers you want (with a hyphen, like 3-6 to print pages 3 through 6).

Tip: You can also type in individual page numbers with commas—like 2, 4, 9 to print only those three pages—or even add hyphens to the mix, like this: 1-3, 5-6, 13-18.

Click Current Page to print only the page that contains the blinking insertion point. Click Selection to print only the text you selected (highlighted) before opening the Print dialog box. (If this option button is dimmed, it's because you didn't highlight any text—or because you're using a program that doesn't offer this feature.)

▶ **Number of copies.** To print out several copies of the same thing, use this box to specify the exact amount. You'll get several copies of page 1, then several copies of page 2, and so on—unless you also turn on the Collate checkbox, which produces complete sets of pages, in order.

▶ **Print.** The Print drop-down list in the lower-left section of the dialog box offers three options: "All pages in range," "Odd pages," and "Even pages."

Use the Odd and Even pages options when you have to print on both sides of the paper, but your printer has no special feature for this purpose. You'll have to print all the odd pages, turn the stack of printouts over, and run the pages through the printer again to print even page sides.

▶ **Application-specific options.** The particular program you're using may add a few extra options of its own to this dialog box. Figure 9-7 shows a few examples from Internet Explorer's Print dialog box.

When you've finished making changes to the print job, click OK or Print, or press Enter. Thanks to the miracle of background printing, you don't have to wait for the document to emerge from the printer before returning to work on your PC. In fact, you can even exit the application while the printout is still under way, generally speaking.

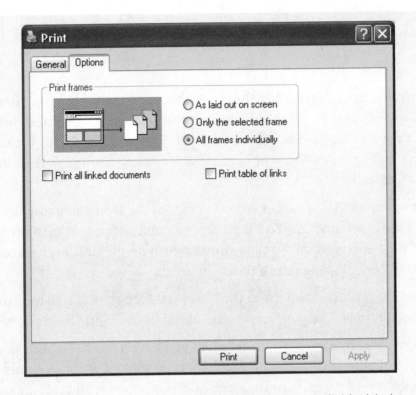

Figure 9-7. The Web page about to be printed uses frames (individual, independent, rectangular sections). The Print dialog box in Internet Explorer recognizes frames, and lets you specify exactly which frame or frames you want to print. If the page contains links to other Web pages (and these days, what Web page doesn't?), you can print those Web pages, too, or just print a table of the links (a list of the URL addresses).

Printing from the Desktop

You don't necessarily have to print a document while it's open in front of you. You can, if you wish, print it directly from the desktop—via an open disk or folder window, or Windows Explorer, for example—in any of three ways:

▶ Right-click the document icon, and then choose Print from the shortcut menu. Windows launches the program that created it—Word or Excel, for example. The Print dialog box appears, so that you can specify how many copies you want and which pages you want printed. When you click Print, your printer springs into action, and then the program quits automatically (if it wasn't already open).

▶ If you've opened the Printers and Faxes window, you can drag a document's icon directly onto a printer icon.

▶ If you've opened the printer's own print queue window (Figure 9-8) by double clicking the Printers icon in your Printers and Faxes window, you can drag any document icon directly into the list of waiting printouts. Its name joins the others on the list.

These last two methods bypass the Print dialog box, and therefore give you no way to specify which pages you want to print, nor how many copies. You just get one copy of the entire document.

Printing from the Internet

If you use Internet Explorer to browse the Web (see Chapter 7), the Print dialog box offers a tab called Options, which contains a few special features for printing Web pages. Figure 9-7 illustrates a few of them.

Controlling Printouts

Between the moment when you click OK in the Print dialog box and the arrival of the first page in the printer's tray, there's a delay. When printing a complex document with lots of graphics, the delay can be considerable.

Fortunately, the waiting doesn't necessarily make you less productive, since you can return to work on your PC, or even quit the application and go watch TV. An invisible program called the print spooler supervises this background printing process. The spooler collects the document that's being sent to the printer, along with all the codes the printer expects to receive, and then sends this information, little by little, to the printer.

Tip: The spooler program creates huge temporary printer files, so a hard drive that's nearly full can wreak havoc with background printing.

To see the list of documents waiting to be printed—the ones that have been stored by the spooler—open the Printers and Faxes window, and then double-click your printer's icon to open its window.

 Tip: While the printer is printing, a printer icon appears in the notification area. As a shortcut to opening the printer's window, just double-click that icon.

The printer's window lists the documents currently printing and waiting; this list is called the print queue (or just the queue) and is shown in Figure 9-8. (Documents in the list print in top-to-bottom order.)

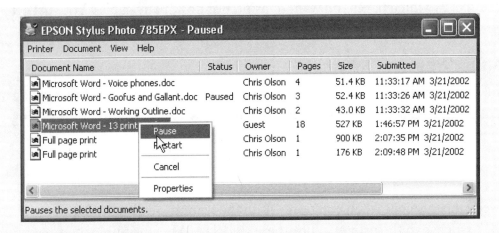

Figure 9-8. The first document, called "Microsoft Word—Voice phones.doc," has begun printing; the second one, you've put on hold (says "Paused" under Status). Several other documents are waiting. By right-clicking documents in this list, you can pause or cancel printing by choosing from the shortcut menu.

You can manipulate documents in a print queue in any of the following ways during printing:

▶ **Put one on hold.** To pause a document (put it on hold), right-click its name and choose Pause from the shortcut menu. When you're ready to let the paused document continue to print, right-click its listing and reselect Pause to turn off the checkmark.

▶ **Put them all on hold.** To pause the printer, choose Printer → Pause Printing from the printer-window menu bar. You might do this when, for example, you need to change the paper in the printer's tray. (Choose Printer → Pause Printing again when you want the printing to pick up from where it left off.)

You can also pause the printer by right-clicking its icon in the Printers and Faxes window and choosing Pause Printing from the shortcut menu. (To undo this procedure, right-click the icon and choose Resume Printing.)

▶ **Add another one.** As noted earlier, you can drag any document icon directly from its disk or folder window into the printer queue. Its name joins the list of printouts in-waiting.

▶ **Cancel one.** To cancel a printout, click its name and then press the Delete key—or, alternatively, right-click its name and choose Cancel from the short-cut menu. Either way, if you click Yes in the confirmation box, the document disappears from the queue; now it'll never print out.

▶ **Cancel all of them.** To cancel the printing of all the documents in the queue, choose Printer → Cancel All Documents. (Alternatively, right-click the printer icon itself in the Printers and Faxes window and choose Cancel All Documents from the shortcut menu, as shown in Figure 9-4.)

Tip: A page or so may still print after you've paused or canceled a print-out. The explanation: your printer has its own memory (the buffer), which stores the printout as it's sent from your PC. If you pause or cancel print-ing, you're only stopping the spooler from sending more data to the printer.

▶ **Rearrange them.** If you're used to, say, Windows Me, it may take you a moment—or an afternoon—to figure out why you can't simply drag docu-ments up or down in the list of waiting printouts to rearrange their printing order. In Windows XP, the procedure is slightly more involved.

Start by right-clicking the name of one of the printouts-in-waiting; from the shortcut menu, choose Properties. On the General tab, drag the Priority slider left or right (documents with higher priorities print first).

Printer Troubleshooting

If you're having a problem printing, the first diagnosis you must make is whether the problem is related to software or hardware. A software problem means the driver files have become damaged. A hardware problem means there's something wrong with the printer, the port, or the cable.

Test the printer by sending it a generic text file from the command line. (Printing a regular printer disk file isn't an effective test, because if there's a problem with the driver, the codes in the file are likely to contain the problem.) To perform such a test, locate a text file, or create one in Notepad. Then choose Start → All Programs → Accessories → Command Prompt; send the file to the printer by typing *copy filename.txt prn* and then pressing Enter. (Of course, remember to type the file's actual name and three-letter extension instead of *filename.txt*.)

If the file prints, the printing problem is software-related. If it doesn't work, the problem is hardware-related.

For software problems, delete the printer driver by opening the Printers and Faxes window, right-clicking the printer's icon, and choosing Delete from the shortcut menu. Then reinstall the printer as described at the beginning of this chapter.

If the problem seems to be hardware-related, try these steps in sequence:

▶ Check the lights or the LED panel readout on the printer. If you see anything besides the normal "Ready" indicator, check the printer's manual to diagnose the problem.

▶ Turn the printer off and on to clear any memory problems.

▶ Check the printer's manual to learn how to print a test page.

- Check the cable to make sure both ends are firmly and securely plugged into the correct ports.

- Test the cable. Use another cable, or take your cable to another computer/printer combination.

Another way to check all of these conditions is to use the built-in Windows troubleshooter—a wizard specifically designed to help you solve printing problems. To run, choose Start → Help and Support. In the Help center, click "Printing and faxing," and on the next screen, click "Fixing a printing problem." Finally, click Printing Troubleshooter.

If none of these steps leads to an accurate diagnosis, you may have a problem with the port, which is more complicated. Or even worse, the problem may originate from your PC's motherboard (main circuit board), or the printer's. In that case, your computer (or printer) needs professional attention.

Hardware

A PC contains several pounds of wires, slots, cards, and chips—enough hardware to open a TruValue store. Fortunately, you don't have to worry about making all of your PC's preinstalled components work together. In theory, at least, the PC maker did that part for you. (Unless you built the machine yourself, that is; in that case, best of luck.)

But adding *new* gear to your computer is another story. Hard drives, cameras, printers, scanners, network adapter cards, video cards, keyboards, monitors, game controllers, palmtop synchronization cradles, and other accessories can all make life worth living for the power user. When you introduce a new piece of equipment to the PC, you must hook it up and install its *driver*, the software that lets a new gadget talk to the rest of the PC.

Fortunately, Microsoft has taken much of the headache out of such installation rituals by its invention of Plug and Play. The rest of this chapter guides you through using this feature—and counsels you on what to do when Plug and Play doesn't work.

Many Drivers

Windows XP comes with the driver software for thousands of different pieces of gear. It keeps many of these drivers, in compacted form, right there on your hard drive (in a file called Driver.cab). The Windows XP CD comes with hundreds of others.

All of these included drivers have been tested to work perfectly with Windows XP. Furthermore, Microsoft adds to this collection as new products appear, and sends you these new drivers via the Automatic Updates feature described on page 301.

Many drivers that were certified for compatibility with Windows 2000 and Windows Me work with Windows XP. But if all you have for a particular gadget is Windows 98 (and earlier) driver software, you're probably out of luck.

Connecting New Gadgets

In books, magazines, and online chatter about Windows, you'll frequently hear people talk about *installing* a new component. In many cases, they aren't talking about physically hooking it up to the PC—they're talking about installing its driver software.

The truth is that you generally have to install *both* the hardware and the software. The ritual goes like this:

1. **Run the installer on the setup disk, if one came with the new equipment.**

   That's right: install the *software first*. Doing so copies the driver file to your hard drive, where Windows will be able to find it in the later steps of the installation.

2. **Physically connect the gadget.**

   That is, connect it to the inside or outside of the computer, according to the instructions that accompanied the equipment.

The beauty of USB gadgets, FireWire gadgets, and PC cards is that they identify themselves to Windows XP the instant they're plugged in. For this kind of gizmo, there is no step 3.

Other kinds of gear aren't so lucky. In general, you must turn off your PC before connecting or disconnecting components from other kinds of connectors. When you turn it on again (after hooking up the new gadget), Windows XP examines every connector, port, and slot on your machine, checking to see whether or not it's now occupied by a piece of equipment it hasn't seen before.

3. **Install the driver software into Windows.**

   If your new gear is Plug and Play–compatible (if its box bears a "Designed for Windows" logo, for example), then skip this step. The simple act of connecting the equipment inspires Windows to find the driver—either the one you copied to the drive in step 1, or one from its own database of drivers.

In either case, your gear is now completely installed—both its hardware and its software—and ready to use.

Using the Add Hardware Wizard

The Add Hardware Wizard fulfills some of the functions of the Found New Hardware process (page 248), but comes in handy in different circumstances. You can use it whenever Windows fails to notice that you've blessed it with new components, for example, or to update the original driver when a better one becomes available.

Begin by connecting the new gear (turning off the computer first, if necessary). Turn the machine on again and then open the Add Hardware Wizard program in the Control Panel (Chapter 10). Click Next to move past the Welcome screen.

The search for Plug and Play

The first thing the wizard wants to do is search for a Plug and Play device. You already know that it won't find one—after all, if the hardware you're trying to install were Plug and Play–compatible, Windows XP would have found it already.

Unfortunately, you can't stop the Hardware Wizard juggernaut. You have no choice but to click Next and proceed as outlined in the next section.

Add Hardware Wizard searches for non–Plug and Play devices

If the search for Plug and Play hardware fails, a new wizard window opens and asks you if the new equipment is already connected to the PC. If you answer no, the wizard closes—its subtle way of telling you that you were supposed to have connected the gadget before even opening the wizard.

If you select "Yes, I have already connected the hardware," on the other hand, you're taken to a list of every component that's already in your computer (Figure 9-9). Scroll to the very bottom of the list and select "Add a new hardware device." Click Next.

Now the wizard asks you to make yet another decision:

▶ **Search for and install the hardware automatically.** If you choose this option and click Next, Windows makes yet another attempt to detect the new equipment and install its driver. If a happy little "Found New Hardware" balloon appears in your notification area, all is well; the wizard's work is done.

If the search succeeds, you've saved a couple of keystrokes; if it fails, you move on to the second option anyway.

▶ **Install the hardware that I manually select from a list.** If you choose this option and click Next (or if the previous option fails), the wizard displays a list of device types (top left in Figure 9-10). From that list, find and select the type of hardware you want to install—"Imaging devices" for a digital camera or a scanner, for example, "PCMCIA adapters" for a PC card, and so on. (Click Show All Devices if you can't figure out which category to choose.)

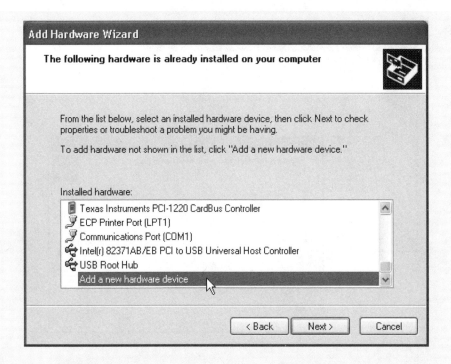

Figure 9-9. Why does the wizard display a list of components you've already successfully installed? Because you can also use the Add Hardware Wizard to troubleshoot PC components you've already installed, using this very screen. Furthermore, Windows may have detected, but not precisely identified, something you've installed.

Then click Next. Now Windows XP opens a two-paned window like the one shown at bottom in Figure 9-10.

To complete the installation, click Next to forge on through the wizard pages. You may be asked to select a port or configure other settings. When you click the Finish button on the last screen, Windows transfers the drivers to your hard drive. (Along the way, you may be instructed to insert the Windows XP installation CD.) As a final step, you may be asked to restart the PC.

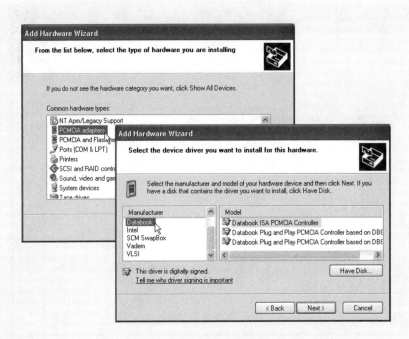

Figure 9-10. Top left: The Add Hardware Wizard asks you to specify which kind of component you're adding.

Bottom: In the left pane, choose the name of your hardware manufacturer. The right pane displays all the models the manufacturer offers. If you can't find your model number, check the hardware's documentation to see if one of the listed models would work just as well.

The Device Manager

The Device Manager is an extremely powerful tool that lets you troubleshoot and update drivers for gear you've already installed. It's a master list of every component that constitutes your PC: floppy drive, CD-ROM drive, keyboard, modem, and so on (Figure 9-11). It's also a status screen that lets you know which drivers are working properly, and which ones need some attention.

You can open the Device Manager two different ways:

▶ Right-click My Computer (in your Start menu or on the desktop); choose Properties from the shortcut menu. In the Systems Properties dialog box, click the Hardware tab, and then click the Device Manager button.

▶ Choose Start → Control Panel; open the System icon. Once again, click the Hardware tab to find the Device Manager button.

In each of these cases, you now arrive at the screen shown in Figure 9-11.

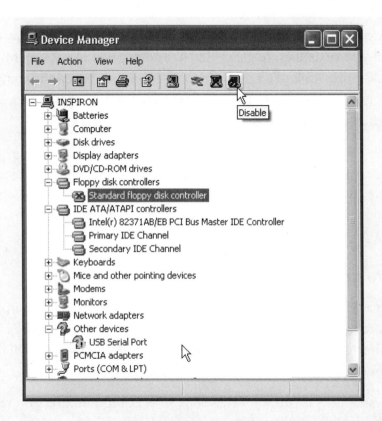

Figure 9-11. The Device Manager lists types of equipment; to see the actual model(s) in each category, you must expand each sublist by clicking the + symbol. A device that's having problems is easy to spot, thanks to the red X's and yellow question marks.

Red X's and Yellow ?'s: Resolving Conflicts

A yellow question mark next to the name indicates a problem with the device's driver. It could mean that either you or Windows XP installed the *wrong* driver, or that the device is fighting for resources being used by another component. It could also mean that a driver can't find the equipment it's supposed to control. That's what happens to your Zip-drive driver, for example, if you've detached the Zip drive.

A red X next to a component's name, meanwhile, indicates that it just isn't working, or that you've deliberately disabled it, as described in a moment. At other times, the X is the result of a serious incompatibility between the component and your computer, or the component and Windows XP. In that case, a call to the manufacturer's help line is almost certainly in your future.

 Tip: To find out which company actually created a certain driver, double-click the component's name in the Device Manager. In the resulting Properties dialog box, click the Driver tab, where you'll see the name of the company, the date the driver was created, the version of the driver, and so on.

Duplicate devices

If the Device Manager displays duplicate icons for a device (for example, two modems), remove *both* of them. (Right-click each and then choose Uninstall from the shortcut menu.) If you remove only one, Windows XP will find it again the next time the PC starts up, and you'll have duplicate devices again.

If Windows XP asks if you want to restart your computer after you remove the first icon, click No, and then delete the second one. Windows XP won't ask again after you remove the second incarnation; you have to restart your computer manually.

When the PC starts up again, Windows finds the hardware device and installs it (only once this time). Open the Device Manager and make sure that there's only one of everything. If not, contact the manufacturer's help line.

Resolving resource conflicts

If the "red X" problem isn't caused by a duplicate component, double-click the component's name, and then click the Resources tab. Here you'll find an explanation of the problem, which is often a conflict in resources (see Figure 9-12).

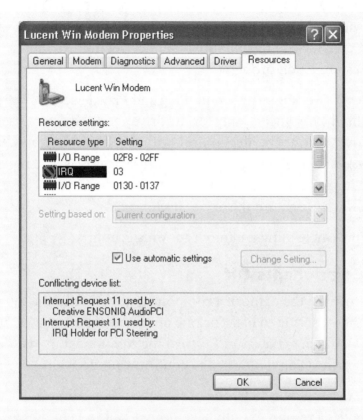

Figure 9-12. The Resources tab should have all the information you need to resolve a problem. Any resource with a conflict is marked with a red circle with a slash, meaning "not working." Selecting a resource with a problem displays information about the conflict.

Click the name of the resource that's having the conflict, and then click the Change Setting button. (If the Change Setting button is grayed out, turn off the "Use automatic settings" checkbox.)

Click the up/down control arrows next to the resource value, keeping an eye on the message in the Conflict Information box. When you select a value that has no conflict (as indicated by the Conflict Information box), move on to the next resource that indicates a conflict, and then click OK.

When Windows XP installs a Plug and Play device, it can modify the settings for both the device and its driver in order to find a combination that works. Windows might even have to reconfigure other devices in the computer, so that the new device can function properly.

But when you're working with a non–Plug and Play device, Device Manager can change the hardware settings only for the driver, not the device itself. In some cases, the driver may not be able to work with the device's settings. In these cases, you have to modify the settings of the hardware device itself using a program supplied by its manufacturer—or for really old gadgets, you'll have to flip jumpers or DIP switches right on the device itself.

Or just sell the whole thing and move to Amish country.

Turning Components Off

If you click to select the name of a component, the icons at the top of the Device Manager window spring to life. The one on the far right is the Disable button (Figure 9-11), which makes your PC treat the component in question as though it's not even there. (You'll be asked to confirm your decision.)

You can use this function to test device conflicts. For example, if a red X indicates that there's a resource conflict, you can disable one of the two gadgets, which may clear up a problem with its competitor.

When you disable a component, a red X appears next to the component's listing in the Device Manager. To undo your action, click the device's name and click the Enable button in the toolbar (formerly the Disable button).

Updating Drivers with the Device Manager

If you get your hands on a new, more powerful (or more reliable) driver for a device, you can use the Device Manager to install it. Newer isn't *always* better, however; in the world of Windows, the rule "If it ain't broke, don't fix it" contains a grain of truth the size of Texas.

In the Device Manager, click the + button for the appropriate type of equipment, and then double-click the component's name to open its Properties box. On the Driver tab (see Figure 9-13), click the Update Driver button. The Update Device Driver Wizard walks you through the process.

Figure 9-13. When you double-click a component listed in your Device Manager and then click the Driver tab, you find four buttons and a lot of information. The Driver Provider information, for example, lets you know who is responsible for your current driver—Microsoft or the maker of the component. Click the Driver Details button to find out where on your hard drive the actual driver file is; the Update Driver button to install a newer version; the Roll Back Driver button to reinstate the earlier version; or the Uninstall button to remove the driver from your system entirely—a drastic decision.

Along the way, the wizard will offer to search for a better driver, or display a list of drivers in a certain folder so you can make your own selection. Ignore the "Install the software automatically (Recommended)" option; you *know* where the driver is, and it's faster to find it yourself. Select "Install from a list or specific location (Advanced)," and then click Next.

If the newer driver is on a disk, turn on the top checkbox ("Search removable media"), and then click Next. If you've downloaded it, turn on "Include this location in the search," and then click the Browse button to find and select it. In either case, you may have to restart the PC to put the newly installed driver into service.

CHAPTER 10:
THE CONTROL PANEL

- ▶ **Navigating the Panel**
- ▶ **Accessibility Options**
- ▶ **Add Hardware**
- ▶ **Add or Remove Programs**
- ▶ **Administrative Tools**
- ▶ **Automatic Updates**
- ▶ **Bluetooth Devices**
- ▶ **Date and Time**
- ▶ **Display**
- ▶ **Folder Options**
- ▶ **Fonts**
- ▶ **Game Controllers**
- ▶ **Internet Options**
- ▶ **Keyboard**

- ▶ Mail
- ▶ Mouse
- ▶ Network Connections
- ▶ Network Setup Wizard
- ▶ Phone and Modem Options
- ▶ Power Options
- ▶ Printers and Faxes
- ▶ Regional and Language Options
- ▶ Scanners and Cameras
- ▶ Scheduled Tasks
- ▶ Security Center
- ▶ Sounds and Audio Devices
- ▶ Speech
- ▶ System
- ▶ Taskbar and Start Menu
- ▶ User Accounts
- ▶ Windows Firewall
- ▶ Wireless Network Setup Wizard

THE CONTROL PANEL is an extremely important window in Windows XP. It's teeming with miniature applications that govern every conceivable setting for every conceivable component of your computer. Some are so important, you may use them (or their corresponding notification-area controls) every day. Others are so obscure, you'll wonder what on earth inspired Microsoft to create them. This chapter covers the most useful portions of the Control Panel.

Navigating the Panel

To see your PC's collection of Control Panel programs, open the Control Panel window by choosing Start → Control Panel. You see nine gigantic icons under the headline, "Pick a category."

First, click the category heading that you think contains the settings you want to change, such as Appearance and Themes. Now you'll see a second screen (Figure 10-1, bottom) that lists a few common tasks in that category: "Change the desktop background," "Choose a screen saver," and so on.

At this point, if you so desire, open the relevant Control Panel program by clicking its icon at the bottom of the screen (Display, in this example). But by clicking the name of the task instead, you're spared a bit of hunting around, since Windows XP takes you directly to the appropriate *tab* of the appropriate program.

If you install software that comes with a Control Panel program of its own, it may not be smart enough to place itself into the correct category. In that case, you'll find it by clicking the link (in the task pane) called Other Control Panel Options (see Figure 10-1, top).

 Tip: In this chapter, the control panels are listed not by category, but alphabetically. To save time, turn on the feature that lets you view the panels alphabetically, as described on page 61.

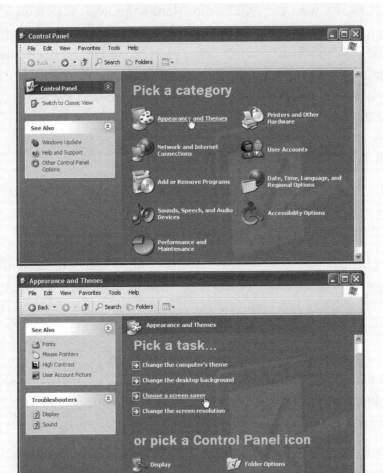

Figure 10-1. Top: This new design is Microsoft's attempt to make the Control Panel look less overwhelming to first-timers. This arrangement groups the existing control panels into functional categories. Clicking one of these headings (like "Appearance and Themes") takes you to another new screen.

Bottom: The next screen lists the corresponding control-panel icons at the bottom. More important, it also lists the useful tasks that those control panels handle under the "Pick a task..." heading.

Restoring the Old Control Panel

If you're a veteran Windows user, the new arrangement of the Control Panel may strike you as just another drag on your efficiency. After all, it places another layer of red tape between you and familiar control panels. Microsoft developed this new design to be friendlier to novices.

Fortunately, it's easy to eliminate the "Pick a category" display forever: Just click "Switch to Classic View" in the task pane. Now your programs appear just as you're used to, as a tidy collection of individual icons, as shown here.

If you're really a speed freak, even the Classic View method of accessing a particular Control Panel program is fairly inefficient. First you have to choose Start → Control Panel and wait for the window to open, then you have to double-click the individual program you want. A faster way is to choose control panels right from the Start menu.

To make this modification to the Start menu is easy: Right-click the Start button and choose Properties from the shortcut menu. On the Start Menu tab of the Taskbar and Start Menu Properties dialog box, click Customize. In the Customize Start Menu dialog box, click the Advanced tab. In the "Start menu items" list, you'll see Control Panel with three options listed under it; turn on "Display as a menu." Click OK twice to close all the boxes. Now your Start menu has a Control Panel *submenu* for you to choose from.

Accessibility Options

Most of the options here are designed to make computing easier for people with disabilities, though some options can benefit almost anyone (Figure 10-2).

Figure 10-2. Double-click the Accessibility Options icon in the Control Panel to open the dialog box shown here. You start out looking at the Keyboard tab, which offers useful ways to adjust keyboard behavior. Clicking any of the Settings buttons allows you to fine-tune many of these features, making it even easier to accommodate special computing needs.

In addition to what's listed on this panel, one of the simplest and most powerful aids to people with failing vision is the "Windows Standard (large)" and "Windows Standard (extra large)" Desktop Themes. You'll find these controls in the

Display program's Appearance tab, as described later in this chapter (page 269). With a single click, you can make Windows enlarge the font used in all of its dialog boxes, menus, icon names, tooltips, and so on.

Don't miss the Mouse program (page 272), either, where you can select much larger arrow cursors.

- **Keyboard Tab.** Three keyboard adjustments make it easier for some people to type without errors. *StickyKeys* is for people who have difficulty pressing two keys (such as Ctrl, Alt, and Shift key combinations) at once; it allows you to press the keys of a keyboard shortcut one at a time. With *FilterKeys* turned on, Windows XP treats a key that is held down as a single keystroke, instead of producing a string of letters like *thissssssss*. Finally, when you turn on *ToggleKeys*, the computer beeps whenever you press the CapsLock, NumLock, or ScrollLock key.

- **Sound Tab.** Turning on SoundSentry instructs Windows XP to make your screen flash or blink when a sound occurs—a useful feature if you have trouble hearing. Turn on ShowSounds if you'd like your applications to display an explanatory caption every time a sound is generated. (Not all programs do, although those specifically advertised as being Windows XP–compatible generally do.)

- **Display Tab.** Here, you can choose Use High Contrast to make text easier to read. You can also make the blinking insertion point fatter, or make it blink faster.

- The **Mouse Tab** lets you use the number keypad to control the arrow cursor.

- The **General Tab** lets you set Windows XP to turn *off* accessibility options if it's been awhile since you've used them. This setup is also useful when several people share the same PC on the same account (see Chapter 12), and only one of them requires these options.

Add Hardware

This icon isn't really a Control Panel program at all; it's a wizard, and it's described in Chapter 9.

Add or Remove Programs

This program, freshly overhauled in Windows XP, is described in Chapter 5.

Administrative Tools

This icon is nothing more than a folder containing a handful of very technical diagnostic utilities that you'll probably never need to use.

Automatic Updates

See page 301 for a discussion of this important security feature.

Bluetooth Devices

Bluetooth is designed to let gadgets communicate within about 30 feet, using radio signals instead of cables. Many PDAs, cellphones, laptops, printers, and even wireless keyboards and mice rely on Bluetooth technology.

In theory, at least, the Bluetooth Devices icon appears on your PC only if it has a Bluetooth transmitter.

Setting up your PC to talk to a particular Bluetooth gadget can be effortless (as with a Microsoft Bluetooth mouse, which comes with an easy-to-use installer) or it can take a Saturday of cruising Web pages for tips and tricks (as when you're trying to make your laptop communicate with a particular cellphone model, and you have to sleuth around until you find the proper modem settings). But it's all in the name of eliminating the world's cables, and that's a very good thing.

Date and Time

This program offers three different tabs:

▶ **Date & Time.** To set the date, choose the month and year from the drop-down lists, and then click the correct calendar day square. To set the time, see Figure 10-3.

- **Time Zone.** This tab presents a world map—one that might tempt you to click to indicate your location on the planet. This display, too, is just for decoration; use the drop-down list above it to specify your time zone.

- **Internet Time.** This tab enables your PC to set its own clock by consulting a highly accurate scientific clock on the Internet. No more worries about resetting your computer's clock for Daylight Savings Time, because it will be updated automatically once a week—if it's connected to the Internet at the time.

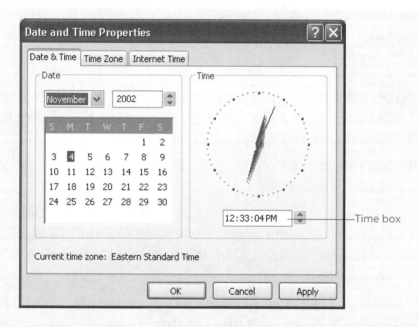

Figure 10-3. To specify the current time, don't bother dragging the hands of the clock—they're just for decoration. Instead, click numbers in the time box (for example, the "12") and then change them by typing numbers, pressing the up or down arrow keys on your keyboard, or by clicking the tiny up or down arrow buttons at the far right of the time box. To jump to the next number, press the Tab key.

Display

Have you ever admired the family photo or Space Shuttle photo plastered across a co-worker's monitor desktop? The Display icon—one of the most important programs on your PC—is your ticket to such interior decoration stunts, and many others.

This icon opens into a window whose controls are then divided into five tabs: Themes, Desktop, Screen Saver, Appearance, and Settings.

 Tip: Here's a quick way to open the Display program: right-click any blank spot on the desktop and choose Properties from the shortcut menu.

▶ The **Themes Tab** lets you change the look of your PC with a color schemes, fonts for your menus and dialog boxes, pictures for use as desktop icons, sounds, cursor shapes, and desktop pictures (Figure 10-4).

▶ The **Desktop Tab** lets you decorate your desktop's background surface with a picture, pattern, or solid color.

▶ Clicking the **Customize Desktop** button at the bottom of the Display Properties dialog box takes you into an absolutely enormous world of additional options. You can change the standard Windows icons, add icons to your desktop, and clean up the desktop.

But the most useful (and most fun) part of customizing your desktop is tucked into the Web tab. Welcome to **Active Desktop** (Figure 10-5), a feature that presents information from the Web directly on your desktop, live and self-updating. If you want to keep an eye on an approaching tornado, the stock market, or a live Webcast, this is the feature for you (provided you have a continuous Internet connection such as a cable modem or DSL line).

Once the Web tab is in front of you, turn on a checkbox in the Web Pages listbox (such as "My Current Home Page"). These checkboxes represent the various Web pages you'd like to see plastered across your desktop. To add to this list, click the New button, type the Web address, and click OK.

Figure 10-4. The Display program's Themes tab lets you change the appearance of all windows and icons on your computer with just one click.

 Tip: Here's something to tuck away for future Web-browsing sessions. Whenever you stumble onto a Web page that might make a good Active Desktop display, right-click its page—right there in Internet Explorer—and choose Set as Desktop Item from the shortcut menu.

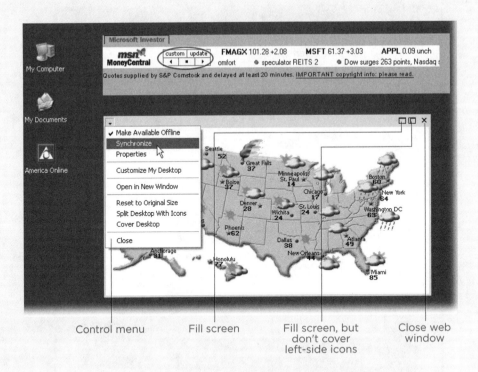

Control menu   Fill screen   Fill screen, but don't cover left-side icons   Close web window

Figure 10-5. The Control menu of each individual Active Desktop window contains useful commands. To make the menu appear, push your cursor close to the top of the mini-page. The Investor ticker (top) works a little bit differently. Click Custom to type in stock symbols you want to track; click the tiny square (circled) to pause the motion of the text. This item doesn't offer the usual mini-menu bar.

▶ The **Screen Saver Tab** lets you pick—you guessed it—screen savers. These entertaining little gizmos kick in a few minutes after you leave your computer, hiding whatever work you were doing; passersby can't see what's on the screen. To exit the screen saver, move the mouse, click a mouse button, or press a key.

Note: Moving the mouse is the best way to get rid of a screen saver. A mouse click or a key press could trigger an action you didn't intend—such as clicking some button in one of your programs or typing the letter whose key you pressed.

▶ The **Appearance Tab** lets you pick from a number of *schemes*: predesigned accent-color sets that affect the look of all the windows you open. (Don't confuse schemes with *Themes*, of which schemes are just one portion.) These color-coordinated design schemes affect the colors of your window edges, title bars, window fonts, desktop background, and so on. They also control both the size of your desktop icons and the font used for their names, and even the fonts used in your menus.

The Settings tab (Figure 10-6) is where you can ensure that Windows XP is getting the most out of your video hardware, by changing the screen resolution and number of colors available.

Folder Options

This program offers three tabs—General, View, and File Types—all of which are described in Chapter 4.

Fonts

This icon is a shortcut to a folder; it's not a program. It opens into a window that reveals all of the typefaces installed on your machine.

Game Controllers

If you're a serious gamer, the Game Controllers program may interest you. You use it to configure and control the joysticks, steering wheels, game pads, flight yokes, and other controllers you've attached to your PC.

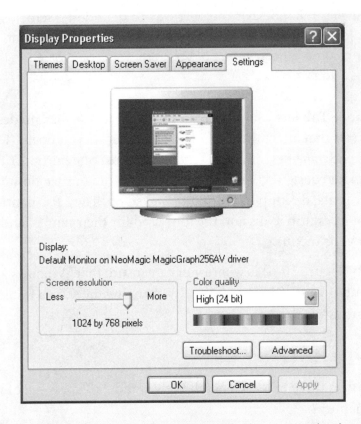

Figure 10-6. The Settings tab of the Display program lets you make the screen picture larger or smaller, thus accommodating different kinds of work. By choosing a higher screen resolution (more pixels), you can see more on the screen at once by making every detail look smaller.

Internet Options

A better name for this program would have been "Web Browser Options," since all of its settings apply to Web browsing—and, specifically, to Internet Explorer. Its tabs break down like this:

▶ **General, Security, Privacy, and Content.** These tabs control your home page, cache files, and history list. They also let you define certain Web pages as off-limits to your kids.

- **Connections.** Controls when your PC modem dials; see page 180 for details.

- **Programs.** Use these drop-down lists to indicate which Internet programs you generally prefer for email, creating Web pages, and so on. For example, the email program you specify here is the one that will open automatically whenever you click an "email me!" link on a Web page. The checkbox at the bottom of the dialog box warns Windows to watch out for the day when you install a browser other than Internet Explorer. At that time, you'll be asked which program—IE or the new one—you want to use as your everyday browser.

  Advanced. On this tab, you'll find dozens of checkboxes, most of which are useful only in rare circumstances and affect your Web experience only in minor ways.

Keyboard

Hold down any key on your PC's keyboard long enough, and you get a long string of repetitions. That's fine if you want to type, "No WAAAAAY!" or "You go, grrrrrl!" but not so fun if you find yourself accidentally typing lengthening wooooorrrrrrrrds.

The Speed tab of this dialog box (Figure 10-7) governs the key-repeating settings.

- **Repeat delay.** This slider determines how long you must hold down the key before it starts repeating (to prevent triggering repetitions accidentally).

- **Repeat rate.** The second slider governs how fast each key spits out letters once the spitting has begun.

After making these adjustments, click in the "Click here and hold down a key" test box to try out the new settings.

Mail

If you have this item, it's because you've installed Microsoft Outlook. The three buttons here offer direct access to the settings you need to teach Outlook about your email account, as described on page 202.

Figure 10-7. The Speed tab of the Keyboard Properties dialog box lets you choose how fast your keys will repeat. This control panel also offers a Hardware tab, but you won't go there very often. You'll use the Hardware tab when you're trying to trouble-shoot your keyboard or its driver.

Mouse

All of the icons, buttons, and menus in Windows make the mouse a very important tool. And the Mouse program is its configuration headquarters (Figure 10-8):

▶ The **Buttons Tab** offers three useful controls: *button configuration* (for making the mouse respond correctly if you're left-handed), *double-click speed* (if you're having trouble opening folders because you're clicking too slowly or too quickly), and *ClickLock* (if you have trouble holding the mouse button down while you drag something across your desktop).

- The **Pointers Tab** lets you choose a different pointer shape. Particularly useful here is the option to choose larger pointers, if you have trouble locating the tiny arrow or blinking insertion point on your screen.

- The **Pointer Options Tab** offers a few more random cursor-related functions. For example, you can make the cursor move faster or slower, or automatically move to the default button (such as "OK" in almost any dialog box).

- The **Hardware Tab** is exclusively for use when your mouse, or its driver, is acting up.

Figure 10-8. If you're a southpaw, you've probably realized that the advantages of being left-handed when you play tennis or baseball were lost on the folks who designed the computer mouse. It's no surprise, then, that most mice are shaped poorly for lefties—but at least you can correct the way the buttons work in the Buttons tab of the Mouse Properties control panel.

Sharing a Computer Between a Lefty and Righty

If a right- and left-hander share a computer, confusion and marital discord may result. If the mouse is set for the righty, nothing works for the lefty, who then may assume that the PC is broken or cranky.

If you're using individual user accounts (see Chapter 12), Windows XP can solve the problem by switching the left- and right-button modes automatically when each person logs on.

But if you're not using user accounts, you probably need a quick way to switch the mouse buttons between lefties and righties. The easiest way is to create a shortcut to the Mouse control panel. Be sure to put it on the desktop or the Quick Launch toolbar, so that the button-switching checkbox is only a click away.

Network Connections

This icon opens up into a window containing icons representing the various network connections you've configured—for America Online, your Internet provider, your network (the Local Area Connection icon), and so on.

Network Setup Wizard

You use this wizard to share one PC's Internet connection on a network, turn on file sharing, or share one printer with other PCs on the network.

Phone and Modem Options

You'll probably need to access these settings only once: the first time you set up your PC or laptop to dial out. Details in Chapter 7.

Power Options

The Power Options program manages the power consumption of your computer. That's a big deal when you're operating a laptop on battery power, of course, but it's also important if you'd like to save money (and the environment) by cutting down on the juice consumed by your *desktop* PC.

The options available in this program depend on your PC's particular features. Figure 10-9 displays the Power Options Properties dialog box for a typical laptop computer.

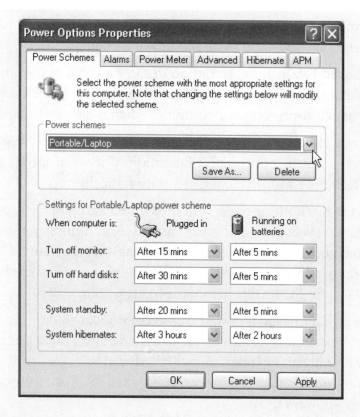

Figure 10-9. The Power Options program is a shape-shifter, meaning the tabs and controls available on each one vary from one PC to the next. Some of these tabs appear if you have a laptop, so you can conserve battery power, for example.

- The **Power Schemes tab** lets you select, change, or create power schemes. A *power scheme* defines which components of your PC shut down since you last used your keyboard, mouse, or processor.

 Tip: You might want to set up your power scheme so that the PC goes into Stand By mode after, say, ten minutes, and then hibernates after 30. That way, if you're only away from your desk for a minute, you can get back to work immediately—but if you get called away longer, or even overnight, everything that was open on the screen is safe—and you're not using electricity while you're away.

- The **Alarms** and **Power Meter Tabs** are for laptops only. Here, you can specify whether and how you want to be warned when you are low on battery power.

- The **Advanced Tab** includes an option to show an icon in the notification area of the taskbar when your laptop is running on battery power. Another option lets you password-protect your computer when it goes into Standby mode.

- If you have a **Hibernate tab**, you can use it to set up the *hibernation* feature (see page 31). Turning on "Enable hibernation" lets you specify the duration of idle time before your PC hibernates automatically.

- The **UPS tab** has nothing to do with the United Parcel Service, even if that's how your PC was delivered. It refers instead to an uninterruptible power supply—a box (about $120) capable of generating a few minutes of battery power in the event of a blackout. This short reprieve provides just enough time for you to save your documents before the lights go out.

  The truth is that this tab is designed to accommodate older UPS devices. Newer devices work with the two tabs—Alarms and Power Meter—that usually show up only on laptops. After all, these dialog boxes are designed to let you monitor and configure battery power—and in effect, your desktop PC is now battery-powered.

Printers and Faxes

This one isn't a program at all; it's a shortcut to your Printers and Faxes folder, described in Chapter 9.

Regional and Language Options

Windows XP is by far the most internationally oriented version of Windows to date. It can accommodate any conceivable arrangement of date, currency, and number formats; comes with fonts for dozens of Asian languages; lets you remap your keyboard to type non-English symbols of every ilk; and so on.

▶ The **Regional Options Tab** lets you change date and number formats (in some countries, 7/4 means April 7, not July 4).

▶ The **Languages Tab** is useful only if you want to use your English keyboard to type in another language (with different symbols, accents, and so on).

Scanners and Cameras

This icon isn't a program at all; it's a shortcut to the Scanners and Cameras window, where there's an icon for each digital camera or scanner you've installed. Fortunately, Windows XP largely automates the operation of these gadgets once you've hooked them up. Still, it's nice to have a central window that contains their icons, so that, if nothing else, you can right-click them to examine their properties.

Scheduled Tasks

Here's another folder masquerading as a program, one that lets you—wait for it—schedule tasks to occur automatically.

Security Center

Chapter 11 describes this command center.

Sounds and Audio Devices

The five tabs within this panel control every aspect of your microphone, speakers, and associated software.

▶ The **Volume Tab** governs the speaker volume for your system, but you'd be crazy to open the Control Panel and this program every time you want to adjust your PC speakers. Fortunately, the "Place volume icon in the taskbar" checkbox puts a speaker icon in your notification area, near the time display. Click that icon to open a much more convenient volume slider.

▶ The **Sounds Tab** lets you fiddle with Windows' little sound effects—the beeps, musical ripples, and chords that play all the time: when you turn on the PC, trigger an error message, empty the Recycle Bin, and so on. And if you like, you can hear them on many other occasions, such as when you open or exit a program, open a menu, restore a window, and so on. This tab lets you specify which sound effect plays for which situation (Figure 10-10).

▶ Use the **Audio tab** to select and configure your microphones and speakers. (Most people have only one gadget for each purpose, so making a choice isn't exactly a brainteaser.)

▶ Use the **Voice tab** to select and configure your microphone.

▶ The **Hardware tab** offers a subset of the Device Manager (see page 250). It presents a list of the sound, video, and movie-related hardware components on your PC, and identifies them by brand and model.

Speech

This little program, new in Windows XP, lets you set up all the speech-related features of Windows. Unfortunately, Windows XP doesn't *have* any speech-related features. So, the only time you'd want to use this program is if you've installed software that has its own speech-recognition or similar features.

Figure 10-10. The Sounds and Audio Devices program presents every conceivable category in which a sound is played: Windows, NetMeeting, Windows Explorer, and so on. A sound scheme is a set of sounds used when certain things occur on your computer (like when you receive an email).

System

This advanced control panel is the same one that appears when you right-click your My Computer icon and choose Properties from the shortcut menu (or press Windows logo key+Break key). Its various tabs identify every shred of circuitry and equipment inside, or attached to, your PC.

General Tab

You can't change anything on this screen, but that doesn't mean it's not useful. Here you can learn:

▶ Which version of Windows XP you have (don't be surprised if the version number contains far more decimal points than you were taught is legal).

▶ The model name and speed of your PC's processor chip (such as Pentium 4, 2.6 GHz).

▶ How much memory your PC has—a very helpful number to know, particularly when it comes time to sell your old computer.

Computer Name

You personally will never see whatever you type into the "Computer description" box here. If you're on a network, however, the blurb you type here is what others see from across the wires. You might use the "Computer description" box to inform your fellow network citizens as to the operating system your PC uses, or what its contents are.

Likewise, the computer description isn't the same thing as your computer *name*, which once again comes into play primarily when you, or your co-workers, view your network connections. (Click the Change button to change the computer's name.)

Hardware Tab

This dialog box is nothing more than a portal. Its four buttons lead to these four other dialog boxes:

▶ **Add Hardware Wizard.** The best way to install the software for a new piece of equipment—a scanner, printer, camera, or whatever—is to use the installation CD that came with it. If you've downloaded a driver from the Internet, however, or in certain other circumstances, you can use this wizard to walk you through the installation.

► **Driver Signing.** After years of grief from its customers for having written an "unstable" operating system, Microsoft went to the root of the problem: buggy software drivers. In response, it created the driver *signing* program, in which the makers of various hardware add-ons can pay Microsoft to test and certify the safety and stability of their drivers. Whenever you install a driver that hasn't received this Microsoft blessing, a frightening dialog box appears to warn you.

By clicking this button, you can specify just how sensitive you want your PC to be when it encounters an installer putting an unsigned driver onto your system, as shown in Figure 10-11.

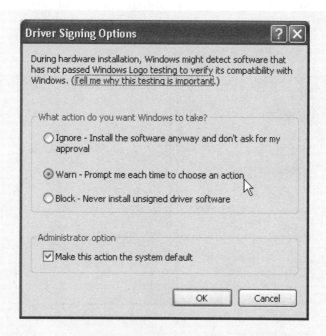

Figure 10-11. The Driver Signing Options box is where you tell your computer if and how to alert you of possible software problems. If you're confident about the hardware add-ons that you install—and the stability of their drivers—instruct Windows XP to stop warning you every time an unsigned driver attempts to infiltrate your hard drive (click the Ignore option button). To protect your PC's stability, however, click the Block option button, so that such software is never allowed to enter your system.

- **Device Manager.** This very powerful dialog box (see Figure 10-12) lists every component of your PC: CD-ROM, Modem, Mouse, and so on. Double-clicking a component's name (or clicking the + symbol) discloses the brand and model of that component. Many of these items are *controllers*—the behind-the-scenes chunks of electronics that control the various parts of your computer, with a technical-looking name to match. For more on the Device Manager, see page 250.

- **Hardware Profiles.** If you're a laptop owner, your add-on equipment list probably changes from location to location. For example, when you're at the office, you may connect your laptop to a docking station—and when you're at 39,000 feet, you probably don't. The hardware profiles feature lets you switch between these configurations relatively easily.

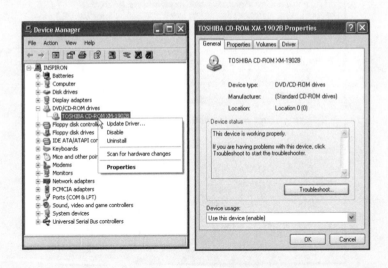

Figure 10-12. Left: The Device Manager dialog box shows you exactly what came with your PC. Click a + sign to see exactly which CD-ROM drive, floppy circuitry, or other hardware you currently have.

Right: Double-clicking a component (or right-clicking it and choosing Properties, as shown at left) lets you read about its specs.

Advanced Tab

Here's another dialog box that's nothing more than a nesting place for five buttons that open other dialog boxes—most of which you will never need to bother with.

System Restore Tab

This dialog box is the control center for the Windows XP System Restore feature, which lets you rewind a balky computer to an earlier date when it was working fine.

Automatic Updates Tab

This tab is a carbon copy of the Automatic Updates control panel.

Remote Tab

This tab controls the settings for Remote Assistance, a new feature that lets a technical-help person connect to your PC (via the Internet) to help you troubleshoot.

Taskbar and Start Menu

This program controls every conceivable behavior of the taskbar and Start menu. You can read all about these options—the same ones that appear when you right-click the taskbar or the Start button and choose Properties from the shortcut menu—in Chapters 2 and 3.

User Accounts

This control panel is the master switch and control center for the user-accounts feature described in Chapter 12. If you're the only one who uses your PC, you can (and should) ignore it.

Windows Firewall

Windows XP has always had a firewall for protection against remote-controlled attacks from the Internet, but it used to be extremely hard to find. Now it has its own icon in the Control Panel.

Wireless Network Setup Wizard

This listing is merely a link to a wizard that helps you set up a wireless network.

CHAPTER 11:
HELP, MAINTENANCE, AND BACKUPS

▶ Navigating the Help System

▶ "What's This?": Help for Dialog Boxes

▶ Getting Help from Microsoft

▶ PC Maintenance: Internet Security

▶ Security Center

▶ Automatic Updates

▶ Microsoft Backup

As you've no doubt noticed, each version of Windows gets bigger and more capable, but seems to come with fewer pages of printed instructions. In Windows XP, Microsoft has relegated more of its wisdom than ever to online help screens—or, even less conveniently, to Web pages on the Internet.

On the other hand, Microsoft has improved the Help window by incorporating links to various diagnostic and repair tools, troubleshooting wizards, and help sources on the Web. It may take all weekend, but eventually you should find written information about this or that Windows feature or problem.

In this chapter, you'll learn how to find your way around the Windows built-in help system. You'll also find instructions to keep your PC running in tip-top shape using Microsoft's Automatic Update program, and instructions for making backups of your files. That's because *prevention* and *insurance* (backups) are the two most important self-help steps you can take when it comes to protecting your computer files.

Navigating the Help System

To open the help system, choose Start → Help and Support, or press F1. The Help and Support window appears, as shown in Figure 11-1. From here, you can home in on the help screen you want using any of three methods: clicking your way from the Help home page, using the index, or using the Search command.

Help Home Page

The home page shown in Figure 11-1 contains three basic areas. In the left column: frequently sought help topics, such as "Music, video, games, and photos" and "Printing and faxing." In the right column: buttons that take you to specialized interactive help systems and utility software. Finally, at the lower right, Microsoft treats you each day to a different "Did you know?" headline.

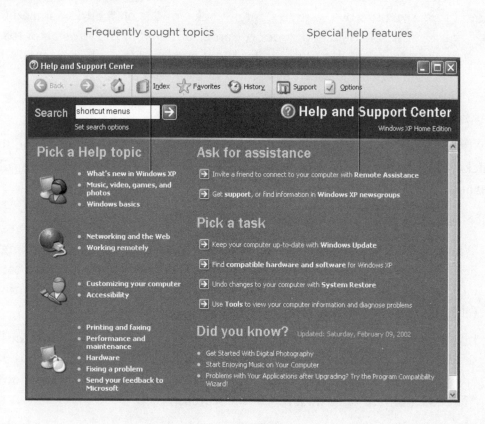

Frequently sought topics   Special help features

Figure 11-1. When working in the Help and Support Center window, you can use the Back, Forward, Home, Favorites, and History buttons on the toolbar. They may look like the corresponding buttons in a Web browser, but these buttons refer only to your travels within the help system. The Favorites button here represents your favorite help pages—they're not the same favorites you see in Internet Explorer.

If one of the broad topics on the left side corresponds with your question, click any topic to see a list of subtopics. The subtopic list will lead you to another, more focused list, which in turn leads you to an even narrower list. Eventually you'll arrive at a list that actually produces a help page.

Tip: If you seem to have misplaced your contact lenses, simply adjust the type size used by the Help Center. Click Options on the toolbar, and then click "Change Help and Support Center options" at the left side of the window. In the right pane, under "Font size used for Help content," you'll see the "Font size" buttons—Small, Medium, or Large.

Search the Help Pages

By typing a phrase into the Search text box at the top of the main page and then clicking the green arrow (or pressing Enter), you instruct Windows XP to rifle through its 10,000 help pages to search for the phrase you typed.

Here are a few pointers:

▶ When you enter multiple words, Windows XP assumes that you're looking for help screens that contain *all* of those words. For example, if you search for *video settings*, help screens that contain both the words "video" and "setting" (although not necessarily next to each other) will appear.

▶ If you would rather search for an exact phrase ("video settings"), click the "Set search options" link underneath the Search text box. The search options page appears; at the bottom, you'll find a "Search for" drop-down menu. Choose "The exact phrase" and then repeat the search.

This same drop-down menu offers choices like "Any of the words," which means that if you type video settings, you'll find help pages that have either of those words. Choosing "The Boolean phrase" from this drop-down menu means that you intend to use the phrases *or*, *and*, or *not* in your search phrase for further specificity. For example, entering *video not settings* would yield all help pages concerning "video" that don't discuss "settings."

▶ Windows displays only the first fifteen topics it finds in each of its help databases. If you'd rather see more or fewer "hits," you'll find an adjustment control on, once again, the "Set search options" page. (That page also lets you turn off the *search highlight*, the dark rectangle shown in Figure 11-2 that appears around your search phrase on the resulting help pages.)

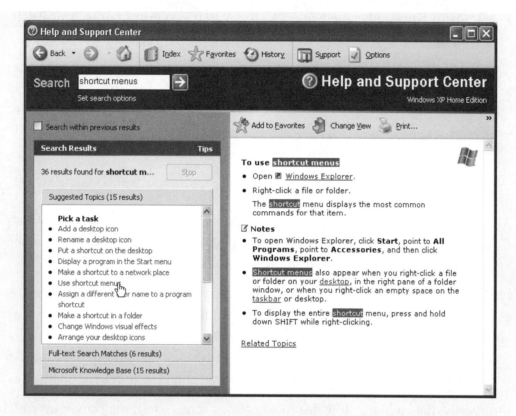

Figure 11-2. When you search for a topic in the Help and Support Center window ("shortcut menus" in this case), you see your results in the list in the left pane. Click a help topic (your cursor turns into a hand pointer, as shown here) to read the help text in the right page.

After each search, the left-side list shows three different categories of help topics:

▶ **Suggested Topics** reveals help pages whose *keywords*, invisibly assigned by Microsoft, match your search phrase. Of course, if you and Microsoft don't happen to use the same terminology, you won't find what you're seeking listed in this group.

▶ **Full-text Search Matches** are help pages on which your search phrase actually appears in the help page text.

▶ **Microsoft Knowledge Base** refers to the massive collection of technical articles on the Microsoft Web site. If you're not online, you can't read them.

 Tip: When you're on a laptop at 39,000 feet, you probably don't have an Internet connection. In that case, you may prefer that Windows not attempt to search the Microsoft Knowledge Base on the Internet. Click "Set search options" just beneath the Search text box, and then turn off the Microsoft Knowledge Base checkbox.

Help Index

The success of the Search command boils down to using the same terminology Microsoft does. Sometimes, you may have better luck unearthing a certain help article by clicking the Index button on the toolbar.

Doing so produces a massive list of almost every help topic in the Windows repertoire, sorted alphabetically (Figure 11-3). Double-click a topic's name to see its corresponding help page in the Help window's right pane. If you type a few letters into the Search box, the Index scrolls to the closest match. But if that doesn't produce a matching entry, you can still scroll through the index manually.

Ordinarily, the Help window fills most of your screen, so it may cover up whichever steps you're trying to follow. However, clicking the Change View button (above the help text in the right pane) hides the list of topics and shrinks the help page so it fills a much smaller window. Click the button again to return to the two-pane view.

"What's This?": Help for Dialog Boxes

If you're ever facing a dialog box (like the one shown in Figure 11-4) while scanning a cluster of oddly worded options, Windows XP's "What's This?" feature can come to the rescue. It makes pop-up captions appear for text boxes, checkboxes, option buttons, and other dialog box elements.

You can summon these pop-up identifiers in either of two ways:

Figure 11-3. *As you type, Windows XP matches each character by highlighting successive index listings. Most of the entries in the index are indented—these are the links to actual help pages. Don't waste your time trying to double-click the category headings. They don't do anything when double-clicked, since you're supposed to open one of the indented subentries.*

▸ Right-click something in the dialog box. In the world's shortest shortcut menu that now appears, click What's This?

▸ Click the question mark in the upper-right corner of the dialog box, and then click the element you want identified.

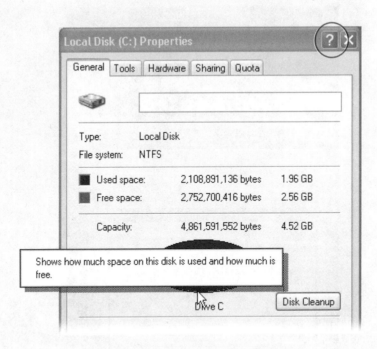

Figure 11-4. After clicking the question-mark icon at the upper-right corner, you can click any control in a dialog box—in this case, a disk-capacity graph—to read about its function. To make the pop-up box go away, click anywhere within its border.

Getting Help from Microsoft

If you run into trouble with the installation—or with any Windows XP feature— the world of Microsoft is filled with sources of technical help. For example, you can consult:

▶ **The Microsoft Help Web pages.** Direct your Web browser (if, indeed, your computer works) to *www.microsoft.com/support*. There you'll find a long list of help resources that handle many of the most common questions: a database of help articles that you can search, a list of known glitches that Microsoft has published, newsgroups (Internet bulletin boards) where you can post questions and return later to read the answers, and so on.

Troubleshooters

When a PC feature isn't working the way you'd hope, or isn't working at all, Windows XP offers a special kind of wizard called a troubleshooter—a series of help screens specifically designed to solve problems.

If you follow all the steps the troubleshooter suggests, and you're unable to fix the problem, the troubleshooter apologizes and suggests another resource for more help.

You won't find troubleshooters for every conceivable problem; Microsoft created only a few. To see a list of them, open the main Help and Support window. Then type *troubleshooter* in the Search text box and press Enter. You can double-click a troubleshooter's name in the resulting list.

Do you have a problem with your sound card?

If you receive an audio error message, or if you have general sound problems, you might have a problem with your sound card or sound card driver. Go to the Sound troubleshooter for more assistance.

Can you play DVDs after you fix a problem with your sound card?

- ◉ No, my sound card is fine, but I still receive an error message.
- ○ Yes, this solves the problem.
- ○ I want to skip this step and try something else.

[Next] [Back] [Start Over]

▶ **Free phone help.** If you bought Windows XP (that is, it didn't come on your computer), you can call Microsoft for free phone help during business hours. The company is especially interested in helping you get Windows XP installed and running correctly—you can call as often as you like for help getting Windows going this way.

After that, you can call for everyday Windows questions for free—twice. You'll be asked to provide your 20-digit product ID number, which you can look up by right-clicking My Computer in your Start menu and clicking the Properties tab. The not-toll-free number is (425) 635-3311.

(If Windows XP came preinstalled in your machine, on the other hand, you're supposed to call the computer company with your Windows questions.)

▶ **Expensive phone help.** Once you've used up your two free calls, you can still call Microsoft with your questions—but it will cost you $35 per incident.

(They say "per incident" to make it clear that if it takes several phone calls to solve a particular problem, it's still just one problem.) This service is available 24 hours a day, and the U.S. number is (800) 936-5700.

 Tip: If you're not in the United States, direct your help calls to the local Microsoft office in your country. You'll find a list of these subsidiaries at *www.microsoft.com/support.*

PC Maintenance: Internet Security

If it weren't for that darned Internet, personal computing would be a lot of fun. After all, it's the Internet that lets all those socially stunted hackers enter our machines, unleashing their viruses, setting up remote hacking tools, feeding us spyware, and otherwise making our lives an endless troubleshooting session. It sure would be nice if they'd cultivate some other hobbies.

This section covers Internet security for Windows. The main idea is that *everyone* should install and maintain three pieces of software for protection:

- A *firewall,* which is a hardware or software shield that protects your PC from unsolicited Internet traffic.

- **Antivirus software,** which is frequently updated to protect you against emerging viruses as they're written.

- **Anti-spyware software,** which helps you clean out your PC once some Web page has installed spyware without your knowledge (see the box on page 296).

It's impossible to overstate the importance of installing and maintaining these three sorts of protection software and keeping them up to date (after all, the hackers aren't resting either). An anti-spam program is a good idea, too.

Unfortunately, all of this means that owning a Windows PC now requires a lot more fiddling, maintenance, and administrative work.

In these regards, the software terrorists have scored a victory. Even so, you really have no choice; maintaining these programs is the only way to be relatively confident that your PC won't be attacked—an event that could be far more disruptive than the preventive efforts described on the following pages.

Security Center

Your Control Panel contains an icon called Security Center. It's an easy-to-understand status report on three important security features: Firewall, Automatic Update, and Virus Protection. If any of these are turned off, dire messages appear on your screen at startup and as balloons in your notification area.

As you can see by Figure 11-5, the Security Center is primarily just a status dashboard; the big ON or OFF "lights" are just indicators, not clickable buttons. But it does contain links to numerous help screens, online resources, and other parts of Windows that let you control its three central functions.

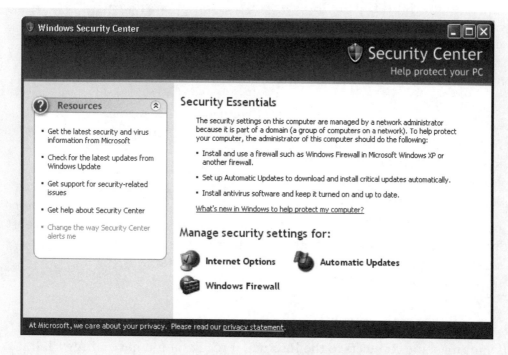

Figure 11-5. The Security Center window gives you an overview of your options for protecting your PC and maintaining its software. Click one of the headings (Windows Firewall, Automatic Updates, Internet Options) to expand that section of the dialog box.

If you're using Windows XP in a corporation where a highly trained network administrator is in charge, you may find that you can't make any changes in the Security Center or Windows firewall. Protecting your PC, in this case, is somebody else's job.

Spyware Defined

Spyware is a program that you don't know you have. You usually get it in one of two ways. First, a Web site may try to trick you into downloading it. You'll see what looks like an innocent button in what's actually a phony Windows dialog box; or maybe you'll get an empty dialog box—and clicking the Close box actually triggers the installation.

Second, you may get spyware by downloading a program that you do want—the free Kazaa file-swapping program is a classic example—without realizing that a secret program is piggybacking on the download.

Once installed, the spyware may surreptitiously hijack your browser's start or search page, make changes to important system files, install ads on your desktop (even when you're not online) or report back to the spyware's creators, letting them know what you're doing online.

As noted later in this chapter, there are both free and commercial programs that can clean your system out after a spyware installation.

But if you'd rather avoid getting spyware in the first place, use a pop-up blocker like the one that's now in Internet Explorer, so you won't fall victim to the fake-dialog-box trick. If you're tempted to download a piece of free software, do a quick search of its name at *http://groups.google.com* to see if other people are reporting it as a spyware container.

The Windows Firewall

If your machine connects to the Internet, it really should have a firewall. If it's connected to the Internet full-time, as with a cable modem or DSL, it really *really* should have a firewall. Most of the people who have fallen victim to snooping attacks from the Internet are people without a firewall.

Windows XP has included firewall software from the very beginning (it used to be called Internet Connection Firewall). Unfortunately, in the original Windows XP, the firewall's factory setting was Off, and finding its deeply buried On switch required three weeks and the assistance of a Sherpa. ("It's like we gave you a car with seat belts that were really well hidden," admits a Windows product manager. "You had to open a secret panel and press three buttons to make them appear.")

In the latest edition of Windows XP, you can't miss the presence of the firewall. It comes already turned on, and, if it somehow gets turned off, the Security Center offers a direct link to the Windows Firewall control panel. (Of course, you can also open it at any time by choosing Start → Control Panel → Windows Firewall.)

All about ports

Now, if you really wanted complete protection from the Internet, you could always just disconnect your PC from the modem. Of course, that might be a little *too* much protection; you'd be depriving yourself of the entire Internet.

Instead, you can open individual *ports* as necessary. Ports are authorized tunnels in the firewall that permit certain kinds of Internet traffic to pass through: one apiece for email, instant messages, streaming music, printer sharing, and so on. (Part of what made the original Windows XP so insecure was that Microsoft left a lot of these ports open, to the delight of evildoers online.)

The Windows firewall works like this: each time a piece of software tries to get onto the Internet, the Windows firewall will pop up a dialog box that lets you know and asks whether it's OK for this piece of software to burrow through the firewall to go about its business. The golden rule: if you recognize the name of the software (for example, an online game), go ahead and grant permission by clicking Unblock. If you don't (for example, PsatNetQuery.exe), click one of the other two buttons.

If you're an online gamer, you'll be seeing a lot of this dialog box. Internet attackers were especially fond of using the ports that interactive online games open.

On the other hand, if you're using a public PC (in a library, say), you might never be asked permission. That's because some administrator has turned on the "Don't allow exceptions" option shown in Figure 11-6 at left. That means, "No holes in the firewall, ever. This is a public terminal, and we can't permit God-knows-what activity to corrupt our system."

If you grant permission, then each time you use that software, Windows will briefly open up a special port for that kind of activity, and then seal the port closed again when you're finished.

The exceptions list

When that little Security Alert box opens up, there will be times when you make the wrong decision. You'll deny permission to something that looks fishy, and then find out that one of your programs no longer works. On the other hand, maybe you'll approve something that has a recognizable name, and then you'll later find out that it was actually a trick—an evil program deliberately named in order to get your approval. That, unfortunately, is life in the Windows fast lane.

Fortunately, you have a second chance. At any time, you can take a look at the list of authorized holes in your Windows firewall, using the Windows Firewall control panel (Start → Control Panel → Windows Firewall). When you click the Exceptions tab, you see something like Figure 11-6 at right: a list of every program that has been granted an open port in the firewall.

Using this list, you can also add a program manually (rather than waiting for it to ask permission at the time of launching). To do so, click the Add Program button, and choose the program's name from the list that appears.

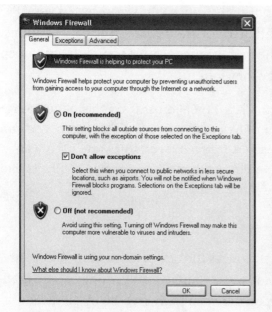
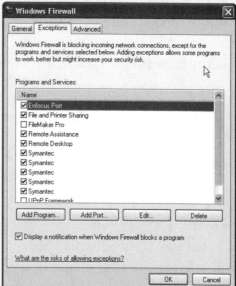

Figure 11-6. Left: Here, in the new Windows Firewall control panel, you can turn the Windows firewall on or off. You should turn it off (despite the stern warning) if you're using a non-Microsoft firewall (like Zone Alarm).

Right: The Exceptions tab and the Advanced tab list all of the programs and ports that Windows Firewall is permitted to open—but only when these programs are actually requesting Internet access. Use the checkboxes to temporarily turn exceptions on or off.

Virus Software

Windows XP also direly warns you if you have no antivirus software installed—but unlike the firewall example, this time Microsoft doesn't provide any. The Virus Protection feature, it turns out, is not an inoculation but simply an alert.

However, if you click the Recommendations button, you're taken online to a Web page filled with free time-limited trials of various antivirus programs.

Once you've installed antivirus software, the Security Center will smile on you with a happy green ON "light" next to the Virus Protection heading. (That is, it will if it *recognizes* the antivirus software.)

You'll have a much more relaxed computing life once you've protected your PC with this kind of software. Consider antivirus software part of the cost of doing business, and remember that *you* are the best defense against viruses. Don't open email attachments, no matter how juicy they look.

 Tip: Some antivirus programs not listed by Microsoft on this page aren't just trials—they're actually free. For example, at *www.grisoft.com*, you can download AVG Free Edition, which is free antivirus software. It's a welcome alternative to better-known but much more expensive products like Symantec Antivirus and McAfee Virus Scan.

Spyware Cleaners

As noted above, the Security Center makes clear the importance of installing firewall, antivirus, and automatic-update software—but, weirdly, doesn't even mention spyware protection. Spyware detectors are generally free, so by all means consider one of them to be part of your essential PC toolkit. You might choose one of these highly regarded programs, for example:

▶ **Ad-Aware.** Free version available to individuals (and commercial versions for corporations) at *www.lavasoftusa.com*.

▶ **Spybot Search & Destroy.** Free at *www.safer-networking.org*.

Current versions of commercial antivirus programs, including those from Symantec, McAfee, and Trend Micro, also include some spyware-cleaning functions.

Having a spyware cleaner available is especially important if you download a lot of programs from the Internet (this means you, file swappers).

 Tip: Here are four telltale signs that your PC has been infected by spyware: the computer suddenly slows down a lot; Internet Explorer doesn't work right anymore; you get a lot of apparently irrelevant, nonsensical error messages; and the PC freezes up a lot. As soon as you notice these behaviors, run one of those spyware utilities.

Automatic Updates

It might come as a surprise to you that most Internet attacks don't occur when online lowlifes discover a hole in Windows' security. As it turns out, they're not quite that smart.

Instead, what usually happens is that *Microsoft* discovers the soft spot. (Actually, some super-brainiac researcher usually finds the hole, and then notifies Microsoft.) Microsoft then puts together a security patch, which it releases to its millions of customers to protect them.

The hackers and virus writers learn about the security hole by studying the *patch*. They leap on the information and create some piece of evilware in a matter of days—yes, *after* Microsoft has already written software that closes the hole.

So how can PCs get infected *after* Microsoft has already created a patch? Because it takes weeks or months for Microsoft's patch to get distributed to all those millions of customers. The hackers simply beat Microsoft to your PC's front door.

The painful part is that Windows XP already *contains* a mechanism for downloading and installing Microsoft's patches the very day they become available. It's called Automatic Updates, and it's yet another icon in your Control Panel (Figure 11-7).

Now, any patches or updates that Microsoft wants to send your way are also available for do-it-yourself download and installation at *windowsupdate.microsoft.com* (or choose Start → All Programs → Windows Update; if you're already surfing in Internet Explorer, you can also choose Tools → Windows Update). As a bonus, this site also reports exactly which bugs are fixed in each update, usually using fairly technical language.

Furthermore, whereas Automatic Update offers you *only* security-related patches, the Windows Update Web page also offers updates that speed up your PC, offers new features, updates Windows Media Player, and so on.

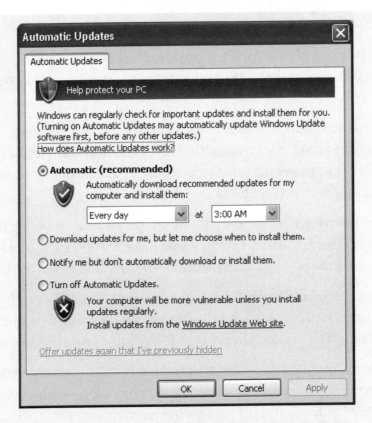

Figure 11-7. If you turn on Windows XP's Automatic Updates installation feature—and Microsoft is practically frantic that you do so—you can ask to be notified either before the software patch is downloaded (third choice) or after it's been downloaded and is ready to install (second choice). You can also permit the updates to be updated and then installed automatically, on a schedule that you specify (top choice).

But a patch won't do you any good if you don't know that it exists. So Automatic Update presents four options, as you can see in Figure 11-7. They correspond to four levels of trust people have in Microsoft, the mother ship:

- **Automatic (recommended).** Translation: "Download and install all patches automatically. We trust in thee, Microsoft, that thou knowest what thou doest." (All of this will take place in the middle of the night—or according to whatever schedule you establish in the control panel—so as not to inconvenience you.)

- **Download updates for me, but let me choose when to install them.** The downloading takes place in the background, and doesn't interfere with anything you're downloading for yourself. But instead of installing the newly downloaded patch, Windows pauses to get your permission, as shown in Figure 11-8.

   This option gives you the chance to conduct a quick search on Google to see if anyone has had trouble with this particular patch. If the coast is clear, *then* you can opt to install.

- **Notify me but don't automatically download or install them.** When Windows detects that a patch has become available, that yellow ! shield icon appears in your system tray. Click the icon to choose which updates to download.

   When the downloading is over, the yellow ! shield appears *again* in your system tray, this time telling you that the updates are ready for installation. From this point on, the cycle goes exactly as shown in Figure 11-8.

> **Tip:** Consider this setting if you're a laptopper. People who use the fully automated option have been known to grab their laptops and head to the airport, only to discover that they're midway through a 25-minute Service Pack installation. Leaving your laptop on as you pass it through the X-ray machine is never a good way to make friends with the security staff.

- **Turn off Automatic Updates.** Microsoft will leave your copy of Windows completely alone—and completely vulnerable to attacks from the Internet. This choice is preferred by people who like to fully research each patch before installing it (at, for example, *www.annoyances.org*).

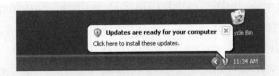

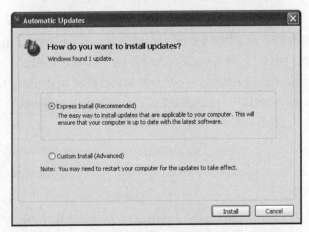

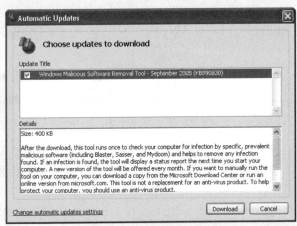

Figure 11-8. Top: When Windows finds an update, a notification balloon lets you know, complete with a yellow ! shield icon.

Middle: Click the balloon to get another choice. You can blindly install whatever Microsoft sent you (click Express Install and then Install). Or you can click Custom Install (Advanced), which really means "Show me a description of what I'm about to install."

Bottom: In that case, this screen lists the patches Microsoft has sent you. It also offers you a link to a Web page containing really specific techno-jargon about the patch.

Microsoft *hates* when people choose anything but the first option, because it's no better than the old system (when hackers attacked *after* a hole was patched but *before* people had installed the patch).

And now a few notes:

▶ You don't get *any* notifications unless you're using an administrator-level account (page 324).

▶ Some updates require that you restart your PC. (Actually, you can decline Windows' invitation to restart your machine, but, of course, the update won't take effect until you do.)

▶ If Windows XP reveals that an update is ready to be installed, but you choose not to install it, Windows makes the updater invisible on your hard drive (if it has space). If, later in life, you decide that you really *would* like to have that particular update, just click the "Offer updates again that I've previously hidden" link at the bottom of the Automatic Update tab. Then, the next time you install an update, those choices become available once again.

Tip: You can find a record of the updates you've installed (and even uninstall them, if you want) in the Start → Control Panel → Add or Remove Programs program.

Turn on the "Show updates" checkbox at the top of the dialog box to reveal the "Windows XP–Software Updates" category, which lists the individual patches and fixes you've installed.

Microsoft Backup

Consider this: the proximity of your drive's spinning platters to the head that reads them is roughly the same proportion as the wheels of an airliner flying at 500 miles per hour, twelve inches off the ground. It's amazing that hard drives work as well, and as long, as they do.

Still, because a hard drive is nothing more than a mass of moving parts in delicate alignment, every now and then disaster strikes. That's why backing up your data (making a safety copy) on a regular basis is an essential part of using a PC. Even if computers aren't your career, there's probably a lot of valuable stuff on your hard drive: all of your digital photos, the addresses and phone numbers you've spent hours typing into your Contacts list, a lifetime's worth of email, the Web sites in your Favorites folder, and so on.

Now, if you use XP in a corporation—a distinct possibility, considering its target audience—you probably don't even have to think about backing up your stuff. A network administrator generally does the backing up for you and your co-workers. (You're probably instructed to save your files on a network server PC instead of your own, so that the administrator can back up all of the employees' files in one swift move.) In that case, you can skip the remainder of this chapter.

If you use Windows XP at home, or in a smaller company that doesn't have network nerds running around to ensure your files' safety, you might be grateful for Microsoft Backup, a very simple backup program that comes with Windows XP. It lacks some of the specialized features of commercial backup programs, but at least it lets you back up entire drives or selected files and folders, at times and under the conditions you specify, to other disks or tapes. You can even schedule it to run at regular intervals (using the Task Scheduler program), so that you always have a recent copy of your data on hand.

Backup Hardware

An external hard drive makes an extremely convenient backup system, since it spares you the hassle of inserting and tracking multiple removable disks (like Zips or CDs).

Still, removable disks are the safest disks of all, because you can store them somewhere else: in a fireproof box, a safe deposit box at the bank, or the trunk of your car—anywhere but in your office, making your data safe even in the case of fire or burglary.

Here's a rundown of popular removable backup disks:

- **Floppy disks.** Forget it. Unless you work with nothing more than a few text files, your stuff will never fit onto floppies.

- **Zip, Jaz, Peerless.** When it comes to removable cartridge drives like these from Iomega, consider capacity and expense. The older Zip cartridges, which hold 100 or 250 MB, may be too small for most backup purposes. The newer 750 MB drives are a better bet.

  Jaz and Peerless cartridges can hold a lot more, but they're expensive. Divide the number of megabytes by the cartridge price to figure out which is the most cost-effective.

- **Recordable CD.** Burning your backups onto blank CD-R and CD-RW (or even blank DVD) disks is another viable alternative—especially since blanks are dirt cheap. Unfortunately—and incredibly—the Windows XP Backup program doesn't recognize CD-ROM or DVD-ROM drives as backup devices.

  Many other backup programs do, however. Your CD/DVD burner may even have come with one. As long as you don't have many gigabytes of files to back up, this system can work well.

- **Tape cartridges.** Magnetic tapes are economical, retain their data for years, and offer huge capacity in a compact package. Better yet, Microsoft's Backup program works with them. Tape drives are available in either external USB versions or internal units that you install yourself.

  The main drawback of a tape system is that you can't use it for anything other than backups. You can't get to a file at the end of the tape without fast forwarding through all of the data that precedes it, so you wouldn't want to use these as everyday disks.

Creating a Backup Job

To launch the Backup program, choose Start → All Programs → Accessories → System Tools → Backup. A wizard walks you through the process of setting up a backup job, as follows.

Backup or restore?

The first wizard screen (Figure 11-9, top) wants to know whether you want to *back up* your files (because you're a shrewd, confident, happy person in a time of PC health) or *restore* them (because you're a desperate, unhappy person whose files have somehow been deleted or corrupted).

To back up your files, of course, click "Backup files and settings" and then click Next.

Create a backup job

The next wizard window asks what you want to back up:

▶ **My documents and settings, Everyone's documents and settings.** These options assume that you're using a PC shared by several people, each with a separate account (see the next chapter). It's asking whether you want to back up just your files and settings, or those of every account holder. (If you're the sole proprietor of *your* machine, just use the first option.)

▶ **All information on this computer.** This option tells Backup to copy every single file and folder on your drive(s), including almost two gigabytes of Windows itself. This is a massive project—and, in general, an unnecessary one. After all, you already have a backup of Windows itself (on your Windows CD) and of your programs (on the original software disks), so there may not be much point in making another copy.

▶ **Let me choose what to back up.** This option leads to a Windows Explorer–like display (see Figure 11-9, bottom) that lets you choose the specific folders and files to be backed up.

Select the backup medium

The next screen asks where you want to store the backup files you're about to create. The drop-down list starts out suggesting that you back up your hard drive onto *floppy disks*—not exactly a forward-thinking choice. Considering the

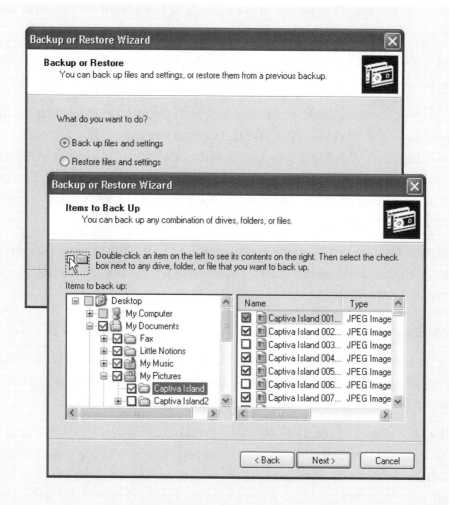

Figure 11-9. Top left: The Backup or Restore wizard lets you either back up or restore your files.

Bottom right: If you choose to back up, this screen appears. Expand the listing of drives and folders by clicking the plus signs. Turn on the checkbox next to any folder or file that you want backed up. To deselect a file, turn off its checkbox. Don't forget that you can drag the gray, vertical divider bar to widen the left panel.

massive size of today's hard drives, you'll be inserting blank floppies for the next three presidential administrations.

Instead, if your PC does, in fact, have a backup disk connected (a magnetic tape drive, for example, or a Zip drive), choose its name from this drop-down list.

The other option, available on all computers, is to back up the selected data to a file on your hard drive. You can use this option to create CD-sized backup files for burning onto CDs later, to back up your data to another hard drive in the same computer, or to back up to another computer on the network. (To use the latter option, click Browse.) In any case, click Cancel if you're asked to insert a floppy disk.

The Save As dialog box that appears asks you to name the backup file you're creating (its filename extension is *.bkf*). Click Save when you've selected a location and typed a name.

Advanced backup options

The final wizard screen now appears (Figure 11-10). If you click Finish, the backup process begins—a process that may take several seconds or several hours, depending on how much you're copying. Your work here is done.

On the other hand, if you click the Advanced button on the final wizard screen, you're treated to yet another wizard. Most people, most of the time, will never need these special-case options. One important exception is the *When to Back Up* screen, which lets you indicate when you want this backup to take place—now or at a specified time and date (click the Set Schedule button shown in Figure 11-10).

Click Finish

When Backup is finished backing up your files, a window shows how many files and bytes were backed up. (If you see a message indicating an error, click Report to see a written record of what happened during the backup.)

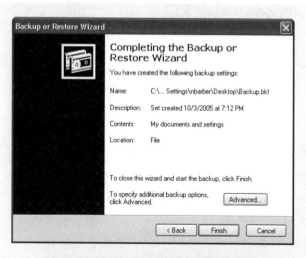

Figure 11-10. Clicking Advanced on the final Backup or Restore Wizard screen (top) launches a whole new series of screens. The screen shown at bottom is the most useful, allowing you to schedule time-consuming backups to take place after you go to bed, for example. You can even back up your PC on an automatic schedule (say, every Saturday at 3 a.m.).

After the backup is complete, click Close to close the Report window. Your data is safe—for now.

 Tip: Most backup errors arise when Backup tries to back up a file that's open. To avoid this problem, exit all your programs before backing up.

Restoring with Microsoft Backup

Restoring files is less complicated than backing them up—a good thing, considering the emotional state of anyone who's just experienced a total hard drive meltdown. That's because, unless you're a spectacularly unlucky individual, you don't perform restores as often as you do backups—and you don't schedule them. The Backup program's Restore Wizard does all the work for you.

Perform regular test restores, to make sure your data is retrievable from the backup disks. (Consider restoring your files to a test folder—not the folder where the files came from—so you don't wind up with duplicates.) There's no other way to be absolutely sure that your backups are working properly.

To restore files using the Restore Wizard, here's the plan (which assumes that, if your whole hard drive was trashed, you have already replaced it and reinstalled Windows XP):

1. **Click Start → All Programs → Accessories → System Tools → Backup.**

   The Backup or Restore Wizard Welcome screen appears.

2. **Click Next. On the second screen, click "Restore files and settings," and then click Next.**

   The What To Restore page contains the now-familiar expanding display that lists your PC's backup devices. The display lists a File icon, too, so that you can restore from a backup file (see "Select the backup medium" on page 308). Backup displays the date and time each backup file was made, making it easy to select the right file. If you use a tape drive or other device for your backups, the display lists the tapes or disks you have created.

Click to select the items you want to restore, exactly as you did when selecting files to back up.

 Tip: Clicking the + button expands a folder so that you can select an individual file inside it. This is also a great trick if you're restoring, from your backup file, a document that you've accidentally deleted from the hard drive.

3. **Select the tape or disk that contains your backup. Select the data to restore.**

When you select the backup disk or tape, the right pane in the What to Restore screen contains an expandable list of its contents. Double-click the folders seen here for a list of individual files. Turn on the checkboxes of the files and folders you want to restore, as shown in Figure 11-11.

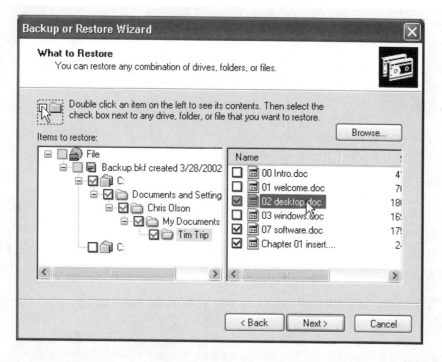

Figure 11-11. The Restore Wizard's What to Restore page is similar in format to Windows Explorer, except that it displays only the contents of a particular backup tape or disk. You can select from the backup tapes, disks, or files you've created.

Whenever Backup backs up your files, it remembers which files it put on which backup disks by creating a table of contents on the disk or tape that was in the drive when the job ended.

That's why, as you browse the files listed on a backup disk, you may be asked to insert that final disk or tape. Only then can Backup show you what's on it.

4. **On the Completing the Backup or Restore Wizard screen, click the Advanced button, if you like.**

   Ordinarily, Backup restores every backed-up file onto your hard drive in exactly the same folder from which it came. If the original file is still *in* that original folder, however, it doesn't bother copying the equivalent file from the backup disk. If that arrangement sounds good to you, skip to the next step.

   But suppose you'd like Backup to put the files in a *different* folder, or you want them to *replace* the duplicate files it encounters. In that case, the Advanced button is just the ticket. It lets you specify where you want the restored files to go: into the folders they came from or some other disk or folder.

   If you choose "Alternate location," you can type in the path to (or Browse to) a different folder (like *C:\Rescued*). If there's no such folder, Backup will create it for you.

   If you turn on "Single folder," Backup dumps all of the selected files directly into one specified folder, loose (not in a hierarchy of folders). Choose this option if you're simply trying to reclaim a few important files, rather than trying to reinstate your entire drive.

5. **Click Next. Indicate whether or not you want Backup to overwrite duplicate files.**

   Backup's file-restoring feature isn't only useful when you've had to wipe out your hard drive completely. It can also be handy when something less drastic went wrong, like a folder accidentally being thrown out. All the rest of your files and folders are OK.

But suppose you've indicated that you want your My Documents folder restored from the backup disks. What should Backup do when it encounters files that are *still in* your My Documents folder, and in perfect shape? You can choose one of three options. **Leave existing files** means that Backup won't restore any file that's already on the hard drive. **Replace existing files if they are older than the backup files** makes Backup replace a file on your hard drive only if it's an older version than the backed-up copy. Finally, **Replace existing files** restores every file, replacing its equivalent on the hard drive, regardless of which is newer.

6. **Click Next.**

   The options on this penultimate screen pertain to specialized security and system files. In general, you should just click past them.

7. **Click Next. If the restore summary page looks good, click Finish.**

   Backup swings into action, asking you to insert backup disks or tapes as necessary, and restoring your backed-up files safely onto your hard drive.

PART FIVE:
LIFE ON THE NETWORK

Chapter 12   User Accounts

Chapter 13   The Home Network

CHAPTER 12:
USER ACCOUNTS

▶ Introducing User Accounts

▶ Setting Up Accounts

▶ Setting Up the Logon Process

FOR YEARS, TEACHERS, PARENTS, tech directors, and computer lab instructors struggled to answer a difficult question: how do you rig one PC so that several different people can use it throughout the day, without interfering with each others' files and settings? And how do you protect a PC from getting fouled up by mischievous (or bumbling) students and employees?

Like the Windows 2000 under its skin, Windows XP is designed from the ground up to be a multiple-user operating system. On a Windows XP machine, anyone who uses the computer must *log on*—click (or type) your name and type in a password—when the computer turns on. And upon doing so, you discover the Windows universe just as you left it, including these elements:

▶ **Desktop.** Each person sees a different set of shortcut icons, folder icons, and other stuff left out on the desktop.

▶ **Start menu.** If you reorganize the Start menu, as described in Chapter 2, you won't confuse anybody else who uses the machine; no one else can even *see* the changes you make.

▶ **My Documents folder.** Each person sees only her own stuff in the My Documents folder.

▶ **Email.** Windows XP maintains a separate stash of email messages for each account holder—along with separate Web bookmarks, MSN Messenger contact list, and other online details.

▶ **Favorites folder.** Any Web sites, folders, or other icons you've designated as Favorites appear in *your* Favorites menu, and nobody else's.

▶ **Internet cache.** You can read about *cached* Web pages in Chapter 7; this folder stores a copy of the Web pages you've visited recently for faster retrieval.

▶ **History and cookies.** Windows maintains a list of recently visited Web sites independently for each person; likewise a personal collection of *cookies* (Web site preference files).

▶ **Control Panel settings.** Windows memorizes the preferences each person establishes using the Control Panel (see Chapter 10), including keyboard, sound, screen saver, and mouse settings.

Behind the scenes, Windows XP stores *all* of these files and settings in a single folder that techies call your user *profile*. It's in your My Computer → Local Disk (C:) → Documents and Settings → [Your Name] folder.

This feature makes sharing the PC much more convenient, because you don't have to look at everybody else's files (and endure their desktop design schemes). It also adds a layer of security, making it less likely for a marauding 6-year-old to throw away your files.

If you're a solo operator, the only person who uses your PC, you can safely skip this chapter. You *will* be using one of these accounts, whether you realize it or not—it's just that there won't be any additional accounts on your PC. You'll be able to use your PC just as you always have.

But when you've got some reading time—perhaps when you're stuck in line at the Department of Motor Vehicles—you may want to skim the concepts presented here. Certain elements of this multiple-user operating system may intrude upon your Windows activities—and the discussions in this book—from time to time.

 Tip: Even if you don't share your PC with anyone and don't create any other accounts, you might still appreciate this feature because it effectively password-protects the entire computer from unauthorized fiddling when you're away from your desk (or when your laptop is stolen).

Introducing User Accounts

When you first installed Windows XP or fired up a new Windows XP machine, you were asked for a name and password. You may not have realized it at the time, but you were creating the first *user account*.

Since that fateful day, you may have made a number of changes to your desktop—fiddled with your Start menu, changed the desktop wallpaper, added some favorites to your Web browser, downloaded files onto your desktop, and so on—without realizing that you were actually making these changes only to *your account.*

Accordingly, if you create an account for a second person, when she turns on the computer and signs in, she'll find the desktop exactly the way it was as factory installed by Microsoft: basic Start menu, Teletubbies-hillside desktop picture, default Web browser home page, and so on. She can make the same kinds of changes to the PC that you've made, but nothing she does will affect your environment the next time *you* log on. You'll still find the desktop the way you left it: *your* desktop picture fills the screen, the Web browser lists *your* bookmarks, and so on.

In other words, the multiple-accounts feature has two components: first, a convenience element that hides everyone else's junk; and second, a security element that protects both the PC's system software and other people's work.

Setting Up Accounts

To see what accounts are already on your PC, choose Start → Control Panel. Open the User Accounts icon; you'll see a list of existing accounts (Figure 12-1).

If you see more than one account here—not just yours—then one of these situations probably applies:

▶ You created them when you installed Windows XP. All of the accounts you create when you first install Windows XP become *Administrator* accounts, as described in the following section.

▶ You bought a new computer with Windows XP preinstalled, and created several accounts when you were asked to do so the first time you turned on the machine.

▶ You upgraded the machine from an earlier version of Windows. Windows XP gracefully imports all of your existing accounts.

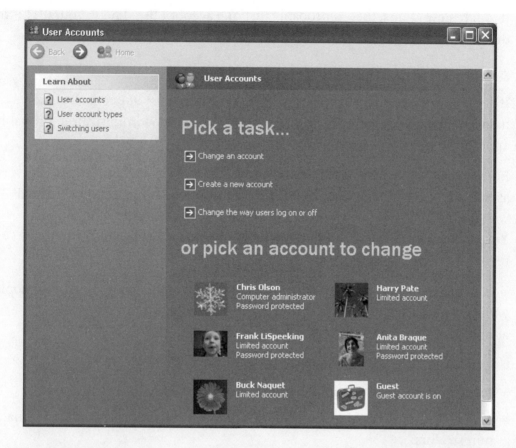

Figure 12-1. The User Accounts screen lists everyone for whom you've created an account. From here, you can create new accounts or change people's passwords. (Hint: To change account settings, just click the person's name from the "pick an account to change" section.

Warning: If you've upgraded from Windows 98 or Me, Windows XP (a) treats all of these imported accounts as Administrator accounts, described below, and (b) wipes out their passwords, which leaves open a security hole the size of Canada. Promptly after upgrading, therefore, you should take a moment to assign passwords and downgrade account types to Limited, as described below.

If you're new at this, there's probably just one account listed here: yours. This is the account that Windows XP created when you first installed it.

Administrator Accounts

It's important to understand the phrase that appears just under each person's name. On your own personal PC, the words "Computer administrator" probably appear underneath yours.

Because you're the person who installed Windows XP to begin with, the PC assumes that you're one of its *computer administrators*—the technical wizards who will be in charge of it. You're the teacher, the parent, the resident guru. You're the one who will maintain this PC and who will be permitted to make system-wide changes to it.

You'll find settings all over Windows XP (and all over this book) that *only* people with computer Administrator accounts can change. For example, only an administrator is allowed to:

▶ Create or delete accounts and passwords on the PC.

▶ Install new programs (and certain hardware components).

▶ Make changes to certain Control Panel programs that are off-limits to nonadministrators.

▶ See and manipulate *any* file on the machine.

As you go about creating accounts for other people who'll use this PC, you'll be offered the opportunity to make each one an administrator just like you. Needless to say, use discretion. Bestow these powers only upon people as responsible and technically masterful as you.

Limited Accounts

Anyone who isn't an administrator is an ordinary, everyday Limited account holder. "Limited" people have everyday access to certain Control Panel settings—the ones that pertain to their own computing environments. But most other areas of the PC are off-limits, including everybody else's My Documents folders, Windows system files, and so on.

If you're a Limited account holder, in other words, your entire world consists of the Start menu, your My Documents folder, the Shared Documents folder, and any folders you create.

If a Limited account holder manages to download a computer virus, its infection will be confined to his account. If an administrator catches a virus, on the other hand, every file on the machine is at risk.

That's a good argument for creating as few computer administrator accounts as possible. (In fact, some Windows pros don't even use Administrator accounts *themselves*. Even they use Limited accounts, keeping one Administrator account on hand only for new software or hardware installations, account or password changing, and similar special cases.)

Adding an Account

Once you've opened the User Accounts program in the Control Panel, it's easy to create a new account: just click the "Create a new account" link, shown in Figure 12-1. (You see this link only if you are, in fact, an administrator.)

A wizard guides you through the selection of a name and an account type (see Figure 12-2).

When you're finished with the settings, click the Create Account button (or press Enter). After a moment, you return to the User Accounts screen, where the new person's name joins whatever names were already there. You can continue adding new accounts forever or until your hard drive is full, whichever comes first.

 Tip: If you never had the opportunity to set up a user account when installing Windows XP—if you bought a PC with Windows XP already on it, for example—you may see an account named Owner, already in place. Nobody can use Windows XP at all unless there's at least *one* Administrator account on it, so Microsoft is doing you a favor here. Just use the User Accounts program in the Control Panel to change the name Owner to one that suits you better.

Figure 12-2. Top: When naming an account in the User Accounts screen, you can keep it simple or get more elaborate. If it's all in the family, the account's name could be Chris or Robin. If it's a corporation or school, you'll probably want to use both first and last names. Capitalization doesn't matter, but most punctuation is forbidden.

Bottom: The "Pick an Account type" screen lets you specify whether or not this unsuspecting computer user will be a computer administrator, as described above.

Editing an Account

Although the process of creating a new account is swift and simple, it doesn't offer you much in the way of flexibility. You don't even have a chance to specify the new person's password, let alone the tiny picture that appears next to the person's name and at the top of the Start menu (rubber ducky, flower, or whatever).

That's why the next step in creating an account is usually *editing* the one you just set up. To do so, once you've returned to the main User Accounts screen (Figure 12-1), click the name or icon of the freshly created account. You arrive at the screen shown at top in Figure 12-3, where—if you are an administrator—you can choose from any of these options:

▶ **Change the name.** You'll be offered the opportunity to type in a new name for this person and then click the Change Name button—just the ticket when one of your co-workers gets married or joins the Witness Protection Program.

▶ **Create a password.** Click this link if you'd like to require a password for access to this person's account (Figure 12-3, bottom). Capitalization counts.

The usual computer book takes this opportunity to stress the importance of having a long, complex password, such as a phrase that isn't in the dictionary, something made up of mixed letters and numbers, and *not* "password." This is excellent advice if you create sensitive documents and work in a big corporation.

But if you share the PC only with a spouse or a few trusted colleagues in a small office, for example, you may have nothing to hide. You may see the multiple-users feature more as a convenience (for keeping your settings and files separate) than a way of protecting secrecy and security.

In these situations, there's no particular need to dream up a convoluted password. In fact, you may want to consider setting up *no* password—leaving both password blanks empty. Later, whenever you're asked for your password, just leave the Password box blank. You'll be able to log on that much faster each day.

If you do decide to provide a password, you can also provide a hint (for yourself or whichever co-worker's account you're operating on). This is a hint that anybody can see (including bad guys trying to log on as you), so choose something meaningful only to you. If your password is the first person who ever kissed you plus your junior-year phone number, for example, your hint might be "first person who ever kissed me plus my junior-year phone number."

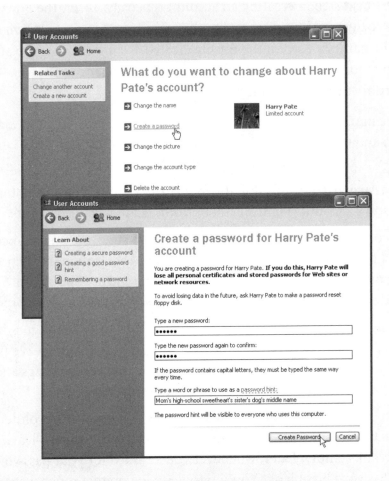

Figure 12-3. Top: Here's the master menu of account-changing options that you, an administrator, can see. (If you're a Limited account holder, you see far fewer options.)

Bottom: You're supposed to type your password twice, to make sure you didn't introduce a typo the first time. (The PC shows only dots as you type, to guard against the possibility that some villain is snooping over your shoulder.)

Later, if you ever forget your password, you'll be offered an opportunity to view this hint at sign-in time to jog your memory.

Tip: It's fine for you, an administrator, to create the *original* passwords for new accounts. But don't change their passwords later on, after they've been using the computer for a while. If you do, you'll wipe out various internal security features of their accounts, including access to their stored Web site passwords and stored passwords for shared folders and disks on the network. See the box on page 328 for details.

▶ **Make your files private.** The first time you make up a password for your own account, another screen asks: "Do you want to make your files and folders private?" If you're using the accounts feature more for convenience than for security—if you and your co-worker are married and have no secrets from each other, for example—click No.

But if you click the button labeled "Yes, Make Private," Windows takes a minute to mark everything in your *user profile folder* off-limits to other account holders. (Your user profile folder is the one bearing your name in the Documents and Settings folder on your hard drive.) Henceforth, if anyone else tries to open any of your files or folders (when they're logged in under their own names), they'll get nothing but a curt "Access is denied" message.

(Technically, making a folder private even shields it from the eyes of the machine's Administrator account holders—but it's a pretty flimsy shield. A determined administrator can burrow past this wisp of protection to examine your files, if she's determined to do so, or even change your password late one night to gain full access to your stuff.)

Note that even if you do make your files and folders private, you'll still be able to share selected files and folders with other people. You just put them into the Shared Documents folder described on page 341.

Tip: You can make *any* of your own folders private—or un-private, for that matter. Just right-click the folder; from the shortcut menu, choose Properties; click the Sharing tab; and turn "Make this folder private" on or off. To make your entire world un-private, for example, you'd perform this surgery on your *user profile folder* in the Documents and Settings folder (page 81).

▶ **Change the picture.** The usual Windows XP sign-in screen (Figure 12-4) displays each account holder's name, accompanied by a little picture. When you first create the account, however, it assigns a picture to you at random—and not all of them are necessarily appropriate for your personality. Not every extreme-sport headbanger, for example, is crazy about being represented by a dainty flower or butterfly.

If you like the selections that Microsoft has provided (drag the vertical scroll bar to see them all), just click one to select it as the replacement graphic. If you'd rather use some other graphics file on the hard drive instead—a digital photo of your own face, for example—you can click the "Browse for more pictures" link (Figure 12-4). You'll be shown a list of the graphics files on your hard drive so that you can choose one, which Windows then automatically scales down to postage-stamp size (48 pixels square).

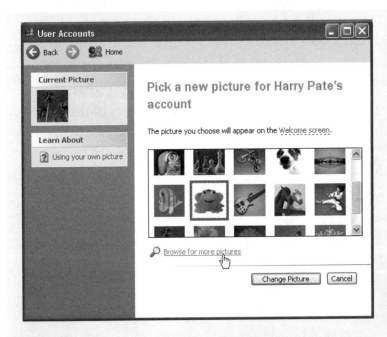

Figure 12-4. Left: Here's where you change your account picture, the one that appears on the Welcome screen and atop your Start menu.

Right: If you like to change your picture whenever your mood changes, there's a shortcut to this dialog box. Just click your account picture at the top of the open Start menu.

- **Change the account type.** Click this link to change a Limited account into an Administrator account, or vice versa. You might want to use this option, for example, after upgrading a Windows 98 or Windows Me computer to Windows XP—a process that otherwise leaves all existing user accounts as Administrator accounts.

- **Delete the account.** See page 334.

You're free to make any of these changes to any account at any time; you don't have to do it just after first creating the account.

 Tip: If the User Accounts program looks nothing like the illustrations in this chapter so far, it's probably because you have only a Limited account. In that case, opening User Accounts in the Control Panel offers only a few certain links: "Create a password" (or "Change my password"), "Change my picture," and "Set up my account to use a .NET Passport". Only a computer administrator can make the other kinds of changes described here.

The Forgotten Password Disk

As described on page 327, Windows XP contains a handy hint mechanism for helping you recall your password if you've forgotten it: the little ? icon that appears after you click your name on the Welcome screen. When you click that little icon, you're shown the hint that you provided for yourself—*if* you provided one—when setting up your account.

But what if, having walked into a low-hanging branch, you've completely forgotten both your password and the correct interpretation of your hint? In that disastrous situation, your entire world of work and email would be locked inside the computer forever. (Yes, an administrator could issue you a new password—but as noted in the box on page 332, you'd lose all your secondary passwords in the process.)

Fortunately, Windows XP offers a clever solution-in-advance: the Password Reset Disk. It's a floppy disk that you can use like a physical key to unlock your account, in the event of a forgotten password. The catch: you have to make this disk *now*, while you still remember your password.

Passwords Within Passwords

The primary password that you or your administrator sets up in the User Accounts program has two functions. You already know that it lets you log on each day, so that you can enter your Windows world of desktop clutter, Start-menu tailoring, Web bookmarks, and so on.

But what you may not realize is that it's also the master key that unlocks all the *other* passwords associated with your account: the passwords that Internet Explorer memorizes for certain Web sites, the passwords that get you into shared disks and folders on the network, the password that protects your .NET Passport (and its Wallet for electronic payments, if you set one up), and so on. The simple act of logging onto your account also unlocks all of these other secure areas of your PC life.

But remember that anyone with an Administrator account can *change* your password at any time. Does that mean that whoever has an Administrator account—your teacher, boss, or teenager, for example–has full access

to your private stuff? After you leave the household, company, or school, what's to stop an administrator from changing your password, thereby gaining access to your electronic-brokerage account (courtesy of its memorized Internet Explorer password), buying stuff with your Passport Wallet, and so on?

Fortunately, Microsoft is way ahead of you on this one. The instant an administrator changes somebody else's password, Windows XP *wipes out* all secondary passwords associated with the account. That administrator can log onto your account and see your everyday files, but not Web sites with memorized passwords, and so on.

Note that if you change your *own* password—or if you use a Forgotten Password Disk, described next—none of this applies. Your secondary passwords survive intact. It's only when *somebody else* changes your password that this little-known Windows XP security feature kicks in, sanitizing the account for your protection.

To create this disk, choose Start → Control Panel. Open the User Accounts program. If you're an administrator, click your account name; if not, you can skip this step.

Either way, you should now see a link in the task pane called, "Prevent a forgotten password." Click that to open the Forgotten Password Wizard shown in Figure 12-5.

When the day comes that you can't remember your password, your attempts to get past the logon screen will be met by a "Use your Password Reset Disk" link.

Figure 12-5. The screens of the Forgotten Password Wizard guide you through the process of inserting a blank floppy disk and preparing it to be your master skeleton key. If you forget your password—or if some administrator has changed your password—you can use this disk to reinstate it without the risk of losing all of your secondary passwords (memorized Web passwords, encrypted files, and so on).

When you click that link or button, Windows asks you to insert your Password Reset Disk, and then gives you the opportunity to create a new password (and a new hint to remind you of it). You're in.

Even though you now have a new password, your existing Password Reset Disk will still be good. Keep it in a drawer somewhere, for use the next time you experience a temporarily blank brain.

Deleting User Accounts

It happens: somebody graduates, somebody gets fired, somebody dumps you. Sooner or later, you may need to delete a user account from your PC.

To delete a user account, you, an administrator, must open the User Accounts program, click the appropriate account name, and then click "Delete the account."

Windows XP now asks you if you want to preserve the contents of this person's My Documents folder. If you click the Keep Files button, you'll find a new folder, named for the dearly departed, on your desktop. (As noted in the dialog box, only the documents, contents of the desktop, and the My Documents folder are preserved—but *not* programs, email, or even Web favorites.) If that person ever returns to your life, you can create a new account for him and copy these files into the appropriate folder locations.

If you click the Delete Files button, on the other hand, the documents are gone forever.

A few more important points about deleting accounts:

▶ You can't delete the account you're already using.

▶ You can't delete the last Administrator account. One account must always remain.

▶ You can create a new account with the same name and password as one that you deleted earlier, but in Windows XP's head, it's still not the same account.

As described in the box on page 332, it won't have any of the original secondary passwords (for Web sites, shared folders, and so on).

▶ Don't manipulate accounts manually (by fooling around in the Documents and Settings folder, for example). Create, delete, and rename them only using the User Accounts program in the Control Panel. Otherwise, you'll wind up with duplicate or triplicate folders in Documents and Settings, with the PC name tacked onto the end of the original account name (Bob, Bob.MILLEN-NIA, and so on)—a sure recipe for confusion.

Setting Up the Logon Process

Once you've set up more than one account, the dialog box that greets you when you turn on the PC (or when you relinquish your turn at the PC by choosing Start → Log Off) looks something like Figure 12-7. But a few extra controls let you, an administrator, set up the logon screen for either more or less security— or, put another way, less or more convenience.

Open the User Accounts program in the Control Panel, and then click "Change the way users log on or off." As shown in Figure 12-6, Windows XP now offers you two extremely important logon options.

"Use the Welcome Screen"

Under normal circumstances, the logon screen presents a list of account holders when the PC is first turned on. If you're especially worried about security, however, you might not even want that list to appear. If you turn off "Use the Welcome screen," each person who signs in must type both his name *and* password into blank boxes—a very inconvenient, but secure, arrangement (Figure 12-7). (You can't turn off "Use the Welcome screen" if Fast User Switching is turned on. Fast User Switching is described in the next section.)

Tip: Strangely enough, even when you're looking at the standard Welcome screen, you can switch to the Classic logon screen: just press Ctrl+Alt+Delete. (If you're having trouble making it work, try pressing down the Alt key before the other ones.)

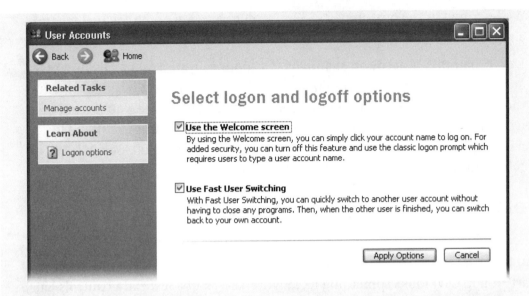

Figure 12-6. The "Select logon and logoff" options have enormous ramifications. The first governs the appearance of the Welcome screen shown in Figure 12-8. The second lets one person duck into his own account without forcing you to log off, as described on page 337. These options are related—you can't turn off the first without first turning off the second.

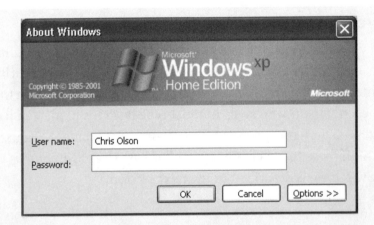

Figure 12-7. If you turn off the new Welcome screen, you sign into Windows XP just as Windows 2000 fans have for years. You're expected to type in your name and password and then click OK.

"Use Fast User Switching"

If you've used any version of Windows before, the business about separate user accounts for everybody who uses a certain PC is old hat. One aspect of this feature, however, is dramatically new in Windows XP—and extremely welcome: Fast User Switching.

How Fast User Switching works

Suppose you're signed in, and you've got things just the way you like them: you have eleven programs open in carefully arranged windows, your Web browser is downloading some gigantic file, and you're composing an important speech in Microsoft Word. Now Chris, a co-worker/family member/fellow student, wants to duck in to do a quick email check.

In the old days, you might have rewarded Chris with eye-rolling and heavy sighs—or a reaction even less suitable for a family book. If you chose to accommodate the request, you would have had to shut down your whole ecosystem, interrupting the download, closing your windows, saving your work and exiting your programs. You would have had to log off completely.

If Fast User Switching is turned on, however, none of that is necessary. All you have to do is press the magic keystroke, Windows logo key+L. (Or, if you've misplaced your keyboard, you can choose Start → Log Off, and then click Switch User in the Log Off dialog box.)

Now the Welcome screen appears, ready for the next person to sign in. Looking at the screen now, you may *think* you've just logged off in the usual way.

But look at it closely (Figure 12-8): You haven't actually logged off at all. Instead, Windows has *memorized* the state of affairs in your account—complete with all open windows, documents, and programs—and shoved it into the background. Chris (or whoever) can now sign in normally, do a little work, or look something up. When Chris logs out again, the Welcome screen comes back once again, at which point *you* can log on again. Without having to wait more than a couple of seconds, you find yourself exactly where you began, with all programs and documents still open and running.

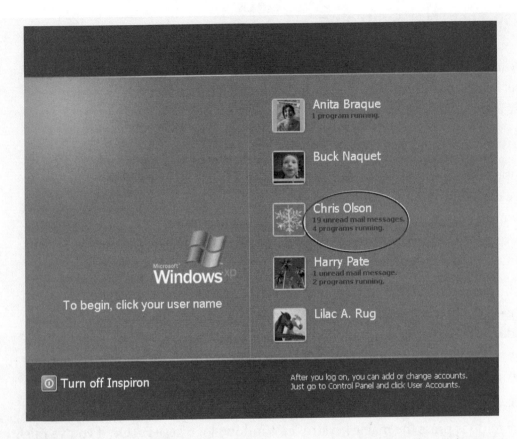

Anita Braque
1 program running.

Buck Naquet

Chris Olson
19 unread mail messages.
4 programs running.

Harry Pate
1 unread mail message.
2 programs running.

Lilac A. Rug

Microsoft
Windows xp

To begin, click your user name

⊙ Turn off Inspiron

After you log on, you can add or change accounts.
Just go to Control Panel and click User Accounts.

Figure 12-8. When Fast User Switching is turned on, you can call up the Welcome screen shown here without even quitting your programs and closing your windows. If Outlook Express or Windows Messenger is running, the Welcome screen even shows you how many unread email messages are waiting for you. (Point without clicking to produce a screen tip that breaks down which email accounts they came in on.)

Tip: When you're logged in under Fast User Switching, you're not allowed to open a file that's open in somebody else's account universe. An "Access is denied" message will tell you so.

Fast User Switching

You can't turn Fast User Switching off if anybody else's account is still open in the background. Before you can turn off the feature, you must first switch to each account in turn (press Windows key+L) and then sign off from each of them.

If Fast User Switching is turned *off*, its special keystroke—Windows logo key+L—is still special. Now it *locks* your PC, hiding all of your open programs and windows. The only thing on the screen is an Unlock Computer dialog box (which looks almost exactly like the one shown in Figure 12-8). At this point, nobody can even get into the machine except you or somebody with an Administrator account.

Here's the power user's version of Fast User Switching (Administrator account required). Press Ctrl+Alt+Delete to open the Task Manager dialog box, whose Users tab reveals the list of logged-on accounts. Right-click the account you want, choose Connect from the shortcut menu, and *boom!* switched. You don't even have to listen to the two-note musical switching theme.

This feature requires a good deal of memory, of course (don't even think about it on a machine with less than 96 MB of RAM). Otherwise, however, it's an enormous time-saver.

How to turn on Fast User Switching

To turn on this optional feature, open the User Accounts program in the Control Panel. Click "Change the way users log on or off"; the dialog box shown in Figure 12-6 appears. Make sure "Use the Welcome screen" is turned on (it's a requirement for Fast User Switching), and then turn on "Use Fast User Switching." Finally, click the Apply Options button.

From now on, you have two options each time you decide that you're finished working for the moment. You can log off normally, closing all of your programs and windows—or you can *fast switch*, logging off temporarily, leaving your work open on the screen behind the scenes. Figure 12-9 shows you the difference.

Figure 12-9. Top: If you choose Start → Log Off when Fast User Switching is turned off, you get this limited dialog box.

Bottom: When you choose Start → Log Off while Fast User Switching is turned on, you get this choice: you can either log off for real (click Log Off), or use Fast User Switching to cede control of the computer to another account holder and put your work into background memory (click Switch User).

Shared Folders

As described earlier in this chapter, the mere act of assigning a password to your user account triggers Windows XP—with your approval—to make all of your files and folders private, so that no other account holders can access them.

If you try to open anybody else's files or folders, you see a dialog box so nice, it tells you twice: "[This folder] is not accessible. Access is denied."

That's all well and good if you'd just as soon prefer your fellow PC users keep their noses out of your stuff. But it doesn't bode well for the kinds of exciting collaboration that computers are supposed to make possible. If your worlds are completely separate, how can you collaborate on a document? What are you supposed to do, email the thing to another account on the exact same computer?

Fortunately, Microsoft has that particular problem licked, thanks to the presence of the *Shared Documents* folder. To find it, just choose Start → My Computer (Figure 12-10). (You might consider making a shortcut of it on your desktop or Start menu.)

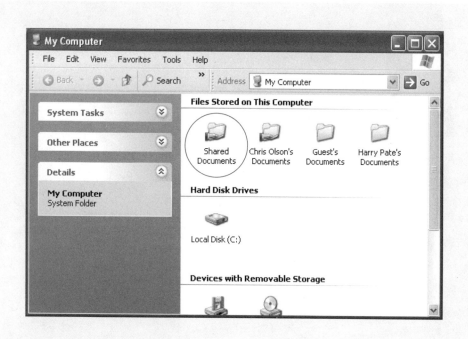

Figure 12-10. The Shared Documents folder (circled) contains files that you're welcome to open, read, and copy to your own folders—stuff that other people have wanted to "publish" for the benefit of their co-workers. You can think of it as sort of a wormhole connecting all accounts. Everybody has full access to everything inside.

Anything you put into this folder is available for inspection, editing, or deleting by anyone else who uses this PC. It's the common ground among all the account holders. It's Central Park, the farmer's market, and the grocery-store bulletin board.

 Tip: You can also create other shared folders, either inside the Shared Documents folder or anywhere you like. The trick: right-click the folder you want to make public. From the shortcut menu, choose Sharing and Security, if that's an option. (If not, choose Properties and then click the Sharing tab.) In the resulting dialog box, turn off "Make this folder private," and then click OK.

CHAPTER 13:
THE HOME NETWORK

▶ The Network Setup Wizard

▶ Simple File Sharing

▶ The Shared Documents Folder

▶ Sharing Your Own Folders

▶ Accessing Other Computers

▶ Working with Network Files

WHEN YOU CONNECT COMPUTERS so that they can access one another's files and equipment, you create a *network*. As millions of PC fans buy second and third computers for their homes and offices, small networks are becoming increasingly common.

When it comes to simplicity, setting up a network has a long way to go before it approaches, say, setting up a desk lamp. It involves buying equipment, installing adapters, and configuring software. Fortunately, Windows XP's Network Setup Wizard makes the software part as painless as possible.

And the payoff is considerable: once you've created a network, you can copy files from one machine to another just as you'd drag files between folders on your own PC. Everyone on the network can consult the same database, phone book, or calendar. When the workday's done, you can play games over the network. Most importantly, you can share a single laser printer, cable modem or DSL, fax modem, or phone line among all the PCs in the house.

The Network Setup Wizard

Once you've set up the networking equipment, you have to inform Windows XP about what you've been up to. You also have to configure your computers to share their files, folders, printers, modems, Internet connections, and so on. Fortunately, the Network Setup Wizard handles this duty for you. (You must have an Administrator account to run this wizard.)

To launch the wizard, choose Start → Control Panel, and then open Network Connections. In the task pane, click the link that says, "Set up a home or small office network. If you've chosen to hide your task pane, you can choose Start → All Programs → Accessories → Communications → Network Setup Wizard instead.

A welcome message appears, as shown in Figure 13-1. Click Next. Then proceed through the remaining screens of the wizard as described on the next few pages.

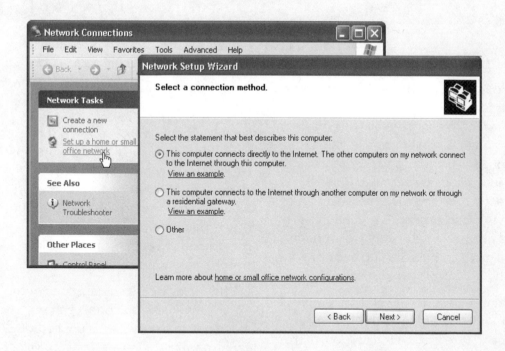

Figure 13-1. Left: Start the Network Setup Wizard by clicking this link in the Network Connections box.

Right: Select the option that best describes this computer's relationship to the Internet. If the PC will be the gateway to the Internet for other PCs on the network, choose the first option. Otherwise, just choose Other to tell the wizard as much.

"Before you continue"

The screen contains a link called "Checklist for creating a network." If you click it, you see a help page that guides you through the steps of setting up a network.

It also reminds you that if you plan to use Internet Connection Sharing, which allows you to share a single Internet connection with multiple PCs, you should ensure that the Windows XP machine whose connection you want to share can get online *before* proceeding with the wizard. When you're finished reading the checklist, close its window, and then click Next.

Connecting Two PCs

If your network has modest ambitions—that is, if you have only two computers you want to connect—all you need is an Ethernet *crossover cable*, costing about $10 from a computer store or online mail-order supplier. Run it directly between the Ethernet jacks of the two computers. Everything else in this chapter works exactly as though you had purchased a hub and were using a "real" Ethernet network.

Of course, even that solution requires a networking card in each PC. If that expenditure is a stretch for you, there's yet another way to connect two machines: a direct connection. You can create this kind of miniature home-made network only if (a) the computers are close to each other, (b) they both have parallel or USB ports, and (c) you've bought a high-speed Direct-Parallel or USB Net-LinQ cable from *www.lpt.com.*

To begin in this fashion, open the Network Connections icon in your Control Panel. Click the "Create a new connection" link to start the New Connection Wizard.

Click Next. On the second screen, click "Set up an advanced connection," and then click Next. Click "Connect directly to another computer," and hit Next again.

Now Windows wants to know if the computer you're using will be the *host* (the machine whose files will be shared) or the *guest* (the one that will be accessing shared resources on the other machine). Choose Host (an option only if you're using an Administrator account), and then click Next.

On the next wizard screen, specify the port you're using to connect the machines (from the list of unused USB, serial, parallel, or infrared ports). Select USB or Parallel, as appropriate. Plug in the cable, if you haven't already.

Click Next again to view the list of user accounts; turn on the checkboxes of the people who should be allowed to tap into your machine via this direct-connect cable. Click Next, then Finish. The host computer starts "listening" for the guest to visit it.

Repeat all of this on the other machine, this time designating it the Guest (you don't need an Administrator account this time). Once the two machines are connected by cable, it's just as though they were connected by a "real" network, as described later in this chapter.

"Select a connection method"

The next wizard window starts the process of setting up Internet Connection Sharing (see Figure 13-1, right).

Your next step depends on your plans for your network and Internet use:

▶ **Each PC will go online independently.** If sharing a single Internet connection isn't the point of your networking efforts, click the Other button; on the next screen, click "This computer connects to the Internet directly or through a network hub." In other words, your various networked PCs will each connect directly to the Internet. No connection sharing is involved.

▶ **This is the computer with the connection.** If the computer you're at now is the one connected to the Internet—that is, if it's the gateway computer—click the first option: "This computer connects directly to the Internet. The other computers on my network connect to the Internet through this computer."

 Note: If your DSL service is for *multiple fixed IP addresses,* then your computers can share the connection without having to choose one single computer as the host.

▶ **This isn't the computer with the connection.** If you like the idea of sharing a PC's Internet connection, but the machine you're using now isn't the gateway machine, choose the second option: "This computer connects to the Internet through another computer on my network or through a residential gateway."

▶ **You have a router.** If you've bought a router (residential gateway) box, you won't be needing the built-in Windows Internet Connection Sharing feature. Once again, you should click the second option ("This computer connects to the Internet through another computer on my network or through a residential gateway").

▶ **You don't plan to use the Internet at all.** If you just want to set up connections among your computers—but none of them ever goes online—click Other, then click the Next button, and then turn on "This computer belongs to a network that does not have an Internet connection."

"Select your Internet connection"

If you indicated that the computer you're setting up will indeed be connecting to the Internet, the wizard now shows you a list of the ways you've set up for your PC to get online (Figure 13-2, bottom). Each represents a different method of getting onto the Internet—via network (Local Area Connection), America Online dial-up, your DSL account, or whatever. Turn on the one you want to use, and then click Next.

"Give this computer a description and name"

On this wizard page (Figure 13-2, top), you see a place to give your PC its own, unique name. For example, if you have a laptop and a desktop PC, you might give them names like *Portegé* and *Millennia* (or *Kirk* and *Spock*, for all Windows cares). Of course, you already gave your computer a name when you installed Windows XP; that should be the name you see here.

"Name your network"

On the screen, you're supposed to make up a name for your *workgroup* (mini-network). Every PC on your network should have the same workgroup name (it doesn't have to be *MSHome*, much as Microsoft might like it).

"Ready to apply network settings"

Click Next. On the next wizard screen, you see a summary of your settings. If it all looks good, click Next, and wait a few minutes while the wizard scurries around, applying various internal settings.

"You're almost done"

Your first PC may now be correctly configured to be part of an office network, but it faces the problem of the first telephone owner: who ya gonna call?

Your next step, therefore, should be to run the Network Setup Wizard again on each of your other PCs. As indicated by the wizard screen before you now,

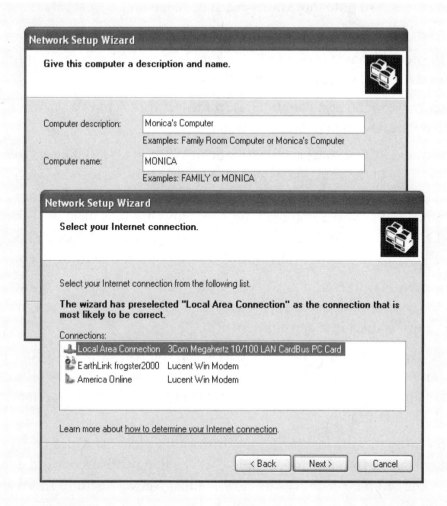

Figure 13-2. *Top: Every computer on a Windows network (even a big network in a business environment) must have a unique name. Computer names and workgroup names are limited to 15 characters, without spaces. Hyphens and apostrophes are OK, but most other punctuation is forbidden.*

Bottom: Tell the wizard how this machine connects to the Internet. See Chapter 7 to find out how these account names got here.

getting the wizard onto those other machines depends on what version of Windows they're using:

- **If the next PC has Windows XP.** Click the bottom option here, "Just finish the wizard." Click Next, and then click Finish.

  Now move to the next computer; start the Network Setup Wizard on *it*, exactly the way you did on the first machine.

- **If the next PC has some earlier version of Windows.** You still need to run the XP version of the networking wizard. XP offers you two ways to go about it. First, you can insert your Windows XP CD-ROM in each of the other PCs. When the Windows Setup program opens up, click the link at the left side called "Perform additional tasks"; on the next screen, click "Set up home or small office networking." The wizard appears, and you're ready to go.

  Second, you can create a *networking setup disk* for your older computers. That is, the wizard will transfer a copy of itself to a floppy disk that you can carry to the non-XP machines on your network.

  If you select this option and then click Next, you're instructed to put a blank formatted disk in the floppy drive. Click Next again to create the disk, which takes only a moment or two. Then eject the disk; for best results, label it for easy identification.

  Now insert the disk into the floppy drive on the older PC. Open the My Computer icon on your desktop, double-click the floppy drive icon, and double-click the Setup.exe icon. The by-now-familiar Network Setup Wizard appears.

No matter how you get the wizard onto the other machines, the experience of using it is precisely as described on the preceding pages—with two exceptions:

- If you've decided to set up the first computer as the gateway for Internet Connection Sharing, you don't see the complex array of choices back in Figure 13-1. Instead, you see only the simplified options of Figure 13-3.

- There's no need to create a network setup floppy disk on the final wizard screen.

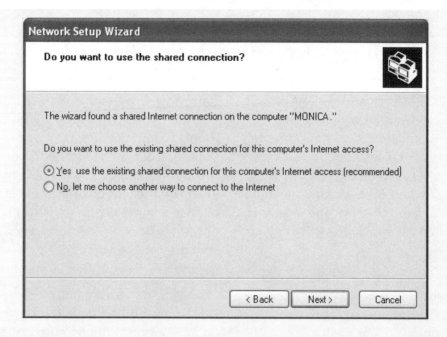

Figure 13-3. If you're using Internet Connection Sharing, the second, third, and subsequent PCs you set up automatically detect the presence of the first one (the gateway computer). Instead of the dialog box shown in Figure 13-1, you get this far simpler version—and in general, you'll want to select the first option.

When it's all over, Windows lets you know that you should restart the computer. At that point, each PC you've visited is ready for network action.

Testing the Network

After all of this setup, here's how you can find out whether or not the gods are smiling on your new network. Seated at your Windows XP machine, choose Start → My Network Places.

The network window opens, revealing the folders and disks that your machine can "see" (detect) on other computers of the network. The first time you try this experiment, there may not be much to see here.

Internet Connection Sharing

The Internet Connection Sharing (ICS) feature of Windows XP is worth its weight in gold—or, to be more precise, it's worth $80. That's about how much you would spend on a piece of equipment called a router, which you would otherwise need to share one Internet connection among all the PCs on your network.

If you have a high-speed connection like a cable modem or DSL, keeping your shared Internet system working is fairly simple. Just remember that the gateway PC must be turned on—and turned on *before* the other computers on the network—in order for the other PCs to get online. Remember, also, that the Windows Firewall feature (page 296) should be turned off for all PCs *except* the gateway computer. (Otherwise, they may not be able to talk to each *other*.)

Another typical problem: the host computer insists on connecting to your Internet service provider 24 hours a day, tying up the household phone line all day long, redialing every time it loses the connection.

Fortunately, it's easy enough to give Internet connection sharing some behavior-modification therapy. On the gateway PC, open the Network Connections icon in your Control Panel. Right-click the connection icon for your Internet service provider; from the shortcut menu, choose Properties, and click the Options tab. Make sure "Redial If line is dropped" is turned off, and set "Idle time before hanging up" to a reasonable number—say, ten minutes.

While you're here, you may as well turn off "Prompt for name and password" and "Prompt for phone number" to streamline the connection process, so that Windows XP won't bother you for this information every time you try to connect.

Note: All recent generations of Windows can "see" each other and work joyously side by side on the same network. On older machines, you would open the equivalent window by double-clicking the My Network Places or Network Neighborhood icon on the desktop instead of using the Start menu.

But if you click "View workgroup computers" in the task pane at the left side of the window, you should see the names and icons of the other computers you've set up (see Figure 13-4). In the next section, you'll find out how to burrow into these icons, using the files and folders of other networked PCs exactly as though they were on your own computer.

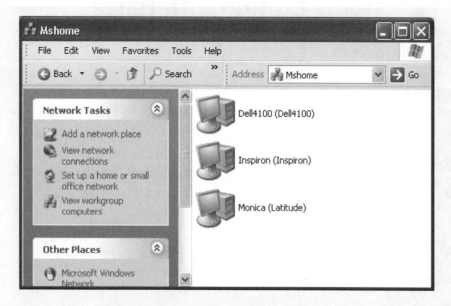

Figure 13-4. After you complete the Network Setup Wizard, your Network Places window (shown in Tiles view here) should reveal the presence of other PCs in your network, complete with the names you gave them.

If you don't see the icons for your other computers, something has gone wrong. Check to see that:

▶ Your cables are properly seated.

▶ Your Ethernet hub (if any) is plugged into an outlet.

► **Your networking card is working.** To do so, open the System program in the Control Panel. Click the Hardware tab; click the Device Manager button. Look for an error icon next to your networking card's name (see Chapter 9 for more on the Device Manager).

If you don't find a problem, rerun the Network Setup Wizard. If that doesn't work, you'll have to call Microsoft or your PC company for help.

UP TO SPEED

Even More Networking Terminology—and Home Edition Differences

A computer running Windows XP Home Edition can't be part of a corporate *domain*—a common corporate arrangement in which one master computer stores the accounts, passwords, and settings for all other machines on the network. Technically, a Home Edition machine can be part of such networks, and can even access shared folders and other resources on them—but you'll have to plug in a name and password each time you want access.

Instead, the form of networking described in this chapter is called *peer-to-peer* networking, in which each PC maintains its own database of account information.

This piece of trivia has been brought to you for the benefit of people who work in corporations, or people who are used to using Windows 2000. Now you'll know what to reply when someone asks you whether you have a *domain* network or the *peer-to-peer* variety.

Simple File Sharing

If you own Windows XP Home Edition, there's a very easy way for anyone on the network to make certain folders available to everybody else on the network. This setup is almost perfect for PCs that are, in fact, at home. If it's just you and your spouse, or you and a co-worker, then you probably want maximum convenience and minimum protection from each other. If you need a peek at the spreadsheet that Harold was working on yesterday, no big deal—you just open up his My Documents folder from across the network.

Tip: If you want to establish individualized control for each person on your network, an upgrade to Windows XP Professional may be in your future. The techniques in this chapter, however, work equally well in both Professional and Home Editions.

The Shared Documents Folder

In the following pages, you'll learn how to *share* certain folders—how to make them public, designating them as available to every PC on the network.

But if you live in a household full of technophobes, you might never need to bother with that business. You're already blessed with a special folder that's ready for this kind of sharing: the Shared Documents folder. It makes a perfect family (or small office) bulletin board.

To have a look at the Shared Documents folder on your own PC, just choose Start → My Computer. There it is, sitting among the other icons in the Files on This Computer section (Figure 13-5).

To peek into the Shared Documents folders on *other* people's computers, putting your network to productive use for the first time, choose Start → My Network Places. (If your Start menu doesn't list My Network Places, take a moment to put it there yourself. Right-click the Start button; from the shortcut menu, choose Properties. Click the Customize button, and then click the Advanced tab. In the scrolling list, turn on "My Network Places." Finally, click OK twice.)

Tip: Technically, and maybe confusingly, the Shared Documents folder on your own PC actually represents the contents of the Local Disk (C:) → Documents and Settings → All Users → Shared Documents folder.

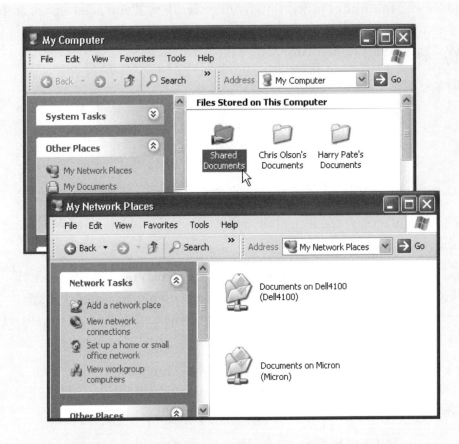

Figure 13-5. Top: Your own Shared Documents folder resides in the My Computer window. To "publish" a document so that everybody else on the network can work with it, just drag its icon into this folder.

Bottom: To access the Shared Documents folders on other computers on your network, simply choose Start → My Network Places. (They show up named "Documents" when viewed across the network.)

As shown in Figure 13-5 at bottom, you've just opened up a window that contains one icon for every shared folder on the network—including the Shared Documents folder on each computer.

At this point, you might consider dragging the Documents folders to your desktop for easier access, for example, where they become something like folder shortcuts. While you're at it, consider renaming them so you know which computers they came from. Or drag these icons directly into your Start menu or onto your Quick Launch toolbar.

In any case, you can open and work with whatever you find inside just as though they were your own documents. The difference, of course, is that these are actually public documents sitting on other people's computers.

 Tip: If you see an error message claiming that the file is in use by "another user," then, sure enough, somebody else on the network is probably working on that same document at this very moment. You'll have to wait until that person closes the document before it's your turn.

Sharing Your Own Folders

The Shared Documents folder is all very well and good, but it's generic. When you feel ready to flex your technical muscles ever so slightly, it's easy enough to "publish" *any* of your folders or disks for inspection by other people on your network. The trick is to use the Properties dialog box, like so:

1. **Locate the icon of the folder or disk that you want to share.**

   Your disk icons, of course, appear when you choose Start → My Computer. You can share any kind of disk—hard drive, floppy, CD-ROM or Zip drive, and so on.

   Sharing an entire disk means that every folder on it, and therefore every file, is available to everyone on the network. If security isn't a big deal at your place (because it's just you and a couple of family members, for example), this feature can be a time-saving convenience that spares you the trouble of sharing every new folder you create.

On the other hand, people with privacy concerns generally prefer to share individual *folders*. By sharing only a folder or two, you can keep *most* of the stuff on your hard drive private, out of view of curious network comrades.

For that matter, sharing only a folder or two does *them* a favor, too, by making it easier for them to find files you've made available. This way, they don't have to root through your entire drive looking for the appropriate folder.

2. **Right-click the disk or folder icon; from the shortcut menu, choose Sharing and Security.**

   The Sharing tab of the Properties dialog box opens (Figure 13-6). (The shortcut menu includes the Sharing command only if you've set up the computer for networking, as described in the previous chapter. And if you don't see a Sharing and Security command, just choose Properties from the shortcut menu—and then, in the resulting dialog box, click the Sharing tab.)

   If you're trying to share an entire disk, you now see a warning to the effect that, "sharing the root of a drive is not recommended." Click the link beneath it that says, "If you understand the risk but still want to share the root of the drive, click here" and then proceed with the next step.

3. **Turn on "Share this folder on the network" (see Figure 13-6).**

   The other options in the dialog box spring to life.

4. **Type a name for the shared disk or folder.**

   This is the name other people will see when they open their My Network Places windows.

   Make this name as helpful as possible. For example, you may want to name the kitchen computer's hard drive *Kitchen Documents Drive*.

   (If any of the other PCs on your network *aren't* running Windows XP, the shared folder's name can't be longer than twelve characters, and most punctuation is forbidden. You can type it here, all right, but—as a warning

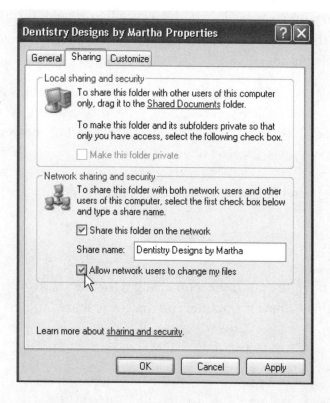

Figure 13-6. Here's the Sharing tab for a disk or folder. (The dialog box refers to a "folder" even if it's actually a disk.) You can turn on "Share this folder on the network" only if "Make this folder private" is unchecked (as is the case here); after all, if a folder is private, you certainly don't want other network citizens rooting around in it.

message will tell you—the other machines won't be able to see the shared disk or folder over the network.)

5. **Turn off "Allow network users to change my files," if you like.**

If the "Allow network users to change my files" checkbox is turned *off*, you create a "look, don't touch" policy. Other people on the network can open and read what's inside this disk or folder, but won't be able to save changes, rename anything, delete anything, or deposit any new files.

Otherwise, your co-workers can theoretically run wild, trashing your files, renaming things at random, and painting a mustache onto your face in the JPEG family photo.

 Tip: Turning off the "Allow network users to change my files" checkbox isn't much of a security safeguard. True, other people on the network won't be able to change what's in your folder—but there's nothing to stop them from saving *copies* of your files on their own hard drives. They can then do with them whatever they like. In other words, if you don't want people to see or distribute what's in your folders, turn off sharing completely.

6. **Click OK.**

As shown in Figure 13-7, the icon changes for the resource you just shared. It's also gained a new nickname: you may hear shared folders geekily referred to as *shares*.

Shared Documents   Local Disk (C:)   CD Drive (D:)

Figure 13-7. When you share a folder or a disk, a tiny hand cradles its icon from beneath—a dead giveaway that you've made it available to other people on the network.

Notes on Sharing

The preceding steps show you how to make a certain folder or disk available to other people on the network. The following footnotes, however, are worth skimming, especially for Windows 2000 veterans:

▶ You can't share individual files—only entire folders or disks.

▶ The "Share this folder on the network" checkbox is dimmed for *all* folders if your PC is not, in fact, on the network—or, more specifically, if you haven't experienced the thrill of the Network Setup Wizard described on page 344.

- Unless you specify otherwise, sharing a folder also shares all of the folders inside it. Your "Allow network users to change my files" setting gives permission to change files in all of those folders, too.

  If you right-click one of these inner folders and inspect the Sharing tab of its Properties dialog box, you'll find the Sharing checkbox turned off, which can be a bit confusing. But you'd better believe it—those inner folders are actually shared, no matter what the checkbox says.

- On the other hand, it's OK to right-click one of these inner folders and *change* its sharing settings. For example, if you've shared a folder called America, you can make the Minnesota folder inside it off-limits by making it private (page 329). Similarly, if you've turned *off* "Allow network users to change my files" for the America folder, you can turn it back *on* for the Minnesota folder inside it.

- You're not allowed to share important system folders like Windows, Program Files, and Documents and Settings. If you've set up your PC with multiple user accounts (Chapter 12), you can't share folders that belong to other people, either—only your own stuff.

Hiding Folders

If a certain folder on your hard drive is really private, you can hide it so that other people on the network can't even *see* it. The secret is to type a $ symbol at the end of the share name (see step 4 on page 358).

For example, if you name a certain folder My Novel, anyone else on the network will be able to see it. But if you name the share My Novel$, it won't show up in anybody's My Network Places window. They won't even know that it exists. (It still shows up on *your* machine, of course. And it will also be visible to other network computers if you shared the *disk* on which the folder sits.)

Accessing Other Computers

So far in this chapter, you've been reading from the point of view of the person doing the sharing. You've read the steps for preparing a PC for sharing by other people on the network.

This section details how to be one of *them*—that is, how to connect to other PCs whose disks, folders, and printers have been shared.

Fortunately, doing so is extremely easy.

My Network Places

Most people view their network contents using a special window:

▶ **In Windows XP or Windows Me:** Choose Start → My Network Places.

▶ **In earlier versions:** Double-click the desktop icon called My Network Places or Network Neighborhood.

The very first time you open the network window (Figure 13-8), you see icons that correspond to the shared folders and files on the computers of your network (including those on your own machine). Just double-click one to open it, in readiness to work with its contents.

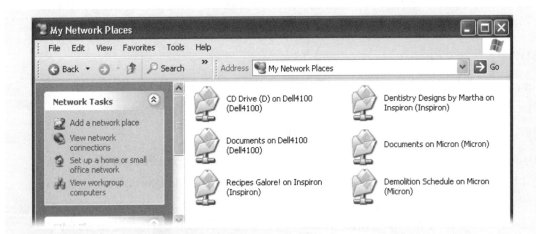

Figure 13-8. Shared disks and folders automatically show up in the My Network Places window—including shared disks and folders on your own PC, which can be a bit confusing. Here, the network-wire logo replaces the usual sharing-hand icon.

"View workgroup computers"

If you find the My Network Places window overwhelmingly crowded as your network grows, you might find clarity in the "View workgroup computers" link at the left side of the window. It shows you the icons of the *computers* on your network—not every last shared folder on all of them. Double-click one of these computer icons to see a list of the shared folders and printers on it (Figure 13-9).

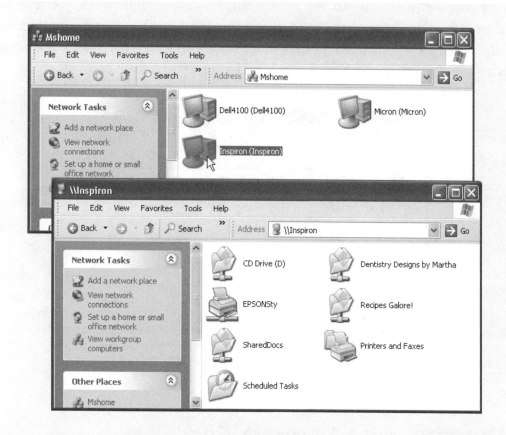

Figure 13-9. Top: If you know that the folder or file you're looking for resides on a particular PC, it's often more convenient to start your quest at this window.

Bottom: When you double-click a computer (Inspiron in this case), you see a list of its shared resources (folders, disks, and printers).

Older PCs: Network Neighborhood

If you're using a networked PC that's still running Windows 95 or Windows 98, you won't find a My Network Places icon on the desktop. Instead, you get its ancestor: Network Neighborhood.

When you open Network Neighborhood, Windows displays an icon in the window for each computer it finds on the workgroup (see Figure 13-10), along with an Entire Network icon. (If you're on a corporate *domain* network, you may see a list of domains here; click the one you want.) Just double-click a computer's icon to see the shared disks, folders, and printers attached to it. (Once again, you may have to type in the correct password before you're given access.)

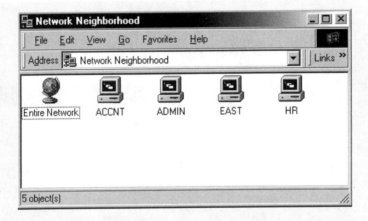

Figure 13-10. This workgroup has four computers. The Entire Network icon in the Network Neighborhood window lets you drill down from the workgroup to the computers—but because you see the networked workgroup PCs immediately, there's not much reason to do so.

Working with Network Files

Now that you know how to open shared drives and folders from across the network, you can start using the files you find there. Fortunately, there's nothing much to it. Here are some of the possibilities.

At the Desktop

When you're working at the desktop, you can double-click icons to open them, drag them to the Recycle Bin, make copies of them, and otherwise manipulate them exactly as though they were icons on your own hard drive. Chapter 3 contains much more detail on manipulating files. (Of course, if you weren't given permission to change the contents of the shared folder, as described earlier in this chapter, you have less freedom.)

 Warning: There's one significant difference between working with "local" icons and working with those that sit elsewhere on the network: when you delete a file from another computer on the network (if you're allowed to do so), either by pressing the Delete key or by dragging it to the Recycle Bin, it disappears instantly and permanently, without ever actually appearing in the Recycle Bin.

Using Start → Search

As noted in Chapter 2, the Windows XP Search program stands ready to help you find files not just on your own machine, but also elsewhere on the network. When the Search window opens up (choose Start → Search), open the "Look in" drop-down list and choose Browse. You will be offered a list of disks and folders to search—and one of them is My Network Places. Click it and then click OK. You've just confined your search to the shared disks and folders on your network. In the Search Results list, you'll be able to see, along with each found file, the name of the PC that holds it.

Inside Applications

When you're working in a program, opening files that sit elsewhere on the network requires only a couple of extra steps. Just summon the Open dialog box as usual (choose File → Open) and then, when it appears, click the My Network Places icon in the left-side panel (or choose My Network Places from the "Look in" drop-down menu.)

Now just double-click your way to the folder containing the file you want to use. Once you've opened the file, you can work on it just as though it were sitting on your own computer.

At this point, using the File → Save command saves your changes to the original file, wherever it was on the network—unless you weren't given permission to make changes, of course. In that case, you can choose File → Save As and then save a copy of the file onto your own PC.

INDEX

Numerics

802.11 access points, 172

A

"A word or phrase in the file" option, 39
access points, 172
accessibility programs
Control Panel options, 262
turning off accessibility options, 263
accounts (see user accounts)
activating Windows, 23
Active Desktop, 266–267
active windows, 58
hiding, 72
Ad-Aware, 300
Add Hardware Wizard, 247–249
searching for non–Plug and Play
devices, 248
searching for Plug and Play devices, 247
Add or Remove Programs, 134
Add Printer Wizard, 232
Address bar, 52, 66, 189
AutoComplete feature, 190
Address Book, 211
addresses, email messages, 205
administrator accounts, 132, 324
changing to Limited, 331

Alarms Tab, 276
All Programs command, 32–36
allmusic.com, 159
Alt key
menu operation, 17
using in dialog boxes, 17, 120
anti-spyware software, 294
antivirus programs
spyware-cleaning functions, 300
antivirus software, 294, 299
Appearance Tab, 269
Application Data folder, 83
application windows, 50
applications (see also programs;
software), 12
printing from, 236–240
Program Files folder, 81
arrow keys, 17
attachments to email, 211
opening, 219
in programs you don't own, 221
audio devices, configuration, 278
AutoComplete feature
Address bar, 190
forms, 191
Internet Options, 191
Automatic Updates, 301–305
Security Center messages about, 295
AutoPlay, 133

B

Back button, 65
  Internet Explorer toolbar, 189
  listing recently opened folders, 121
background (inactive) windows, 58
  hiding, 72
background printing process, 241
Backspace key
  backing out of open folder, 124
backups, 286
  Microsoft Backup, 305–315
    advanced options, 310
    creating backup job, 307
    hardware for, 306
    restoring with, 312–315
    selecting medium, 308
  searching tape-backup system, 41
base station, 172
blind carbon copies (BCC), 207
Bluetooth Devices, 264
bookmarking Web sites, 197
borders, dragging to resize windows, 52
burning CDs
  from the desktop, 102–103
  in Media Player, 162
buttons
  Mouse program, Buttons Tab, 272
  standard buttons toolbar, 65
    Internet Explorer, 188
  taskbar
    button grouping, 112
    window buttons, 71–74

C

C: drive, 80
cable modem service, 170–171
Camera and Scanner Wizard, 153
cancel, 17
canceling printouts, 243
cascading menus, 28
cascading windows, 73
case-sensitive searches, 40
CC: (carbon copy) field, email, 207
CD Writing Wizard, 105
CD-R drive (CD recordable), 102
CD-RW drive (CD rewriteable), 102
CDs
  burining from the desktop, 102–103
  burning in Media Player, 162
  installing software from, 133
  music
    copying to hard drive, 156–160
    playing in Media Player, 155
    track names, 159
  recordable CDs, 307
Classic View, Control Panel, 261
Clear History button, 190
clicking, 7
Clipboard, 125
clock, 265
close button, 51
command line, sending file to printer, 244
commands
  triggering, 7

compressed files, 135
computer sharing, 48
connection icons, 176
Contacts list, 205
context menus (see shortcut menus)
control icon, 52
Control Panel, 18, 259–284
  Accessibility Options, 262
  Bluetooth Devices, 264
  categories, 259
  Classic View version, 261
  Date and Time, 69, 264
  Display program, 266–269
  Game Controllers, 269
  Internet Options, 180, 185, 270
  Keyboard, 271
  Mail, 271
  Mouse, 272
  Network Connections, 274
  Network Setup Wizard, 274, 344
  Phone and Modem Options, 274
  Power Options, 30, 275
    Hibernate feature, 32
  Printers and Faxes, 234
  Regional and Language options, 277
  Scanners and Cameras, 277
  Scheduled Tasks, 277
  Security Center, 295–300
  Sounds and Audio Devices, 278
  Speech program, 278
  starting, 45
  System, 279–283
  User Accounts, 283, 322
  Windows Firewall, 284

controllers, 282
Copy command, 96, 126
COWS (Cluttered Overlapping Window Syndrome), 71
crashes, 114–117
  sending error report to Microsoft, 116
Ctrl+Alt+Delete, 115
Cut command, 96, 126

D

Data files dialog box, 90
Date and Time program, 264
  opening from taskbar time display, 69
Delete button, 121
Delete command
  Tools menu, 122
  Windows Media Player, 162
Deleted Items folder, 214
deleting files, 15
desktop
  burning CDs from, 102–103
  Customize Desktop, 266–267
  Desktop Tab, 266
  dragging and dropping data, 128
  elements, 24
  printing from, 240
Desktop Themes, 262
desktop windows, 50
  customizing, 58–64
    sorting order, 61–63
    standard folder views, 64
    views, 59
  task pane, 52–55

Details area, 54
Details view, 63
    displaying filename extensions, 131
Device Manager, 250–255, 282
    disabling components, 254
    duplicate devices, 252
    resolving conflicts, 252
    resolving resource conflicts, 253
    updating drivers, 254
dialog boxes
    overview, 120
    triggering options with Alt key and
        underlines, 17
    underlines, 16
    "What's This?" feature, 290
dial-up Internet accounts, 172–177
dial-up modems, 170
    connecting to Internet, 180–185
    dialing up to the Internet
        automatic dialing, 181
        disconnecting, 183
        manual connections, 180
        notification-area icon, 181
    manual connection setup, 178
digital cameras
    connecting to PC, 140
    Scanners and Cameras program, 277
digital subscriber line service, 170–171
discussion groups (mailing lists), 216
Disks dialog box, 90
disks, removable backup disks, 306
Display, 266–269
    Appearance Tab, 269
    Customize Desktop, 266–267

    Desktop Tab, 266
    Screen Saver Tab, 268
    Themes Tab, 266
documentation (Microsoft), 3
documents
    closing, 123
    dragging and dropping to desktop,
        128
    filename extensions, 130–131
    finding with Search menu, 38
    moving data between, 125–129
        Cut, Copy, and Paste, 96, 126
        drag-and-drop method, 126
    My Recent Documents, 47
    My Recent Documents folder, 83
    opening, 124
    opening My Documents from Start
        menu, 47
    Properties dialog box, 90
    saving, 117–123
        into My Documents, 118
        Save As dialog box, 119–123
        Save File dialog box, 117
    Shared Documents folder, 83
    in Startup folder, 34
Documents and Settings folder, 81
    your account folder, 83
domains, 23
    My Computer window and, 80
    results of Ctrl+Alt+Delete and, 115
downloaded software, installing, 135
drag-and-drop method, 126–129

dragging icons
   copying and moving files and
      folders, 93
   in Windows Explorer, 94
   out of Recycle Bin window, 100
drivers (see also hardware), 20, 245
   included with XP, 246
   troubleshooting with Device
      Manager, 252-254
   updating with Device Manager, 254
DSL service, 170-171
DVDs
   playing with Windows Media
      Player, 164-165

E

Easy CD Creator, 103
editions of Windows XP, 3
email (see also Outlook Express)
   addresses, 205
   filters (see message rules)
   formatting body text, 208
   HTML formatting, 208
   opening attachments, 221
   plain-text formatting, 208
   sending photos, 150
   spell checking in Microsoft Word, 210
   standard reply, 215
   Subject: field, 208
   user accounts, 202
emulation feature, printers, 235
Enter key, 17
   using in dialog boxes, 120

error reports, sending to Microsoft, 116
Esc key, 17
   closing dialog boxes, 120
ESP Internet connections, 180
Even pages option, 239
Explorer bar, 192

F

Fast User Switching, 28, 337-340
Favorites folder, 123
   adding files with Save As dialog, 122
**Favorites menu, bookmarking Web
   sites**, 197
File and Folder Tasks, 53
file format menu, 123
File menu
   Open command, 117, 124
   Save command, 117
   Send To command, 97
filename extensions, 89, 130-131
   displaying, 130
   searching by, 38
files
   attaching to email, 211
   copying and moving, 91-97
      Copy and Paste, 95-97
      copying by dragging icons, 93
      dragging icons in Windows Ex-
         plorer, 94
      right mouse button, using, 93
   deleting, 15
   finding, 36
   found files, managing, 41

files (*continued*)

    moving to Recycle Bin, 98

    naming, 89

    organizing on Windows, 12

    paths, 42

    restoring from Recycle Bin, 98

    Search subfolders option, 40

    searching for a word or phrase, 39

    searching for by name, 38

Files Stored on This Computer, 80

Filmstrip view, 59, 152

FilterKeys, 263

filters for email (see message rules)

Firefox, 186, 199

firewalls, 179, 294

    Windows Firewall, 284, 296–299

Flag commands, 219

floppy disks

    as backup medium, 307, 308

    saving documents to, 119

.fnd filename extension, 44

folders

    copying and moving, 91–97

        Copy and Paste, 95–97

        copying by dragging icons, 93

        dragging icons in Windows Explorer, 94

        right mouse button, using, 93

    creating, 78, 121

    creating in Outlook Express, 217

    displaying contents, 52, 66

    finding, 36

    found folders, managing, 41

    mail folders, Outlook Express, 203

    making private, 329

    moving to Recycle Bin, 98

    My Computer, 78–88

    naming, 89

    navigating into with Save As dialog, 119

    Properties dialog box, 90

    restoring from Recycle Bin, 98

    Search subfolders option, 40

    shared, 340–341

    standard folder views, 64

    viewing contents with Windows Explorer, 87

Folders button, 66

Fonts folder, 83

Fonts icon, 269

fonts, enlarging for Windows displays, 263

forgotten passwords, 331

forms, AutoComplete and, 191

Forward button, 65

    Internet Explorer toolbar, 189

free software

    antivirus programs, 300

    spyware contained in, 296

    Windows Media Player, 154–165

freezes, 114–117

    sending error report to Microsoft, 116

frozen programs, exiting, 115

G

Game Controllers program, 269
games, security and, 297

H

hard drive, 80
hardware (see also drivers), 245
  backup, 306
  drivers, 20
  Hardware Profiles, 282
  installing new, 246-249
    Add Hardware Wizard, 247-249
hardware problems, printers, 244
Hardware Tab
  Mouse program, 273
  Sounds and Audio Devices, 278
help, 286-294
  for dialog boxes, 290
  from Microsoft, 292-294
  navigating the Help system, 286-290
    help index, 290
    home page, 286
    searching help pages, 288
  Remote Assistance, 283
  troubleshooting wizards, 293
Help and Support, 44, 286
help screens, shortcomings of, 3
hibernation
  Hibernate command, 31
  Hibernation Tab, 276
hidden files, searching, 39

hidden folders, 83
high contrast for text, 263
highlighting icons, 91
  all icons in a window, 92
  several icons, 92
  specific icons only, 92
Home button, 189
hot spots, 172
HTML (Hypertext Markup Language), 208
  email formatting and, 208

I

Icon view, 59
icons, 12, 88-90
  adding to Favorites, 123
  adding to Quick Launch toolbar, 75
  adding to Startup folder, 34
  connection icon, 176
  copying and moving, 91-97
    Copy and Paste, 95-97
    copying by dragging, 93
    dragging icons in Windows Explorer, 94
    highlighting icons, 91
    in Windows Explorer, 94
    right mouse button, using, 93
  creating a folder to hold, 78
  deleting from Startup folder, 34
  My Computer folder, 78
  printer, 234
  properties, 90

icons (*continued*)
  Recycle Bin, 98–100
    emptying, 100
    restoring from, 98
  renaming, 88
  sortcut, 101–102
  sorting, 61–63
IE (see Internet Explorer)
image toolbar, 195
inactive windows, 58
  hiding, 72
Indexing Service, 42
Internet
  connecting to, 180–185
  dialing up to
    automatic dialing, 181
    disconnecting, 183
    manual connections, 180
    notification-area icon, 181
  establishing new dial-up
    account, 172–177
  how to get online, 170–172
    cable and DSL, 170–171
    wireless networks, 171
  manually setting up a
    connection, 178–179
  security, 294
  surfing the Web, 185
  switching between cable and dial-up
    connections, 185
Internet clock, setting PC clock by, 265
Internet Connection firewall, 179

Internet Connection Wizard, 202
Internet Explorer, 186–200
  Address bar, 189
  AutoComplete feature, 191
  browsing basics and toolbars, 186
  Explorer bar, 192
  history list and cache file, 83
  launching from Quick Launch tool-
    bar, 75
  Links toolbar, 67
  printing Web pages, 241
  searching the Web, 193
  Status Bar, 192
  tips for better surfing, 194–200
    adjusting Web page text, 194
    blocking pop-ups and pop-unders,
      200
    bookmarking favorite sites, 197
    full-screen browsing, 194
    resizing online photos, 195
    turning off graphics, 195
    viewing Web pages offline, 197
  toolbars, 188
    Links, 191
    standard buttons, 188
Internet Options, 180, 185, 270
  clearing history of Web sites visited,
    190
ISP (Internet service provider), 176
  establishing an account with, 172
ISP Signup Wizard, 174

K

keyboard
accessibility options, 263
key-repeating settings, 271
navigating dialog boxes, 120
navigating Save As list, 122
underlined letters in menus and
dialogs, 16
keyboard shortcuts, 7
All Programs command, 32
bringing different program to foreground, 112
closing windows, 51, 57
Cut, Copy, and Paste commands, 96,
126
menu bar, activating, 51
menus, opening, 51
minimizing all windows on your
screen, 74
opening minimized windows, 50
restoring windows to previous size, 50
rotating through open windows and
programs, 58
saving documents, 57
Search command, 36
Windows Explorer window, 87
keywords, 289
Knowledge Base, 290

L

Languages Tab, 277
laptops
Alarms and Power Meter Tabs, 276
hardware profiles, 282
Power Options Properties, 275
switching between cable and dial-up
connections, 185
last-modified date, searching by, 39
Limited accounts, 324
changing to Administrator, 331
links
to frequently accessed locations on a
PC, 53
to multimedia tasks, 55
Links toolbar, 67, 191
List view, 59
Local Disk (C:) window, 80
Local Folders icon, 217
Local Settings folder, 83
Log Off command, 31
logging off, 28
dialog box, 29
logging on, 320
setting up process, 335-341
Fast User Switching, 337-340
shared folders, 340-341
Welcome screen, 335
Look-in option, 39

M

mail folders, 203

Mail program, 271

Mail Sending Format, 208

mailing lists, 216

Map Network Drive, 122

maximize button, 50

MDI (multiple-document interface)
    programs, 113

Media Player (see Windows Media
    Player)

menu bar, 51

menu commands
    choices for triggering, 7
    keyboard shortcuts, 7
    Properties, 19

menus
    underlines, 16

message rules, 222–225
    creating spam filter, 226
    naming and choosing sequence, 224
    sending automatic replies to email, 226
    specifying action to take with filtered
        mail, 224
    specifying words or people to look
        for, 222, 224

microphones, configuring, 278

Microsoft Backup, 305–315
    advanced options, 310
    creating backup job, 307
    hardware, 306
    restoring with, 312–315
    selecting backup medium, 308

Microsoft documentation, 3

Microsoft Help Web pages, 292

Microsoft Knowledge Base, 290

Microsoft Word, spell checking
    email, 210

Microsoft's Internet service (see MSN)

minimize button, 50

minimizing all windows on desktop, 73

mixed-mode CDs, 106

modems, 170

modification date, searching by, 39

most frequently used programs list, 26

mouse
    Mouse program, 263, 272
    right mouse button, 14
        using while dragging icons, 93

Mozilla Firefox, 186, 199

MP3 files
    burning music CDs, 106
    creating in Windows Media Player, 157
    ripping for portable players, 158

MSN, 172
    establishing account, 172

MSN Groups, 148

multimedia files, searching for, 38

multimedia task links, 55

multiple-document interface (MDI)
    programs, 113

music
    burning CDs, 162
    copying CDs to hard drive, 156–160
    finding with Search command, 38
    Internet sites selling downloadable
        files, 160

music (*continued*)
    naming tracks on CDs, 159
    opening My Music with Start menu, 45
    organizing your library, 160
    playing CDs with Windows Media
        Player, 155
    playlists, 162
    transferred to a CD, information
        loss, 103
My Computer, 78–88
    differences in appearance of
        window, 80
    icon properties, 90
    icons, 78
    Local Disk (C:) window, 80
    navigating, 84
      with Windows Explorer, 84–88
    searching, 39
    Shared Documents folder, 83
    starting, 45
    your account folder, 83
My Documents
    displaying someone else's
        documents, 48
    opening with Start menu, 47
    saving new documents into, 118
**My Music, opening folder with Start
    menu**, 45
My Network Places, 45
**My Pictures, opening with Start
    menu**, 45
My Recent Documents, 47, 83

N

naming files and folders, 89
NetHood folder, 83
Network Connections, 274
    Internet connection, 176
network printers, installing, 231
Network Setup Wizard, 274, 344
networks
    logging off, 28
    logging on, 23
      workgroups vs. domains, 23
    My Computer window, 80
    My Network Places window, 45
New Connection Wizard, 172, 202
notification area, 68
    icon for Internet connection, 181
    turning off auto-hiding, 70
number keypad, 263

O

Odd and Even pages options, 239
online services, 176
Open dialog box, 124
operating system, Windows overview, 12
**Outbox folder, placing messages in be-
    fore sending**, 211
Outlook Express (see also email), 202–226
    Address Book, 211
    attaching files to messages, 211
    composing and sending
        messages, 205–211
    creating new folders, 217

Outlook Express (*continued*)

    flagging messages, 219

    folders, working with, 218

    forwarding messages, 216

    mail folders, 203

    message rules (see message rules)

    moving messages into folders, 217

    opening attachments, 219

    printing messages, 217

    reading email, 212–214

    replying to messages, 215

    sending email, 202

    setting up, 202

P

Page Up and Page Down keys, 53

passwords

    creating for user accounts, 327

    hints for remembering, 327

    Password Reset Disk, 331

    primary and secondary, 332

Paste command, 96, 126

paths, 42

    Search Results, In Folder column, 43

pausing printouts, 242

personal firewall, 179

Phone and Modem Options, 274

phone help from Microsoft, 293

photo-manipulation features, 144

phrases

    finding in files, 39

    searching online for, 67

pictures

    attaching to email messages, 212

    digital photos in XP, 140–152

        creating photo screen saver, 151

        emailing, 150

        manipulating downloaded photos, 144

        posting on the Web, 147

        transferring from digital camera, 140–143

        viewing in Windows Picture and Fax Viewer, 152

    finding with Search command, 38

    My Pictures folder, opening, 45

    resizing online photos, 195

    saving from the Web, 188

    scanning, 153

    transferred to a CD, information loss, 103

pinned items list, 26

plain text, email message format, 208

playlists, 162

Plug and Play

    Add Hardware Wizard and, 247

    automatically detecting and installing printer, 232

pointer, mouse, 273

pop-ups and pop-unders, blocking, 200, 296

ports, 297

Power Meter Tab, 276

Power Options program, 30, 275

    Hibernate feature, 32

power schemes, 276

previewing email messages, 212

Print dialog box, 236-240
    application-specific options, 239
    number of copies, 239
    page range, 238
    Preferences/Properties, 237
    Print drop-down list, 239
    Select Printer, 237
print queue, 242
    manipulating, 242
print spooler, 241
printer drivers, 230
    not included in Windows XP, 235
printer emulation, 235
printers
    installing, 230-235
        existing printers, 230
        network printers, 231
        printer icon, 234
        USB printers, 231
    troubleshooting, 244
Printers and Faxes, printer icon, 234
printing, 236-241
    controlling printouts, 241-244
    from applications, 236-240
    from the desktop, 240
    from the Internet, 241
Printing Troubleshooter, 245
Program Files folder, 81
    Properties dialog box, 90
programs (see also applications;
    software)
    closing documents, 123
    crashing or freezing, 114-117
    exiting, 114

    filename extensions, 130-131
    launching, 110
    managing multiple open programs, 111
        bringing different program to fore-
            ground, 112
    MDI and SDI, 113
    most frequently used, 26
    moving data between documents,
        125-129
    opening documents, 124
    recent documents list, 47
    saving documents, 117-123
    starting all, 32-36
properties
    changing for Windows, 18
    defined, 90
Properties command, 122
Properties dialog boxes, icons, 90

Q

Quick Launch toolbar, 74
quitting programs, 114, 124
    closing the window, 57
    crashed or frozen programs, 114-117

R

rearranging printing order, 243
recently used list (documents), 47
Recycle Bin, 98-100
    emptying, 100
    restoring deleted files and folders, 98

Refresh button, 189
Regional Options, 277
Remote Assistance, 283
removable backup disks, 306
Rename command, 122
renaming files found with Search
          command, 44
renaming rectangle, 88
Reply button, 215
Reply to All button, 215
resource conflicts, resolving, 253
Restart command, 31
restore down button, 50
Restore Wizard, 312
restoring files, with Microsoft
          Backup, 312-315
right mouse button, using while drag-
          ging icons, 93
right-clicking, 14
ripping, 156
     for a portable MP3 player, 158

S

Save As dialog box, 119-123
     additional buttons in some
               programs, 121
     file format menu, 123
     navigating list of files and folders, 122
Save File dialog box, 117
Scanner and Camera Wizard, 153
Scanners and Cameras icon, 277
scanning, 153
Scheduled Tasks, 277
schemes, 269

Scrap file, 128
     dragging onto document taskbar
               button, 129
Screen Saver Tab, 268
screen saver, creating from photos, 151
scroll bars, 52
     using, 53
scrolling, Web pages, 188
SDI (single-document interface)
          programs, 113
Search button, 66
Search command, 36
     all files and folders option, 39
     file names, typing, 38
     managing found files and folders, 41
     pictures, music, or video, finding, 38
     results list, 43
     saving setup, 44
     Search Results panel, 42
     starting a search, 36
search engines, 193
Search the Web, 121
searches, 67
security
     Automatic Updates, 301-305
     Internet, 294
     passwords, 332
Security Center, 295-300
     Virus Protection feature, 299
     Windows Firewall, 296-299
     Windows Firewall control panel, 297
security holes, Administrator
          accounts, 323
selecting icons (see highlighting icons)

selecting multiple email messages, 214
Send Error Report button, 116
Send To command, 97
sending found files to another
 location, 44
Service Packs, 13
Setup Wizard, 23
Shared Documents folder, 83, 341
shortcut menus, 14
 task pane, 52
shortcuts, 101–102
 creating and deleting, 34–35, 102
 creating for found files, 44
ShowSounds, 263
Shut Down command, 30–32
 Hibernate option, 31
 Log Off option, 31
 Restart option, 31
signatures, email messages, 210
single-document interface (SDI)
 programs, 113
size of files, searching by, 39
sleeping
 Hibernate command, 31
 Standby command, 30
slide shows, 59
software (see also applications;
 programs), 12
 drivers (see drivers)
 installing, 132–137
 Add or Remove Programs, 134
 downloaded from Internet, 135
 from a CD, 133
 preloaded software, 135
 Windows components, 136

Internet security, 294
 uninstalling, 137
software problems, printers, 244
sorting
 changing order for desktop
 windows, 61–63
 files found with Search, 44
sound effects, Windows, 278
sound files, adding to Media Player database, 160
Sounds and Audio Devices, 278
SoundSentry, 263
Space bar, scrolling Web pages, 188
spam filter, creating, 226
spam, protecting yourself from, 225
speakers, configuring, 278
speech, Speech program, 278
spell checking email, 210
Spybot Search & Destroy, 300
spyware
 anti-spyware software, 294, 300
 defined, 296
standard buttons toolbar, 65
Standby command, 30
Start menu, 24
 All Programs command, 32–36
 Control Panel, 45
 Taskbar and Start menu, 283
 Control Panel submenu, creating, 261
 Help and Support, 44, 286
 Log Off command, 28
 My Computer, 45
 My Documents, 47
 My Network Places, 45

Start menu (*continued*)
My Recent Documents, 47
opening with Windows logo key, 17
Search command, 36
Shut Down command, 30-32
submenus, 28
Turn Off Computer command, 30-32
Startup folder, 34
Status Bar, 192
StickyKeys, 263
stop, 17
Stop button, 189
stopping a program from launching, 34
subfolders, searching, 40
Subject: field, email messages, 208
submenus, 28
Switch User/Log Off dialog box, 28
symbols not allowed in folder or file names, 89
System, 279-283
Device Manager, 282
Hardware Profiles, 282
System Restore, 283

T

Tab key
menu operation, 17
navigating dialog boxes, 120
tabbed dialog boxes, 20
tape backups, 307
searching, 41
Task Manager dialog box, 115
task pane, 52-55
Details area, 54

taskbar, 68-74, 283
bringing a different program to the front, 112
managing multiple open programs, 111
notification area, 69
notification-area auto-hiding, turning off, 70
window buttons, 71-74
taskbar toolbars, 74
Quick Launch, 74
templates, 55
text, high contrast for easier reading, 263
Themes Tab, 266
Thumbnails view, 152
tiling windows, 73
time display, 69
time zones, 265
title bars, 50
active and inactive windows, 58
dragging to move windows, 56
To: field, email messages, 205
ToggleKeys, 263
toolbars, 51, 64-68
Address bar, 66
Internet Explorer, 188
Links, 191
standard buttons, 188
Links bar, 67
standard buttons, 65
taskbar toolbars, 74
Tools menu, Save As dialog box, 122
troubleshooters, 293
Turn Off command, 30

U

underlines, 16
Undo command, 74
uninstalling software, 137
uninterruptible power supply (UPS),
   276
Universal Serial Bus (USB), 231
unread email messages, 213
Up button, 66
URLs
   typing into Address bar, 189
   visited during browsing session, 190
USB printers, installing, 231
Use High Contrast, 263
user accounts, 283, 320–342
   account folder, 83
   adding an account, 325
   administrator accounts, 132, 324
   deleting, 334
   editing, 326–331
      changing account picture, 330
      changing account type, 331
      changing name, 327
      creating password, 327
      making files private, 329
   forgotten password disk, 331
   introduction to, 321
   Limited accounts, 324
   logging off, 28
   logon process, setting up, 335–341
      Fast User Switching, 337–340
      shared folders, 340–341
      Welcome screen, 335

passwords, primary and secondary, 332
setting up, 23, 322–324
user profile, 321
users
   access to software, 133
   Fast User Switching feature, 28

V

video
   adding files to Media Player
      database, 160
   finding with Search command, 38
video CDs, 106
View menu, toolbars, 65
views
   Details view, 63
   Save As dialog box, 121
   standard folder views, 64
   windows, 59
Views button, 66
Virus Protection message, 295
virus software, 299
visualization, 155
Volume Tab, 278

W

Web
   information on desktop, 266–267
   searching, 193
   surfing, 185
Web addresses, 52
   typing into Address bar, 66

web browsers
    Internet Explorer (see Internet Explorer)
    Mozilla Firefox, 186, 199
Web page addresses (see URLs)
Web pages
    adjusting text size, 194
    bookmarking in Favorites, 197
    forms, AutoComplete and, 191
    interesting and important, 193
    links to, 67
    printing, 241
    viewing offline, 197
Web Publishing Wizard, 148
Welcome screen, 335
"What size is it?" option, 39
"What's This?" feature, 290
"When was it modified?" option, 39
WiFi networks, 171
window buttons, 71-74
Windows
    changing properties, 18
    overview of, 12
windows, 50-68
    closing, 56
    components of, 50-52
    customizing desktop windows, 58-64
        Details view, 63
        folder views, 64
        sorting order, 61-63
        views, 59
    desktop and application categories, 50
    manipulating from the taskbar, 72

MDI programs, 113
    moving, 56
    multiple, working with, 57
        active and inactive windows, 58
    sizing, moving, and closing, 55
    toolbars, 64-68
        Address bar, 66
        Links, 67
        standard buttons, 65
Windows 2000, 2
Windows Components Wizard, 136
Windows Explorer, 84-88
    dragging icons, 94
    keyboard shortcuts, 87
    navigating folders on your PC, 84
    too-narrow panel, 86
    viewing folder contents, 87
Windows Firewall, 296-299
    exceptions list, 298
    ports, 297
Windows folder, 83
Windows logo key, 17
Windows Media Audio (WMA) format, 157
Windows Media Player, 154-165
    burning CDs, 162
    copying CDs to hard drive, 156-160
    deleting things, 162
    DVD movies, 164-165
    launching from Quick Launch toolbar, 75
    organizing your music libarary, 160
    overview of functions, 154
    playing music CDs, 155

Windows Media Player (*continued*)
  playlists, 162
  sound and video files, adding to
    database, 160
Windows Picture and Fax Viewer, 152,
  154
Windows Security dialog box, 115
Windows Update, 301
Windows XP
  documentation shortcomings, 3
  Professional and Home editions, 3
WINNT folder, 83
wireless devices, 264
wireless networks, 171
  setup wizard, 284

wizards, 15
words, finding in files, 36, 39
workgroups, 23
  Files on This Computer icon, 79
  My Computer window, 80
  results of Ctrl+Alt+Delete, 115
  Shut Down (Turn Off) command, 30
World Wide Web (see Web)

Z

Zip disk, saving a document onto, 119

COLOPHON

Sanders Kleinfeld was the production editor and proofreader for *Windows XP for Starters: The Missing Manual*. Adam Witwer and Claire Cloutier provided quality control. Ellen Troutman-Zaig wrote the index.

Nicole Skillern created the series cover design. Linda Palo produced the cover layout. Marcia Friedman designed the hand lettering on the cover.

Tom Ingalls designed the interior layout. Andrew Savikas converted the text and prepared it for layout. Robert Romano, Jessamyn Read, and Lesley Borash produced the illustrations.

Better than e-books

Buy *Windows XP for Starters: The Missing Manual* and access the digital edition FREE on Safari for 45 days.

Go to www.oreilly.com/go/safarienabled
and type in coupon code JJLG-8M1M-9MUQ-G8N7-AJ6T

Search
thousands of
top tech books

Download
whole chapters

Cut and Paste
code examples

Find
answers fast

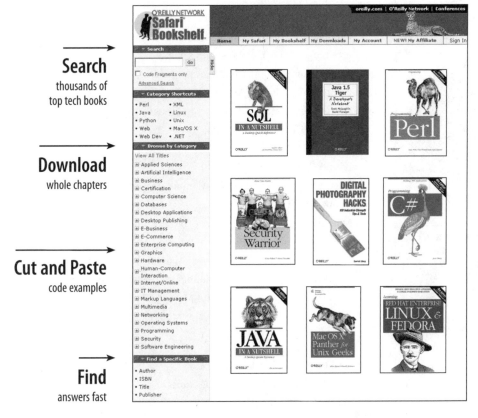

Search Safari! The premier electronic reference
library for programmers and IT professionals.

Related Titles from O'Reilly

Missing Manuals

Access: The Missing Manual, *Startup Edition*

AppleWorks 6: The Missing Manual

Creating Web Sites: The Missing Manual

Dreamweaver MX 2004: The Missing Manual

eBay: The Missing Manual

Excel: The Missing Manual

Excel for Rookies: The Missing Manual

FileMaker Pro: The Missing Manual

FrontPage 2003: The Missing Manual

GarageBand: The Missing Manual

Google: The Missing Manual, *2nd Edition*

Home Networking: The Missing Manual

iLife '04: The Missing Manual

iMovie HD & iDVD 5: The Missing Manual

iPhoto 5: The Missing Manual

iPod & iTunes: The Missing Manual, *3rd Edition*

iWork '05: The Missing Manual

Mac OS X: The Missing Manual, *Tiger Edition*

Office 2004 for Macintosh: The Missing Manual

Windows 2000 Pro: The Missing Manual

Windows XP: The Missing Manual, *Startup Edition*

Windows XP Pro: The Missing Manual, *2nd Edition*

Windows XP Home Edition: The Missing Manual, *2nd Edition*

Pogue Press

Mac OS X Panther Power Hound

Switching to the Mac, *Tiger Edition*

Windows XP Power Hound

Our books are available at most retail and online bookstores.

To order direct: 1-800-998-9938 • *order@oreilly.com* • *www.oreilly.com*

Online editions of most O'Reilly titles are available by subscription at *safari.oreilly.com*

Keep in touch with O'Reilly

Download examples from our books

To find example files from a book, go to: *www.oreilly.com/catalog* select the book, and follow the "Examples" link.

Register your O'Reilly books

Register your book at *register.oreilly.com* Why register your books? Once you've registered your O'Reilly books you can:

- Win O'Reilly books, T-shirts or discount coupons in our monthly drawing.
- Get special offers available only to registered O'Reilly customers.
- Get catalogs announcing new books (US and UK only).
- Get email notification of new editions of the O'Reilly books you own.

Join our email lists

Sign up to get topic-specific email announcements of new books and conferences, special offers, and O'Reilly Network technology newsletters at:

elists.oreilly.com

It's easy to customize your free elists subscription so you'll get exactly the O'Reilly news you want.

Get the latest news, tips, and tools

www.oreilly.com

- "Top 100 Sites on the Web"—PC Magazine
- CIO Magazine's Web Business 50 Awards

Our web site contains a library of comprehensive product information (including book excerpts and tables of contents), downloadable software, background articles, interviews with technology leaders, links to relevant sites, book cover art, and more.

Work for O'Reilly

Check out our web site for current employment opportunities:

jobs.oreilly.com

Contact us

O'Reilly Media, Inc.
1005 Gravenstein Hwy North
Sebastopol, CA 95472 USA
Tel: 707-827-7000 or 800-998-9938
    (6am to 5pm PST)
Fax: 707-829-0104

Contact us by email

For answers to problems regarding your order or our products:
order@oreilly.com

To request a copy of our latest catalog:
catalog@oreilly.com

For book content technical questions or corrections: **booktech@oreilly.com**

For educational, library, government, and corporate sales: **corporate@oreilly.com**

To submit new book proposals to our editors and product managers:
proposals@oreilly.com

For information about our international distributors or translation queries:
international@oreilly.com

For information about academic use of O'Reilly books:
adoption@oreilly.com
or visit:
academic.oreilly.com

For a list of our distributors outside of North America check out:
international.oreilly.com/distributors.html

Order a book online

www.oreilly.com/order_new